Is He All That?

Is He All That?

Great Footballing Myths **SHATTERED**

talkSPORT ⚽

ADRIAN DURHAM

**SIMON &
SCHUSTER**

London · New York · Sydney · Toronto · New Delhi

A CBS COMPANY

First published in Great Britain by Simon & Schuster UK Ltd, 2013
A CBS Company

1 3 5 7 9 10 8 6 4 2

Simon & Schuster UK Ltd
1st Floor
222 Gray's Inn Road
London WC1X 8HB

www.simonandschuster.co.uk

Simon & Schuster Australia, Sydney
Simon & Schuster India, New Delhi

A CIP catalogue record for this book is available
from the British Library

ISBN 978-1-47113-159-2
ebook ISBN 978-1-47113-161-5

Typeset in UK by Hewer Text UK Ltd, Edinburgh
Printed and bound by CPI Group (UK) Ltd, Croydon, CR0 4YY

For Grace and Jamie. Love those guys.

CONTENTS

Acknowledgements

Thanks to the following: Jonathan Conway for seeing this through. Ian Marshall and Tom Whiting at Simon & Schuster. Calum Macaulay, Bill Ridley and Liam Fisher at talkSPORT for support, stories about Cher, and time off to finish it respectively. To Guillem Balague for the advice – I owe you dinner and I will turn up this time. Special thanks to Jamie Carragher for not bottling it when I asked him to write the foreword! Thanks to Mark Alford and Lee Clayton at the *Daily Mail* for backing me. The best producers and co-presenters I've worked with at talkSPORT are the ones who can be trusted totally; thanks to you guys, you know who you are. And most of all thanks to Amanda who makes sure life is brilliant every day.

Foreword
by Jamie Carragher

The first time Adrian Durham came into my life it's fair to say we were both at our passionate and angry best. It was a clash of two football lovers who can both get het up over the game – I like to think I showed the listening nation that some footballers do care and some presenters do back down when challenged!

Anyone who listens to *Drive* on talkSPORT on a regular basis (like I do) will know that Adrian can make you laugh out loud or shout at your radio in despair almost in the same breath. That's why this book is an essential read for football fans throughout the country; he has an opinion, and whether you agree or not, sitting on the fence is something that can never be done when Durham's in town.

I listen to him and Goughy at least three times a week, when I'm travelling with my dad and son to the Liverpool FC academy in Kirkby. The debates on the show will spark debates in our car, and that's the whole point. My son's favourite is 'The Daily Arsenal' – typical of the show, it's set up to get Gooners on to vent their spleens at Adrian. And when they do, he's won! That's exactly what happened to me during a lovely afternoon drive to training in pre-season, when my listening pleasure was interrupted when I heard the word 'bottler'.

Not sure who this applied to, I was looking forward to hearing until I realised it was yours truly. My blood started to boil. *How can I get on?* was my first thought. I had to wait for the phone number to come on at the breaks while listening to myself getting slaughtered! I eventually phoned in – Quinny was on and his only advice was 'don't swear'. That was the call that put Adrian on the map! Our 'chat' was passionate, funny and entertaining . . . I'm sure I don't need to go into that as Adrian will have the transcript in the book and milked it for all it's worth.

This call started an unlikely relationship which consists of Adrian phoning me every few weeks to come on the show. After a Liverpool game, we met up in the players' lounge and at my restaurant in Liverpool to do a radio show, for which he gave his fee to my charity.

This book is a real page-turner: reading it is like listening to the Adrian Durham I know and you'll probably feel like phoning him too! That's the point; he's always got something to say.

Introduction

FOOTBALL IS BRILLIANT. I love it so much I decided to watch it and talk about it for a living, and that's why I host radio shows on the nation's only sports radio station, talkSPORT. The *Drive* show every weekday is all about opinions, and *Matchday Live* on Saturdays takes me out and about to Premier League grounds to bring you all the goals as they go in.

The beautiful game has been a big influence on my life. I never met my dad, and was brought up in Peterborough by a single mum, so things weren't easy. Growing up, football was massive for me. I got so nervous on World Cup final day in both 1974 and 1978 that I threw up on the living room carpet. In between, I went to my first game in 1976 when I was six – Peterborough United 3 Shrewsbury Town 2 – after which I was totally hooked on Posh. One of the houses I lived in as a boy had a window at the top of the stairs from which I watched Sunday football matches played on the nearby pitches. From the age of four I would commentate on these matches to myself, making up names as I went along. The early signs of a future career in radio emerged right there; I had no idea I would go to World Cups and Champions League finals for talkSPORT. I am still so excited to be watching Premier League games every week, and one of my most vivid childhood memories is hurriedly writing down the football results every Saturday tea-time and reading them out loud over and over again. I still do that today – it's my job!

I've had the high of presenting a show from a play-off final won by my beloved Peterborough United, as well as being on air presenting *Matchday Live* on talkSPORT for the devastation of relegation as Posh lost at Palace in the last minute in May 2013. I still don't know how I managed to hold it together.

Talking about football on the radio on *Drive* every day is literally my boyhood dream come true. My other ambition was to write a book. My house is overflowing with books, including hundreds on football. I've had a burning desire to add my own work to this growing library for a long time, and here it is. It's been four years of stopping and starting, researching and writing, and I've loved every second.

This book challenges some of football's accepted wisdom – was Sir Alf Ramsey actually a good manager? To quote my own catchphrase on talkSPORT, 'Is he all that?' Why doesn't anybody ask the obvious question about Gary Lineker? Did Italy really deserve all four of their World Cups? There are chapters on the kind of thing you might expect if you listen to my show regularly: Michael Carrick, Jamie Carragher and of course, Arsenal. And it's packed with some truly unbelievable facts and stories you might never have found out about the game if you hadn't picked this up.

Read this book and find out about the dog who barked to tell a top-flight manager not to accept a derisory bid from Real Madrid for one of his players . . . the keeper who claimed he let in four goals in a World Cup final to save the lives of the opposition . . . why a top footballer chose true love over a World Cup . . . the FA Cup winner who taped his medal to his forehead for a whole training session to prove a point to his manager . . . the England record-breaker who turned his back on his country . . . and why a former Aston Villa manager was searching for alligators.

Like I said: Football is brilliant!

PART 1

'It was clear to Mourinho that despite walking into the Bernabeu and finding he had a stack of cash as well as the world's most expensive player at his disposal, he needed to start a fight off the field to become successful on it.'

Arsene Wenger
– a great football manager?

It's often said that Arsene Wenger is a great manager, but for me the evidence doesn't confirm that.

If you want a manager guaranteed to tell his team to play entertaining football then he fits the bill. The quality has been breathtaking at times. If you want a manager prepared to take a teenage boy from abroad (Fabregas, Anelka, Clichy etc) for next to nothing (because he hasn't signed a professional contract with the club who taught him how to play), and turn him into a footballer worth millions, then Wenger is that man.

But he is no trophy machine. Arsenal great he may well be, but not an all-time great. And he is not a born winner.

Wenger has reached three different European finals, and three times he's failed. He's the only manager with that dubious record. At least he's consistent. The first time was with Monaco in the now defunct Cup Winners' Cup. In 1991–92, they thrashed Welsh Cup winners Swansea, then a lower division side, 10–1 on aggregate. Easy start. Swedish side IFK Norrkoping were next – another easy tie. They overcame a tough hurdle in the quarter-final, squeezing past Roma 1–0. They couldn't get the better of Feyenoord in either game of the two-legged semi-final, but they won through on away goals. In the final Monaco faced Otto

'Wenger has had success, but has he had enough success? World Cup winners, and world-class players have been and gone.'

Rehhagel's Werder Bremen; Rehhagel would go on to manage Greece to their unlikely European Championship success in 2004. Wenger had some serious talent at his disposal at Monaco: Manu Petit, George Weah, Youri Djorkaeff and Lilian Thuram, who was an unused substitute; keeper and captain Ettori had played at the 1982 World Cup for France (he was in goal when Bryan Robson scored after 27 seconds in England's 3–1 win in the first game of the group stage); and Rui Barros was a Portuguese international who had won the UEFA Cup with Juventus.

Weah was the jewel in the team. Wenger brought him to Europe, and Weah credits Wenger as a huge influence on his career. But it was only after Weah moved on to Paris St Germain and then AC Milan that he started to win the honours his talents deserved.

But Wenger's Monaco were comfortably beaten by Bremen. It finished 2–0 – Klaus Allofs on 40, and Wynton Rufer on 55 minutes scored in Lisbon, with sloppy defending to blame for both goals.

To be fair to Wenger, France as a nation had been rocked by the Bastia tragedy in which 17 football fans died, and hundreds were injured, when a temporary stand built for the French Cup final collapsed. This happened 24 hours before Monaco's final in Lisbon.

Wenger won the title with Monaco, and the French Cup, and he took them to the semi-finals of the old European Cup and the Champions League. But in the end he was sacked when Monaco finished ninth in 1994–95.

Despite reports that he was wanted by Bayern Munich and the French national team, the best job he could get was in Japan. He was awarded manager of the year in Japan, won the Cup but not the title.

So let's fast forward to Highbury. Unknown when he arrived, he won the double in his first full season,1997–98, which is impressive.

But in 2000 Wenger's Arsenal were in the middle of three years without a trophy. He had assembled an amazing team: Petit, Vieira and Henry all had World Cup winners' medals; Dennis Bergkamp had won the UEFA Cup with Inter Milan; Marc Overmars and Nwankwo Kanu had won the Champions League with Ajax; Davor Suker had won the Champions League with Real Madrid; Tony Adams, Ray Parlour, David Seaman, Lee Dixon and Nigel Winterburn had all won the Cup Winners' Cup with Arsenal under George Graham in 1994. In short Arsenal were a team of winners, while their UEFA Cup final opponents Galatasaray had Gheorghe Hagi, his brother-in-law Gheorghe Popescu and that was about it. Hagi was 35 and Popescu was 32 – both were past their best. Actually they did have World Cup winner Claudio Taffarel in goal, but honestly, a Brazilian keeper?

The game was poor, and despite the creative qualities of most of their squad, Arsenal ran out of ideas. It finished goalless after 120 minutes and the Gunners lost the penalty shoot-out. Two foreigners – Vieira and Suker – missed for Arsenal. The only Gunner to score was the Romford Pele – Englishman Ray Parlour, one of my favourite talkSPORT colleagues. Maybe Wenger should have put more of his faith in English players over the years. With an incredible team, Arsenal failed to beat an average Galatasaray.

Arsenal had become a bit of a joke in the Champions League up to 2006. As kings of England, they went out in the group stages in 1998–99. They did the double over Panathanaikos, but couldn't beat Lens and Dynamo Kiev, even somehow losing at home to the French club. Manchester United won the final that year.

In 1999–2000 the Gunners again failed to get out of the group stage. Once again the minnows – AIK Solna – were beaten home and away, but having done the hard work of drawing away to both Barcelona and Fiorentina, Wenger's team lost to both at home and went out.

The following season Arsenal won their first three games comfortably, seeing off Sparta Prague, Shakhtar Donetsk and Lazio. Progressing smoothly through to the second group stage (although a 3–0 thrashing in the Ukraine on matchday six was a concern), the Gunners started off by being hammered 4–1 away to Spartak Moscow. In fact they won only two of their six games in that group, but it was enough to progress by virtue of the fact they beat Lyon in the head to head. Arsenal beat Valencia 2–1 in the first leg of the quarter-final, but went out on away goals after Tony Adams momentarily lost John Carew and the big Norwegian scored the only goal in the Mestalla.

The next season Arsenal lost to Schalke, Mallorca and Panathanaikos in the group stage but still scraped through. But in the second group stage they lost home and away to Deportivo la Coruna, lost to Juventus and went out.

Arsenal won their first three group games in 2002–03, but then lost at home to Auxerre, were beaten in Dortmund, and couldn't beat bottom club PSV at home. Thankfully they'd already done enough to get through. A Thierry Henry hat-trick in Rome kicked off the second group stage in style. But they didn't win another game and went out, defeat in Valencia in the final game sealing their fate.

The 2003–04 European campaign started terribly for Wenger – thrashed 3–0 at home to Inter Milan. Arsenal were so bad even Andy van der Meyde scored, and a new viral swiftly did the rounds on the internet showing Arsenal's new shirt sponsors to be O3 rather than O2. The Gunners would answer the critics with a stunning 5–1 win in the San Siro later in the group. Before that stunning win in Milan Ashley Cole's late goal had actually saved Arsenal from going out at Highbury against Dynamo Kiev. A comfortable matchday six win against Lokomotiv Moscow sealed their passage.

Arsenal had no problems seeing off Celta Vigo in the first knockout stage, but then came Chelsea in the quarter-finals. A 1–1 draw at Stamford Bridge looked like being followed by a 1–1 draw at Highbury until Wayne Bridge popped up to score an excellent goal late on to take Chelsea through. Even Blues fans say Arsenal were brilliant in the first leg, but that is exactly the point. They played brilliant football, had brilliant players, but still the manager couldn't shape all this into a formula resulting in domestic and European domination. With the players he had, Wenger should have turned Arsenal into the best team in Europe.

The following season Arsenal went unbeaten in the group stage (drawing four and winning two). But they were beaten 3–1 in Munich by Bayern in the first knockout stage, and could only win 1–0 at home. Liverpool performed miracles to win the final that year.

Then we come to the season they eventually made the final. After just two quarter-finals, and no semi-final appearances, the Gunners got their act together in 2006. In an easy group stage Arsenal were brilliant and won five out of six. The first knockout stage saw them go to Real Madrid and win 1–0. A goalless draw at home was enough. Fabio Capello's Juventus were easily seen off 2–0 on aggregate. And in the semi-finals Arsenal were extremely fortunate. They beat Villarreal 1–0 at home, and drew 0–0 away, although Juan Riquelme saw a late penalty saved by Arsenal keeper Jens Lehmann.

Arsenal made it to the final and Lehmann was a hero. But some serious questions had been raised over the years about Lehmann's temperament and his decision-making. Wenger stood by him, but was he really the top-level keeper Arsenal needed? In fact, after being gifted David Seaman when he arrived at Highbury, Arsene Wenger's ability to pick a good keeper had been flawed. Arsenal never had a Van der Sar, a Cech or a Reina; and Lehmann was about to cost the Gunners dear.

In the final in Paris Lehmann came charging out of his goal to bring down Samuel Eto'o. He became the first player to be sent off in a Champions League final. It was a poor decision from the German. To be fair to Wenger, a manager has a quick and unexpected decision to make when a keeper is sent off. Almunia would go on, but who would come off? Wenger took off Pires, a potential match-winner. I remember sitting in the press box wondering how the Arsenal manager thought that was a good idea. Either Ljungberg or Hleb would have been my choice.

Down to ten men, Arsenal went ahead before half-time with Sol Campbell heading in from a free-kick, although even Wenger admitted afterwards that Eboue had dived for the free-kick. Wenger actually told the press: 'It is clear there was no foul. I condemn and regret the attitude of Eboue. I have always risen up against cheating. I detest simulation.' (His policy on simulation seems to have changed by the time Eduardo was 'fouled' against Celtic in the 2009–10 qualifier.)

Arsenal were leading with 16 minutes left. Some think Henrik Larsson's introduction on 61 minutes changed the game. Others look at Juliano Belletti replacing Oleguer on 71. But for me the turning point was Wenger inexplicably taking Cesc Fabregas off on 74 minutes, and putting Matthieu Flamini on. It was a change which invited Barcelona to attack. Arsenal's midfield consisted of Gilberto Silva and Flamini – they could win the ball, but couldn't create anything with it. Consequently Barça kept getting the ball back. Two minutes later Eto'o equalised, four minutes later Belletti got the winner. (Almunia should have saved this, the ball going through his legs at the near post. Almunia is another keeper Wenger stuck by with no reward. Like Lehmann he is not a bad keeper, but he is below the standard Arsenal require to dominate domestic and European football.)

The final whistle went and Arsenal were left complaining that Barcelona's tackles had been nasty. It was pathetic. No Arsenal fans seemed to want to mention that while the game was being thrown away by Lehmann and Wenger, Dennis Bergkamp and Robin van Persie – both had won UEFA Cup finals at their previous clubs – stayed on the bench unused. Wenger's reasoning behind that would have been double Dutch. A football crime.

The following season Arsenal didn't make the quarter-finals, losing to a PSV side who were then thrashed by Liverpool.

The Gunners were beaten 5–3 on aggregate by Liverpool in the quarters the next season. And then in 2008–09, Arsenal reached the semis before being totally outclassed and humiliated in their own stadium by Manchester United. In 2009–10 they were outclassed by Barcelona in the quarters, and have failed to make the quarter-finals since.

In short, at the time of writing, Arsenal have never won the Champions League under Wenger. In his years at the club he has had truly world-class players in his team – Henry, Pires, Gilberto Silva, Vieira, Bergkamp, Van Persie, Overmars and Petit among others. These players should have been the tools any great manager would need to produce a team capable of dominating the Premier League and the Champions League. But Wenger did neither.

If we look at his signings his record gets slowly worse. It seems to me he had a list of top players to sign when he came to the club, but once that supply was exhausted he ran out of ideas.

Andrey Arshavin had a great Euro 2008 for Russia, so Wenger signed him for huge amounts of money, and he turned out to be a shocking buy.

The signing of the Brazilian midfielder Denilson was bizarre. As a teenager he hardly played for Sao Paolo, and if someone tells you he was a key part of their success when they won the World Club Championship in 2005 (beating Liverpool 1–0 in the final) they're wrong – he didn't play a minute.

Denilson arrived at Arsenal for £3 million in 2006 but was never special. In the summer of 2013, after two years on loan at Sao Paolo, he went back there permanently (he actually won a trophy there during his original loan spell).

So the Brazilian Under-17 captain went to Arsenal, and his talent either didn't exist or was completely flattened out by Wenger. To date, Denilson has never played for the full national team. Did Wenger sign a player just because he was a junior representative captain? That is not a great reason to spend money on a footballer in my book.

Denilson is one of many thought to have earned wages of around £45-50,000 a week at Arsenal. Almunia, Djourou, Squillaci, Bendtner are others on what is apparently a long list of very average players who in my opinion are paid far more than they were worth at the Emirates.

Wenger has had success, but has he had enough success? World Cup winners, and world-class players have been and gone. And although Chelsea and Manchester City have taken transfer fees and wages to amazing levels in the Premier League, the budget has been there for Wenger. When Arsenal should have been dominating Europe, Vieira and Campbell were two of the top three earners in the Premier League.

If you don't believe that Wenger had the budget, and the board were to blame, then maybe the manager should have said something about that. He arrived in 1996, so had built up enough 'credit in the bank' to be open with the supporters. Working with a tight budget always makes it difficult to compete for major honours. But nobody told the fans this, so they carried on paying top price for season tickets year after year.

In February 2013 Arsene Wenger went on a rant about how Arsenal fans will 'miss him' when he is gone. It was days after the club lost at home to Blackburn in the FA Cup, and just before they lost at home to Bayern Munich in the Champions League. It was a season in which the Gunners had also gone out of the League Cup thanks to Bradford of League Two.

Wenger promised that when he retires he will reveal a list of top clubs who have wanted to appoint him in the years he has been at Arsenal. He added that after so long at Arsenal, he deserves some respect.

Fans only want you to be loyal if you're good. There is no doubt Wenger has shown loyalty, but in the period after the Champions League final in 2006 you could question how good he has been in the job. Some Arsenal fans still stand by him and defend his record. Others don't. I suspect that Wenger's astonishing salary might be a reason he was reluctant to leave. Reports range from £6 million to £7 million a year. Not many across Europe could match that salary. Not many would want to pay Wenger such a salary given the trophy-less years he's forced the fans to endure at the Emirates.

No back-to-back Premier League titles, no Champions League, years and years without a trophy in the second half of his reign in north London but a host of highly paid, world-class players at his disposal for a large chunk of his time at Arsenal. Is that the sign of a truly great football manager?

The 2003–04 Invincibles

This Arsenal title-winning side were officially hailed as the best ever Premier League team but I think that is an absolute joke. In fact it's an insult to those who were better.

The Arsenal Invincibles – the side that went unbeaten in the 2003–04 season – saw that campaign out with tedious draws at Spurs and Portsmouth and at home to Birmingham to preserve the record. Arsenal played for draws – not the mark of a great side. Hard to criticise them going unbeaten in a season (and I won't mention Pires' dive for the equaliser against Pompey early in the season), but defeats in the FA Cup to Manchester United and in the Carling Cup to Middlesbrough (Toure, Parlour, Keown, Edu, Gilberto Silva, Ashley Cole, Reyes and Vieira all played a significant part over the two legs, so Wenger didn't 'play the kids') actually mean Arsenal were not totally unbeatable that season. They also lost to Chelsea in the Champions League. So the 'Invincibles' lost to *three* Premier League sides.

They weren't invincible then.

In that season Arsenal scored 73 goals. 20 less than champions Man City scored in 2011–12. Not impressive.

Arsenal ended up with 90 points at the end of their unbeaten campaign, five points less than Chelsea accumulated the following season. Makes a mockery of the Gunners' 2003–04 side being nominated as the best side in the first 20 years of the Premier League. How can they be the best when the following season another club amassed more points?

It's not hard to go unbeaten – New Zealand did it at the World Cup in 2010. Technically a side can get relegated if they go unbeaten in a whole season – 38 draws means 38 points and that spells relegation from the Premier League.

The Invincibles' greatness is a total myth. The 2002 Arsenal champions were a better side in my view.

David Beckham . . . was terrific

I'm writing this chapter on the evening David Beckham announced his retirement from football. On talkSPORT today we devoted the whole three hours of *Drive* to him, and from the announcement onwards the station's airtime was wall-to-wall Beckham.

I've been watching some of his best moments, and I wish we had a young English player of that quality coming through now. During the show I watched his first United goal – at Aston Villa on the first day of the season in 1995 (the game which inspired Alan Hansen to say Fergie 'won't win anything with kids' – they won the title). A square ball from the left reaches him in the middle of the pitch, Beckham controls it in an instant, is aware he has the space to flip it out of his feet, and he tees himself up for a 30-yard shot that flies past the goalkeeper into the back of the net.

In Manchester United's first game of the following season, Beckham launched himself into the football stratosphere. Receiving the ball just inside his own half, Beckham looked up, saw Wimbledon keeper Neil Sullivan off his line, and fired the ball into the net. It was a stunning goal. His body shape, the technique, the connection with the ball all contributed to making it the perfect strike. Imagination and execution both faultless. In 1999 Manchester United won the treble, and Beckham was runner-up to Rivaldo as World Player of the Year.

Beckham played in central midfield in the Champions League final against Bayern Munich because Scholes and Keane were both suspended. Many felt Beckham didn't play well, but not Sir Alex Ferguson who said in his autobiography: 'Unlike many reporters, I was happy with my decision to use Beckham in central midfield and Giggs on the right. Anybody who doesn't think Beckham was the most effective midfielder on the park was taking a strange view of the action. By comparison Stefan Effenberg was anonymous.'

Beckham took the two injury-time corners that led to the goals which won the Champions League for United.

Two years later he was World Player of the Year runner-up to Luis Figo, with the intricacies of the voting system failing to fully acknowledge that Beckham received more votes as the best player in the world. This was the year of the goal against Greece.

I was at Old Trafford for talkSPORT covering that World Cup qualifier. England were useless but David Beckham was keeping everybody's head above water. He covered every blade of grass that day; he worked non-stop, he was fantastic, the perfect captain. England were trailing when Beckham twisted and turned, taking on two Greece defenders down the left. He was fouled, he floated in a perfect ball, right-footed, inswinging towards the goal, really hard to defend and the keeper couldn't come for it. Teddy Sheringham got his head on it, and that was the equaliser.

But Greece went in front again and England had 20 minutes to find the goal to send them to the World Cup finals. The clock ticked by.

A 60-yard pass from Beckham to Andy Cole led to an England free-kick. Beckham grabbed the ball, but fired wide into the side-netting, when the crowd thought it was in.

'As he retired, David Beckham said he wanted to be known as a "hard worker". He was that, and so much more.'

Then another foul, this one close on 30 yards out. Beckham grabs it again, despite Sheringham's protests. It's in a central position; as he steps up the Greek keeper watches the body shape of Beckham and thinks he's going to put it to the keeper's left. So he steps that way, but Beckham's unique ability to disguise the direction comes to the fore again. He almost wraps his right boot around the ball and swings it to the keeper's right. Brilliant. Deceiving the keeper from those free-kicks became his trademark, especially at Real Madrid. If keepers didn't anticipate, they were dead. If they anticipated, he sent them the wrong way. To an extent, those Beckham free-kicks became unsaveable.

Also in 2001 Manchester United found themselves 3–0 down at half-time at Tottenham. Beckham came out for the second half like a man possessed. He passed to the overlapping Neville who crossed for Andy Cole to pull one back. His corner was headed in by Laurent Blanc for 2–3. And Beckham capped a superb display with a fearsome strike to complete the scoring – Solskjaer's pass, Beckham hanging out at the edge of the box having lost his marker, chests it down and fires home. United won 5–3.

Fast forward to 2002 at Upton Park and another 5–3 away win for United. This is probably my favourite Beckham goal. Scholes passes it perfectly into Beckham's path as he runs down the right. Just as he meets the ball on the corner of the box, he slows up, straightens his back, and lobs the ball over David James into the net. I could watch it over and over again. As the commentator said at the time: 'Just brilliant from England's captain, just brilliant.'

Big goals at big moments in big games from David Beckham. I've not even mentioned the passes and the crosses yet.

Over the years Beckham must have caused more arguments on talkSPORT than any other player. I think he's been a world-class footballer, and I get fed up with people having a go at him. Some ex-professionals are just jealous of Beckham – his money, his profile, his looks, his ability or his England caps. Whatever the reason it is obvious they don't like him and it's also blindingly obvious that it's down to pure jealousy. Maybe they didn't make the most of the talent they had and are jealous of someone who did.

Chris Waddle, for example, is one of my favourite players ever. He claimed Beckham wouldn't make it into the top 1000 Premier League players ever. I'm still waiting for him to name the long list of players ahead of Beckham. It's a ridiculous statement that cannot be backed up. He's entitled to an opinion, but he needs to name all those better players and back up each claim for his view to be taken seriously. Dare I suggest Waddle played at a time when he didn't earn the kind of money his talents would have commanded in the modern game? Let it go, Chris, you were a terrific player, don't bring others down for no reason.

But I do accept there are also some who actually don't think Beckham was a very good player. They're totally wrong though. I could point to medals and trophies but then the cynics might argue team-mates contributed more than Beckham. I could point to the fact that he played for three of the world's biggest clubs – Manchester United, Real Madrid and AC Milan. But then the cynics might say he was with those clubs to sell shirts.

If you're looking for the speed and skill of Lionel Messi then Beckham isn't your man. If you want a player who can torment defenders with his blistering pace, that's not Beckham.

But he had serious qualities.

He was heavily criticised after England's failed attempt to win the World Cup in 2006, but apart from a stunning display from Owen Hargreaves (he even scored a penalty, the only England taker to do so) after Wayne Rooney had been sent off against Portugal in the quarter-final, nobody played well. But let's focus on Beckham, who had to come off injured during that quarter-final.

In the opening game for England they played Paraguay. Beckham's free-kick was touched in by a Paraguayan defender and that was the winning goal.

In the second game we played a Trinidad & Tobago side who had held Sweden to a goalless draw in their first game, and who had absolutely no intention of doing anything but defend. The most negative side the World Cup has seen. They didn't score a goal in their three games, but shut up shop enough to take that draw against the Swedes. So England were frustrated until Peter Crouch broke the deadlock with a header towards the end of the game. David Beckham's cross was perfect. Beckham then passed to Gerrard who slammed in the second goal.

For England the stats read two games, three goals, three assists for David Beckham. England had qualified for the knockout phase.

On to Stuttgart for a game against Ecuador. England can't get their game together at all, there is no fluency. Ten minutes into the second half, with Sven-Goran Eriksson considering changes, England get a free-kick on the edge of the box. David Beckham has been in this situation before, and he takes responsibility again. His curling shot beats the keeper and goes in off the inside of the post, and Beckham's goal wins the game for England.

So he ended the tournament with three assists and a match-winning goal. Not a bad return for someone who had a poor tournament. The truth is no England players performed at the World Cup in 2006, but for me David Beckham's contribution was a positive.

And this to me is the mark of a great player: even when he wasn't on top of his game, even when he wasn't fully fit, David Beckham still made a significant contribution.

Somehow there are people who ignore that, and focus on the fact that he hasn't got blistering pace, and it's as if they believe you cannot be a top player unless you're lightning quick. Or they go on about the so-called 'Beckham circus', or 'Brand Beckham'. Let's judge him on his football ability. Top player. And after being jettisoned by Steve McClaren in 2006, Beckham never gave up on England, never spat his dummy out. He was prepared to play for the foolish McClaren once the manager had admitted his mistake. By then it was too late to save England's Euro 2008 qualifying campaign.

Beckham gave up valuable time with his family to follow Fabio Capello's orders and play in Europe (for AC Milan, twice), after his main season with LA Galaxy had ended.

Total commitment to the England cause – and don't tell me he did that for 'Brand Beckham'. He's a multi-gazillionaire and one of the most recognisable men on the planet, so money and profile play a part but are not the motivation. He loves football and he loves England. Passionate England fans appreciate that, and that's why Beckham always got the biggest cheer at Wembley for England games. No one else came close. Even if he was just a sub warming up, the England fans at Wembley loved him.

Some Manchester United fans debate whether he is a legend at Old Trafford. The sceptics point to the fall-out with Sir Alex Ferguson and question his commitment to the club.

The truth about his relationship with Sir Alex is clear: United were knocked out of the Cup by Arsenal, Fergie blamed Beckham for the second Gunners goal, Beckham felt bullied and swore at the manager who then kicked a boot which hit Beckham above the eye, causing it to bleed. Beckham lunged at Sir Alex and had to be restrained. The boss apologised to Beckham as he left the dressing room after getting changed. But a few months later he moved to Real Madrid. Both parties behaved in a way which was unacceptable. Beckham's lasting issues were two-fold: firstly he wanted the apology from Sir Alex to be public, not just a quiet word in the dressing room. Secondly Sir Alex had told Beckham's mother Sandra around that time that 'the trouble with David is that everyone sucks up to him now.' Beckham felt the Manchester United manager was no longer judging him on his football ability.

He may have fallen out with Sir Alex but I think it's hard to make a case supporting the belief that Beckham isn't a Manchester United legend. I was at the Champions League tie at Old Trafford when he came on as a substitute for an already well-beaten AC Milan side. The United fans gave him a fantastic ovation and sang '*Fergie sign him up!*' After almost setting up a goal for United with a poor backpass, Beckham then forced a decent save from Edwin van der Sar with a well-struck volley. The United fans were almost willing it to go in. As he walked off the field, Beckham returned the applause he was given, and then in a moment of unplanned spontaneity, he picked up a green and gold 'anti-Glazers' scarf that had been thrown onto the field and wrapped it round his neck. He knew what it meant. True United fans acknowledge his legendary status at the club.

At Real Madrid the club was desperate to win something. They had been European Champions in 1998, 2000 and 2002. They had won La Liga in 2001 and 2003. Beckham arrived in the summer of 2003 and the trophies dried up.

His England career seemed finished after the World Cup in 2006 when he was left out by Steve McClaren, his coach at Manchester United during the treble season in 1999, and his coach with England for the previous six years. Beckham decided that with no international commitments he was free to quit Europe and head for the USA two years ahead of schedule. The decision was made around Christmas 2006 and Real Madrid were so angry, Capello was ordered to drop him by the President Ramon Calderon, and the Sporting Director Predrag Mijatovic. But with Barcelona on course for the title, Beckham was recalled by Capello and Madrid went on a run to seal the title on the final day, the club's first major title for four years.

His contribution to the run of form was unquestionable, and he was popular with fans and team-mates for his work ethic as well as ability. The sceptics sneered when he hobbled off in the crucial final game against Real Mallorca, and was replaced by Jose Antonio Reyes, whose two goals confirmed Madrid as champions. But most fans thought it was tough luck on a player who had shown character on and off the field.

The MLS beckoned for Beckham and the attention was,

according to his first coach at LA Galaxy, Frank Yallop, 'wild'. He said that for the first time there were hundreds of photographers at games and that 'everyone's head was spinning' and 'it was difficult to concentrate on the soccer'.

Yallop's view is that David Beckham made a 'bold' and 'brave' move heading to America, and that it was a success. He said: 'The MLS wasn't as big before David came. I don't think the interest from non-soccer people was as high. He filled stadiums and made people aware of the game and the Galaxy brand. It was a fantastic move getting him here and a big move from David himself.'

One of Beckham's team-mates in LA, Mike Magee, said: 'This league wouldn't be close to where it is today without him. It's 100 per cent because of him.'

On the pitch, Yallop and then Ruud Gullit lost their jobs coaching LA Galaxy, and then former USA coach Bruce Arena arrived and found the formula for success. It included Beckham, sometimes wide, sometimes in central midfeld, but always impacting games. The standard of the league is questionable of course, but the quality of Beckham's contribution isn't.

Galaxy won back-to-back MLS Cups in Beckham's final two years at the club. Bruce Arena said of his on-field contribution: 'He performed under pressure and the magnificent skill he demonstrated in free-kicks and passing was very special and something we'll never forget.'

Magee also said this about Beckham: 'On the field things speak for themselves. I think a lot more needs to be made of the kind of man he is, the person he is, and the father and the friend and everything. It's a pleasure to know him.'

So after success in the USA with the Galaxy and blasting 'soccer' into the consciousness of everyone Stateside including Tom Cruise, Beckham came back to Europe. Signing for Paris St Germain might have seemed like an easy choice to make but this club wanted him, and they didn't need to sell shirts. The previous season PSG had been expected to win the title in France but were pipped at the end by little Montpellier. It was a shock, and Carlo Ancelotti didn't want it to happen again. So he brought in Beckham, a proven winner, to help see PSG over the finishing line. And they sealed the title. He wasn't the standout player, but his experience, his gravitas and his calmness in the middle of the pitch, helped them hugely. In a key game at home to Marseille, PSG were leading 1–0, but looked certain to concede; Marseille had them on the back foot. Beckham came on and his first three touches sent Paris forward, they were key balls into the opposition half that found a team-mate. That's exactly what PSG needed at that time of the game, and they went on to win it 2–0.

The French title was Beckham's 19th major honour.

He gave his salary to charity whilst at Paris. Somehow people still contrived to turn that into something he deserved criticism for. What a mean and vindictive world it can be sometimes.

I'm not bothered about sarongs and mohicans. I'm not bothered who he's married to. I'm interested in the football. Having said that, I interviewed him once and we spoke at length about our children and the joys of fatherhood. He seemed pretty normal to me.

As he retired, David Beckham said he wanted to be known as a 'hard worker'. He was that, and so much more.

We all love football. But we all know some professionals see it as a job and they somehow lose the passion for the game that fans will never lose.

The story goes that Beckham cried when he heard Manchester United wanted to sign him for six years as a teenager. In his autobiography he says he 'choked back tears' after one row with Sir Alex Ferguson. Whilst on loan to AC Milan he says he 'almost cried' when he heard they had been drawn with Manchester United in the Champions League. And as he walked off a football pitch for the final time at the Parc des Princes after captaining PSG to a 3–1 victory over Brest, the tears flowed again.

Football only makes grown men cry if they really love the game; and despite being worth millions and being ascribed celebrity status, David Beckham truly loved football.

Wales' World Cup side 1958

The last time Wales reached the World Cup finals was way back in 1958, and the passing of time means that there are people in villages in Welsh valleys who would have you believe that the Welsh side in 1958 was the best football team in the history of the game.

It's a total myth.

The truth is astonishing. Sure, in the quarter-final against Brazil injury had deprived Wales of the services of three-times Scudetto winner John Charles, a true great of the game, unquestionably. But those boyos who claim that Wales would have thrashed Pele and Brazil had Charles been fit, are living in a dreamland waving leeks and daffodils.

Wales were incredibly lucky to get out of the initial group stage at that World Cup. Drawn in a group with

Hungary, Mexico and host nation Sweden, Wales drew all three of their games. After the Mexico match the Welsh press described the display as 'shocking' and said Charles had 'flopped'. And in the final group game, where Wales needed a win to qualify against a Sweden side who were already through, manager Jimmy Murphy played a defensive game to guarantee a 0–0 draw and the prospect of a play-off, rather than make certain with victory. Wales were jeered off and Charles himself said that he 'felt sorry for the people who had paid to see the game'. Even the Swedish press called Charles the 'flop' of the World Cup.

Wales ended up level on three points with Hungary in the group, behind leaders Sweden. Two qualified, and nowadays goal difference would apply: the Hungarians had scored six, and conceded three, whilst the Welsh had scored two and conceded two. However, World Cup rules at that time meant goal difference was ignored and the two teams level on points had a play-off, and Wales won 2–1 against a Hungary side forced to make four changes after thrashing Mexico 4–0 two days earlier.

So at the tournament Wales didn't exactly wow the crowds. But Wales shouldn't have even been at that World Cup. They were drawn randomly from a list of runners-up from European qualifying games to face a newly born Israel side who had no opponents in the African–Asian group after a flurry of withdrawals on political grounds. The Welsh beat Israel in that play-off, although *The Times* reported that 'what little football there was came from Israel', and went on to criticise the Welsh: 'The less said about Wales the better . . . they gave a perfect exhibition of what not to do.'

Some will tell you about the heroic Wales team of 1958, deprived of Charles, gallantly bowing out to eventual winners Pele and Brazil in the quarter-finals. But don't forget Wales didn't even qualify properly, and shouldn't have even made it out of their group once they'd jammed their way to Sweden.

Italy's four World Cup wins

1934 – With fascism at its height under Mussolini, Italy hosted and won the World Cup in 1934. But not without controversy. First of all, holders Uruguay refused to travel to Europe to defend their trophy in protest at the Europeans not travelling to Uruguay four years earlier.

Italy and Czechoslovakia met in the final in the National Stadium in Rome, with Swede Ivan Eklind chosen to referee the game. Eklind had refereed at only three games prior to the final, and shortly before kickoff he visited Mussolini in his private box.

Frantisek Planicka was the Czech goalkeeper, and he was quoted as saying: 'We have been cheated out of victory. The atmosphere in the stadium was tense. Eklind was in Mussolini's box. We didn't know what was discussed there. But we had an inkling. The man stopped clean passes, blowing his whistle, and overlooked bad fouls.'

Another key member of the Czech team, tournament top scorer Oldrich Nejedly, said: 'This man was anything but impartial.'

Italy won the game 2–1 after extra-time. Not convinced that Italy had a helping hand from the man in the middle?

Well, Eklind was banned from refereeing for life after the final. Let's get real, Mussolini wanted Italy to win, he was after world domination on and off the pitch. And a man who killed thousands to achieve his aim was always going to be able to 'persuade' a shop manager from Sweden to give a few decisions against the Czechs.

'Italy should be embarrassed about those two World Cup wins in the 1930s. An evil fascist bully won them, not the best football team.'

Italy's Luis Monti was starting his second successive World Cup final. Remarkably he had played for Argentina when they lost the final in 1930. He switched countries and then represented Italy, who also had a Brazilian in their squad. Anfilogino Guarisi had played and indeed scored for the Brazil national team before he signed for Lazio in 1931. The rules were so relaxed back then that he was allowed to play for Italy and became the first Brazilian to win the World Cup.

1938 – This one is truly horrible. Held in France, where many Italians had fled from fascism, Mussolini wanted to show the refugees that they could not hide. France was desperate to hold out against fascism. When the French played Italy in the quarter-final, Mussolini's side wore black shirts – fascist colours – and gave the fascist salute before kickoff.

Italy made it to the final in Paris where they faced Hungary. Prior to kickoff Mussolini sent a message to the Italy players saying simply: 'Win or die!' It could have been a message of support, a motivational mantra. But would you take a chance with a murderer like Mussolini?

No, me neither. He had executed all sorts of people – artists, actors and entertainers – so why should footballers be exempt?

Italy took an early lead, but two minutes later Hungary equalised. Rumour has it that at this point the Italians got scared and told the Hungarian players about Mussolini's threatening message. Italy were leading 3–1 at half-time, and eventually won the game 4–2. Hungarian goalkeeper Antal Szabo reportedly said after the game: 'I may have let in four goals, but at least I saved their lives.' A Hungarian journalist in the 1970s tracked down those members of the Hungary team for the final in 1938 who were still alive. According to his report, all of them said they had deliberately thrown the game to save the lives of the Italian players.

Italy should be embarrassed about those two World Cup wins in the 1930s. An evil fascist bully won them, not the best football team.

Now this may be controversial, but I don't count World Cups before the Second World War. That's because England didn't enter. I'm not so arrogant that I assume England would have won those tournaments, but without doubt they would have made some sort of significant contribution.

In 1928, FIFA announced that it would be holding the first World Cup in Uruguay in 1930. The FA's representative there was Charles Sutcliffe, and he apparently said: 'I don't care a brass farthing about the improvement of the game in France, Belgium, Austria or Germany. FIFA does not appeal to me. An organisation where such football associations as those of Uruguay and Paraguay, Brazil and Egypt, Bohemia and Pan Russia are co-equal with England,

Scotland, Wales and Ireland seems to me to be a case of magnifying the midgets.'

That's right, he said 'magnifying the midgets'. Up the empire, Mr Sutcliffe, Rule Britannia! But that attitude robbed England of three chances to win the World Cup when the team was arguably at its strongest.

Anyway, back to Italy . . .

1982 – The year Brazil should have won the World Cup. But Italy, thanks to the goals of a man caught up in a football betting scandal, somehow lifted the trophy. Zico, Socrates, Falcao, Junior and Eder . . . all awesome talents worthy of winning the World Cup under Tele Santana. While Brazil's movement, passing, individual skill and finishing brought them ten goals in the group stage, Italy were rubbish. They didn't win any of their three games, scoring only two goals, and scraped through by virtue of the fact that Cameroon were only slightly worse than Italy. In fact in the final group game a victory over the Africans would have guaranteed Italy safe passage through, but they couldn't even manage that, surrendering the lead less than 60 seconds after taking it. In the end 1–1 was enough for the Italians although it should have been a different story. Earlier in the group Peru and Cameroon had drawn 0–0; Roger Milla had a goal ruled out that was clearly onside and should have stood.

After scraping through Italy got their act together and beat Argentina (with Maradona) and Brazil (thanks to some astonishingly bad defending), before going on to beat West Germany 3–1 in the final. The consolation for the football purists who believe Brazil were the 'true' winners was the awesome goal celebration of Marco Tardelli in the final. He summed up how we would all feel if we scored a goal for our country in a World Cup final. Having said that, Brazil scored 15 goals, while Italy scored 12 despite playing two more games.

So in short, the best team in the world did not win the World Cup in 1982.

And what about Paolo Rossi, the Italian hero of the tournament?

The first article in a December 1982 edition of *Shoot!*, the popular football magazine in England of the time, highlights the contenders for European Footballer of the Year. The final winner by a landslide – he secured more than double the votes of the runner-up, the Frenchman Alain Giresse – was Paolo Rossi, who took the Ballon d'Or thanks to three decent weeks of football and six goals. Rossi had hardly played for two years prior to the 1982 World Cup.

Back then any form of betting on football matches was illegal in Italy so in the late 1970s two friends, Trinca and Cruciani – one ran a restaurant the other had a fruit and veg shop – were acting as bookies. They kept losing money, and they thought certain games were fixed. So they decided to start bribing players. But those players didn't deliver the results, and others in the undercover betting world in Italy started getting suspicious, so the two guys went public.

They claimed they had paid Rossi two million lire – around £1,000 – to ensure a game finished 0–0. But it finished 2–2 and Rossi scored. With little evidence against him Rossi was cleared by a criminal court, but a soccer tribunal banned him from playing for two years. His supporters said he had been made a scapegoat. Rossi always maintained he was innocent.

In the middle of his ban he moved from Perugia to Juventus for £1.1 million, and after his ban he played the last three games of the 1981–82 season when Juve won the title. Rossi had played well at the 1978 World Cup when Italy finished fourth, and the national team manager Enzo Bearzot picked him for Spain 1982, saying Rossi was 'an opportunist in the box', but the press were critical, especially after Rossi didn't deliver in the group games. Italy drew against Poland, Cameroon and Peru and scraped through because they scored one more goal than the Africans. But then came Rossi's moment of glory.

The second phase in Spain consisted of four groups of three, and only the winners went through to the semifinals. Rossi again failed to score in the first game when Italy beat Argentina 2–1. Brazil then beat their South American neighbours 3–1, which meant Italy had to win the final game in the group.

Only five minutes had gone when Rossi ended his drought, heading home a wonderful Cabrini cross to the far post. Brazil captain Socrates started a move in his own half which led to him beating Zoff at his near post to level seven minutes later. Then Rossi capitalised on a Brazilian blunder to fire home from the edge of the box to give the Italians a half-time lead.

Halfway through the second half Brazil equalised again through a shot from 18 yards out from Falcao – who my mother for a long time believed was actually called Fat Cow. But Rossi would not be denied. He got his hat-trick, and the winner, with 16 minutes left. Tardelli fired in a shot, Rossi flicked it past the keeper. Some thought Zoff clawed Oscar's late header back from over the line but Italy won 3–2.

This was possibly the second-best Brazil side ever, behind the 1970 winners, and Paolo Rossi's goals had beaten them. He then scored both in the 2–0 win against Poland in the semi – he tapped in a free-kick from close range for the first, and then headed in Bruno Conti's perfect cross for the second. In the final against West Germany he opened the scoring, heading home Gentile's cross. Italy won 3–1, Rossi ended the tournament as top scorer. A man banned from Italian football for two years had turned into a national hero and World Cup superstar just a couple of years later. Doesn't sit right, does it?

2006 – On the face of it there wasn't a lot wrong with Italy's win here. OK, it was won thanks to a penalty shoot-out, which is hardly ideal, but that's within the rules. OK, it's true that arguably their best player at the tournament was Mauro Camoranesi, who's about as Italian as Yorkshire pudding. Born in Argentina, he moved to Italy to play for Verona when he was 23. He didn't get a call-up for Argentina so he played for Italy instead. He didn't sing the national anthem, and when he spoke into a TV camera in the midst of the celebrations in Berlin, he spoke in Spanish and dedicated the victory to the people back in his neighbourhood on the outskirts of Buenos Aires – around 7,000 miles from Rome. He even said he still felt Argentine.

That's probably because he was.

But in the crazy world of FIFA rules on international football (when it is actually possible for the Nigerian Emmanuel Olisadebe to play for Poland, for the thoroughly Brazilian Eduardo Alves da Silva to pretend to be from Croatia, and for the paella-eating, San Miguel-drinking, siesta-taking Manuel Almunia to be eligible to keep goal for England), Camoranesi and Italy are breaking no rules.

You could look at the way Italy were given a penalty in the last minute against Australia earlier in the tournament, Grosso literally falling over Lucas Neill, and claim the Italians didn't deserve to go through. But also in that game, Marco Materazzi was wrongly red-carded so it's not even for that reason that Italy's 2006 World Cup win is under the spotlight.

In fact I'll pay tribute to Italy. I was in Dortmund for the semi against Germany and it was the best game of football I have ever witnessed. It was brilliant, open football, from both sides.

No, the real reason I can't have Italy's World Cup win in 2006 is because of Zinedine Zidane. The French hadn't exactly set the tournament alight under Dommenech, but in Zidane they had a player capable of magic on the big stage – two goals in the 1998 World Cup final, a goal in the quarter and a goal in the semi of Euro 2000, and an unbelievable finish for the winner in the 2002 Champions League final for Real Madrid. Zidane had already coolly chipped a penalty in off the underside of the bar in the final, but with the match all square and extra-time running out, Zidane lost the plot. After Materazzi pulled his shirt for the millionth time during the game, Zidane asked him if he wanted the shirt. Materazzi said he'd rather have Zidane's 'whore of a sister', so Zidane, in his last ever act on a football field, headbutted the Italian in the chest and was sent off. Both sides saw out the remaining ten minutes of the game and Italy won the shoot-out.

The football romantics had written a different script with Zidane scoring a stunning last-minute winner in his final game, rather than being sent off for violent conduct. We'll never know what would have happened had he stayed on, but we do know Zidane was more than capable of something special, especially in a big game.

It is pure luck for Italy that Zidane saw the rouge mist. It wasn't inspired management from Lippi, and certainly wasn't part of any Italian game-plan (although cynical Italian tactics are nothing new).

So in short, Italy's Mussolini-inspired wins in 1934 and 1938 should be wiped from the record because the evidence of cheating is overwhelming; in 1982 they were not the best side in the world and their top scorer had just completed a two-year football ban; and in 2006 they won it because one of the best players the world has ever seen, well, how can I say, 'il a perdu le plot.'

Italy's four gold stars really aren't all that.

FOOTNOTE – EURO 68

I must throw in Italy's ridiculous European Championship victory in 1968. Astonishingly before penalty shoot-outs arrived, drawn games were decided by the toss of a coin. This may seem hard to believe but it is absolutely true. Imagine that happening today? Imagine Liverpool's 2005 Champions League final in Istanbul being decided by Steven Gerrard calling heads and the coin landing tails. That incredible fightback rendered meaningless by the way a coin falls. Absurd.

In the 1968 European Championships, Italy drew 0–0 after extra-time with the USSR in the semi-final. The referee tossed a coin and the USSR captain Albert Shesternyov called it wrong and Italy – the hosts – went through. That was it! USSR went home! Their defeat had nothing to do with football. The final finished Italy 1 Yugoslavia 1 after extra-time, but rather than tossing a coin they came back two days later for a replay which the Italians won 2–0. So the semi was decided on the coin toss, but the final went to a replay. Can Italy honestly say they were worthy European champions in 1968?

Ashley Cole – spoilt brat or brilliant footballer?

He shot someone at the Chelsea training ground with an air-rifle, he has been at the centre of some shockingly disgusting tabloid stories about his private life, he called the Football Association 'a bunch of twats', he's tweeted abuse to fans, he was found guilty in the tapping-up row before his move to Chelsea, and he admitted he nearly swerved off the North Circular when he was offered 'only' £55,000 a week by the Arsenal board of directors.

But Ashley Cole is a brilliant footballer, and has won everything – literally everything – you can win at club level. Three Premier League titles, seven FA Cups, a League Cup, a Champions League and a Europa League. He has been in the PFA Team of the Year four times, in the UEFA Team of the Year twice, and he's won Chelsea's players' Player of the Year award twice as well as being England's Player of the Year in 2010.

Surely nobody questions how good he is? Read this from Carlo Ancelotti, who managed him at Chelsea: 'He is highly motivated, a very good player and a very good professional. I think everyone who appreciates football should appreciate him because he is also a very fair player. He never shouts at referees or makes bad tackles on opponents. On the pitch he is an example.' He even won Chelsea's Goal of the Season against Sunderland in the 2009–10 season. He ran in behind the right-back, onto a long ball into the box, controlled it, dummied and sent the centre-half out of the ground before flipping a shot beyond the keeper.

Ashley Cole has been first choice at two clubs at a time when both were winning trophies and competing at the top. In fact, it may be pure coincidence but Arsenal stopped competing at the serious end when Ashley Cole left – his last game for the Gunners was the Champions League final in 2006. He then won two trophies in his first season at Chelsea.

So why did Arsenal sell him? We'll come to the tapping-up row later but first let's address the issue of Cole nearly crashing his car because Arsenal offered him £5,000 a week less than he wanted. There are two sides to every story and when presented in such dramatic fashion, this version of events, albeit from Cole himself in his book *My Defence*, makes Cole look like a spoilt brat who doesn't know how lucky he is to be offered loads of money to play football.

When put into context though, the story is very different and I actually have some sympathy for him.

Cole had signed his first professional contract aged 19 and it was worth £25,000 a week. He thought he was in dreamland earning that kind of money. But he also became a first-team regular at Highbury at that age – 33 appearances (29 starts) for Arsenal in the 2000–01 season – and made his England debut in March 2001 in a World Cup qualifier in Albania alongside the likes of Scholes, Beckham and Owen. It wasn't until the end of the 2003–04 Invincibles season that Arsene Wenger said to the board that Cole's wages were behind the other players and needed to be reviewed.

Arsenal's first offer made by David Dein to the player in June 2004 was a £10,000-a-week increase to £35,000 a week. Cole wasn't impressed: 'I couldn't understand why, according to David Dein, I was worth only about half the wage of the players around me . . . Mr Dein carried on, telling me how I would be set for life and it was a huge wage for a lad my age. I wondered if I was going to get a pat on the head and a lollipop for being good if I accepted it.'

Dein told him it was 'a generous offer'; Cole wondered if they 'would treat Thierry or Patrick in this way'. Cole was left to conclude that 'maybe Arsenal drew a distinction between a son of the club and one of the foreign imports.' He said: 'I was discovering that if you're on apprentice wages and come through the ranks, you don't get a bigger jump in wage than if you'd been scouted and transferred in. If the dressing room was supposed to be a level playing field, and my input was to be recognised, the new offer was a slap in the face, not a pat on the back.'

In fact the new offer was much less than half the weekly wage of some of his team-mates: certainly Patrick Vieira and Sol Campbell were earning £99,000 a week – they were two of the top three earners in the Premier League (the other was Roy Keane).

The new season started with 24-year-old Cole still earning £25,000 a week – a deal he had signed as a teenager. The Gunners started the season on fire, continuing where they had left off. Cole even scored the winner at Manchester City with a 'deft flick from the outside of his boot' in a game where he was described by the *Guardian* as Arsenal's 'most menacing attacker'. High praise considering Bergkamp, Henry, Ljungberg and Reyes were all playing.

By December 2004 Cole told his agents that he wanted a five-year contract and £60,000-a-week wages. They told him he was a £20 million player and could command more than £80,000 a week. Beckham, Lampard, Terry, and Rooney were all earning £80,000 a week or more – and plenty of Arsenal players were on significantly higher wages than what Cole was asking for. Even Patrick Vieira told him he should ask for more. In his book, Cole says Vieira told him: 'Don't be stupid. Don't sign for anything less than between £80,000 and £100,000 a week.' The day after Arsenal won 1–0 at Portsmouth (Sol Campbell scored a 25-yard winner) it was Cole's birthday, 20 December. According to Cole in his book *My Defence*, that was when his agent told him he had 'shaken' on a £60,000-a-week deal. Dein would recommend that to the board and had apparently said he was confident the board would approve it. Dein later said no agreement was made. In mid-January the board met and decided to offer Cole £55,000 a week. Before that offer was made to the player, Cole told the *London Evening Standard*: 'As for the contract, what I want is to be paid on my ability and what I've achieved. I am not greedy – I want to make that clear.'

It is of course open to interpretation, but an Arsenal regular winning trophies and a firm fixture in the national side on £25,000 a week in 2005 was unquestionably being underpaid. And while all those around Cole – team-mates and agents – were telling him to ask for £80,000 a week at least, he asked for £60,000 a week. In everyday life it's a lot of money, but in football terms Cole was being underval-ued by Arsenal. In a purely footballing context it is hard to say he was being greedy given all the factors. And for their own reasons, the Arsenal board seemed prepared to sell Cole over the 'missing' £5,000 a week he believed he had been promised. Yet he was a player making a significant contribution to Arsenal's success.

'. . . he's an excellent footballer, one of the most successful English footballers in the game and I prefer to judge him on that.'

Cole's agent was standing alongside David Dein when he phoned to tell the player £55,000 a week was Arsenal's 'best and final offer'. Given that Cole had told his mother about the £60,000-a-week offer, he was obviously shocked that Dein had, he felt, gone back on this promise. Hence the line in the book: 'I nearly swerved off the road.'

Did he nearly crash because he was offered *only* £55,000 a week? No, of course not. He nearly crashed because he felt a promise had been broken. He also felt the club were saying he wasn't as valuable as other players in the team. In 2003–04 and 2004–05, the time all the contract negotiations were being thrashed out, Ashley Cole was selected by his fellow professionals in the PFA Team of the Year. The only other Arsenal player to appear in both was Thierry Henry.

Cole felt he had no future at Arsenal, but on 27 January 2005 he told his agent, Jonathan Barnett, he couldn't imagine playing against them. So they decided to look at the possibility of a move abroad. There and then, Barnett quickly arranged a meeting with international agent Pini Zahavi, and off they went to see him at a London hotel.

Cole's meeting ended, the Chelsea duo Mourinho and Kenyon walked in and Cole admitted they chatted for '15–20 minutes'.

Maybe Cole and Barnett should have left sooner; maybe they shouldn't have chatted at all. It's clear there were some serious mistakes in what some newspapers reported about the meeting – for example the car Cole was in and the time he arrived at the hotel. But it wasn't a good situation for Cole to find himself in – unhappy but under contract at Arsenal, and then being seen in a hotel room with the manager of Chelsea, the chief executive of Chelsea, and two agents wasn't his brightest moment. Does it constitute what Cole was eventually found guilty of, approaching another club while under contract with a different club and without that club's written consent? Possibly.

Arsenal's pursuit of the case was understandably robust and relentless. They wanted to get Chelsea. But at the same time they also 'got' Ashley Cole. He became a demon in the eyes of the fans and Arsenal were quite happy to let him take the heat and be the villain.

At the end of the tapping-up scandal he was fined £100,000 – four week's wages. It was later reduced on appeal to £75,000.

There is plenty of reason to believe Cole was guilty, but plenty of evidence to suggest he wasn't. But even if he did approach Chelsea, if you felt your employer had broken a promise to you, it's fair to say you would feel less loyal to that employer. With the £55,000-a-week offer, Cole felt he was being told to go. So he was sorting out his future.

I can't and won't defend the kind of immaturity that led to an intern at the Chelsea training ground, 21-year-old Tom Cowan, being shot in the side in February 2011 as Cole handled an air-rifle. Cole, who reportedly took the gun into the training ground, was said to have been 'larking around' with the gun. I'm absolutely not defending him but it has been blown out of all proportion. It wasn't like that. It was the kind of gun you don't need a licence for, and he didn't intend for it to go off. It was still incredibly stupid.

And those tabloid stories? The stuff with Cheryl? It's either lies or not really any of our business. He didn't sleep with a team-mate's wife now, did he? Some of the tabloid stuff simply isn't true. And why their marriage broke down isn't fully known – who knows exactly what is said and done in a private relationship? I'm pretty certain that when a relationship is breaking down people do things they regret, make bad decisions, and sometimes find themselves in so much despair they are unable to take the right and proper course of action. You're a very lucky person if you've never been in that place.

As for his tweets to fans, again he has acted stupidly. But a good number of Twitter users are horrible, nasty, foul-mouthed, jealous individuals and sometimes, if your skin isn't thick enough, that can get to you. I can imagine the abuse he takes on Twitter, and what he gave back would be amoebic by comparison with the volume of insults he receives. Maybe he shouldn't be on Twitter, but how sad is it if a top player's best course of action is to cut off communication between himself and the fans?

As for calling the Football Association a 'bunch of twats', I would be fairly certain that at some point in the life of every football fan in England they have also had similar feelings towards our FA. We applauded Brian Clough for being forthright and honest, so why would we castigate Ashley Cole for being exactly the same?

Critics have banged on about the 'right behaviour',

what he should and shouldn't do, but at the end of it all he's an excellent footballer, one of the most successful English footballers in the game and I prefer to judge him on that.

When he captained England after his 100th cap against the Republic of Ireland in May 2013 many questioned whether he was fit for the role, given all the controversy surrounding him during his career. I felt sorry for him again – here was a top player, who had all the club medals he could wish for but with no desire whatsoever to give up on England. He had even been booed after giving away a goal with a wayward pass against Kazakhstan in October 2008. He said at the time: 'It was difficult when they booed. I'm a normal person, I'm just like you and just like everyone else – I have feelings and thoughts. So of course it hurt, I'm not going to sit here and say it didn't.'

Ashley Cole almost always plays well for England, always shows commitment and passion; I don't remember him pulling out of squads too often, even for friendlies.

And after captaining England that night against Ireland, he said it was 'the number one' moment in his career. In the post-match interview on ITV, Cole said: 'It was a very proud moment for me and one I'll never forget. I wanted to be captain, it was a dream come true. I've lived a little boy's dream today.'

My son Jamie, 12 at the time, was watching it with me. He heard Cole's words, turned to me and said: 'That was inspirational. He's basically saying you can do anything if you put your mind to it.'

He's not exactly a role model, Ashley Cole. But he's far from the demon some make him out to be.

Jose Mourinho's
. . . a lucky manager

If it's all about medals and trophies and winning the undying love and respect of some of the players you manage, then Jose Mourinho is the king.

There have been coaches in the past who have been winners and have been rightly applauded for the quality of football their teams played. Rinus Michels with Ajax is perhaps the best example, Johan Cruyff at Barcelona, and later Pep Guardiola at the Nou Camp, and Sir Alex Ferguson at Manchester United are others.

Mourinho cannot be put in the same category. His style is rigid and formulaic. Sometimes it's labelled negative or defensive, and then you look at the amount of goals his teams score and that accusation is hard to substantiate.

So all I can give you is my interpretation.

Mourinho's teams basically have a top-quality playmaker, and a great finisher, and he demands that the rest become defenders.

At Chelsea he had Frank Lampard and Didier Drogba and the rest were defenders. This is why Arjen Robben decided he had to leave. Ahead of the 2010 Champions League final between Jose's Inter Milan and Robben's Bayern Munich, the Dutchman said of his old boss: 'He puts out a winning team, it doesn't matter if it's done with nice football or not.'

Inter won that final 2–0. Mourinho had his goalscorer – Argentine Diego Milito got both and was second highest scorer in Serie A that season as Inter won the treble – and he had his playmaker, the brilliant Dutchman Wesley

'Mourinho is a winner, but he wins without loving football.'

Sneijder. The rest were defenders. Take Samuel Eto'o as an example. At Barcelona he had scored over a hundred goals in five seasons, and scored in each of their Champions League final victories (against Arsenal in 2006 and Manchester United in 2009). The Cameroonian's international scoring rate is a goal every other game.

But Mourinho turned him into a defender. Any attacking Inter did in the final in 2010 centred around Sneijder and Milito. At one point I forgot Eto'o was playing. In his first season at Inter he scored 12 goals in 32 league games and two goals in 13 in the Champions League.

I've seen worse, but compare those figures with what he was doing at Barcelona: 30 goals in 36 league games in 2008–09, and six in 12 in Europe. In fact Eto'o always averaged more than a goal every other game in La Liga for Barça. His goal glut came to an abrupt end under Mourinho. As former Republic of Ireland captain, and my former colleague at talkSPORT, Andy Townsend said during ITV's coverage of the Champions League final, at times Eto'o was 'playing like a full-back'.

And as a proud England fan I feel particularly disappointed about Joe Cole's development under Jose. At West Ham United, Cole – in my opinion – showed enough to suggest he would be the player around whom future England teams would be built. A gifted passer, he could run with the ball, and control the ball. All that was needed was some physical development which would come with age. But at Chelsea Joe Cole was asked to be defensive. In October 2004, Cole was fighting for a regular place in the Chelsea team under Mourinho. A Sunday afternoon

Premier League game at home to Liverpool saw Cole on the substitutes' bench. But Drogba was injured in the first half, and Cole seized his chance. After 64 minutes, he flicked a header from a Lampard free-kick past Chris Kirkland, and that was the winning goal.

But it wasn't enough for Mourinho, who said after the game: 'Joe Cole scored a goal which was very important. He played really well in terms of attacking dynamism. When he scored the goal the game finished for him. After that I needed 11 players for my defensive organisation but I had just 10. Joe can be a regular but he has to improve when the team needs him to be part of a defensive organisation.'

Joe Cole was substitute for the next game at Manchester City. Chelsea lost 1–0.

Mourinho has a system which can win honours. Most of his players love it because they get medals at the end of it. And he perfected this system at Chelsea where Lampard cost £12 million (although he was already at Stamford Bridge when Jose arrived), and Drogba cost an astonishing £24 million.

Then at Inter, Sneijder cost £15 million, and Milito £22 million – at the age of 30. So Mourinho's methods rely on having considerable sums of money to spend on the only two attacking players in his team. The emphasis is very much on defending, which of course is part of the game. But to Mourinho it is the key. His teams defend and defend, and then hit on the counter with their expensive players. His philosophy is to stop the opposition, rather than control the game.

In the Champions League final 2010, Bayern Munich had 66 per cent possession. Inter just put men behind the ball to stop the German champions doing anything with it. It worked, but it was impossible to enjoy as a neutral. You may say that doesn't matter, but it does in the context of this debate. The truly great managers win trophies with style. I'm not saying Mourinho isn't a winner – his record is irrefutable. But he's no tactical master. That Inter side will not be remembered as one of the great champion teams of Europe. Whereas Real Madrid 2002, Barcelona 2009 and Bayern Munich 2013 all gave a footballing masterclass; they won with style in a way which will remain in the memory.

Mourinho arrived at Real Madrid tasked with dethroning Barcelona from the very peak of world football. His first game in La Liga ended 0–0.

His first Clasico ended 5–0 to Barcelona in the Nou Camp; Madrid president Florentino Perez described it as the worst defeat in the club's history.

It was clear to Mourinho that despite walking into the Bernabeu and finding he had a stack of cash as well as the world's most expensive player at his disposal, he needed to start a fight off the field to become successful on it. So we had the horrible sight of Mourinho charging towards Barça's then assistant Tito Vilanova on the touchline and deliberately poking him in the eye.

From this moment on, Pep Guardiola, a man who lived for football, loved the game, and worked tirelessly at it, lost a little bit of heart. Pep loved to engage with Real Madrid on the pitch, but once Mourinho turned it into a battle off the pitch, Pep lost interest.

It was a despicable act from Mourinho, and one for which he later apologised. By then the damage was done.

With Pep's heart not in it, he announced he would quit

Barça at the end of the 2011–12 season as Real Madrid won the title.

With Pep gone, Madrid might have been expected to retain their title. But under Vilanova (who spent a large part of the season undergoing treatment for cancer) Barcelona won it back in style, suggesting that the title win the previous season was down more to the demotivation of Guardiola, than the magic of Mourinho.

His time at Real Madrid ended with a Copa del Rey final defeat to neighbours Atletico Madrid; Cristiano Ronaldo was sent off and so was Jose Mourinho. He then compounded the disgrace by becoming the first manager to refuse to accept his medal from the King.

There was nothing correct about Mourinho's behaviour – he showed he was unfit for the privileged position as manager of a great club like Real Madrid.

Mourinho is a winner, but he wins without loving football.

He makes friends with players – Essien, Sneijder and Drogba have all called him 'daddy'. There is nothing wrong with that, it's good man-management. But it is very short term because at the same time he is friends with some, others feel isolated or ostracised. This for me is one of the biggest reasons why he never stays at clubs. It's a short-term hit – he has no longevity. And just because a manager is loved by players doesn't mean he is a great manager. Chelsea players Frank Lampard and Ashley Cole made a point of hugging Phil Scolari at half-time during England's friendly in Brazil in June 2013. They clearly loved the guy – Cole ran the width of the pitch to cuddle up to Big Phil. Yet Scolari had a terrible time at Chelsea, one fan describing his reign to me as 'disastrous'. He was sacked after seven months. Making friends with players means nothing.

For me Mourinho won't go down as one of the game's great tacticians; he's simply not at that level when it comes to coaching.

The biggest problem I have with Mourinho is how he controls referees. A lot of managers do it of course, but nobody in the modern game has done it to the damaging level Mourinho has.

Referees are now scared of Jose in my opinion.

In 2005, Chelsea met Barcelona in the Champions League and Mourinho accused Anders Frisk, a very experienced Swedish referee, of inviting Barça coach Frank Rijkaard into his room at half-time.

This didn't happen. Rijkaard asked Frisk if he could talk to him in the ref's room, but Frisk had refused to let him in and said: 'This is not the place or the moment to talk about the match.'

Mourinho made the appalling decision to go public with his accusation. Within a matter of days Frisk suffered death threats, and he later decided to quit refereeing prematurely. Since then officials have always been aware of how the Mourinho incident was followed by the end of the career of a referee who was highly respected and at the top of his game.

Mourinho is clever, and always manages to deflect that kind of attention away. Only Jose could suggest that Barcelona's link with UNICEF was a reason why they, according to him, 'get all the power – and no one else has a chance.'

I love the beautiful game, so a coach whose approach is to not even want the football, to not even trust his players with the football, doesn't sit right with me.

It is impossible to knock Mourinho's winning habit. He

wins because he man-manages, undermines the opposition off the field, and controls referees. I wish I could say he has brought a fantastic new innovative tactical approach to the beautiful game. But he hasn't. He's a winner. But he's not a football genius.

His career successes at Porto, Chelsea and Inter should never have happened. Porto should almost certainly have gone out to Man United in the knockout stage of the Champions League competition they won in 2004. Paul Scholes' goal at Old Trafford in the second leg was wrongly ruled out; had it stood United would have been 3–2 up on aggregate going into the second half of the game.

Mourinho's a lucky manager who wins. But he came unstuck when he had the chance to manage a truly global club. He was an abject failure at Real Madrid, and neither they nor Barcelona would go near Mourinho ever again.

New Wembley

The 80,000 capacity Stade de France in Paris cost £230 million.

The 94,000 capacity Soccer City Stadium in Johannesburg cost £284 million.

The 69,000 capacity Allianz Arena in Munich cost £278 million.

The 60,000 capacity Emirates Stadium, Arsenal's home, cost £390 million.

The 90,000 capacity New Wembley Stadium cost nearly £800 million.

That is an inexplicably high price for a stadium where you get a decent view from every seat but which is actually no more special than any of the others in the list.

And the original estimated cost of a new Wembley Stadium back in the mid-1990s? £200 million.

In May 1998 Ken Bates was made chairman of Wembley National Stadium Limited. Fourteen months later the costs had risen to £475 million. By December 2000, with the old Wembley closed down, costs were estimated at £710 million. Two months later Ken Bates stepped down. Bates claimed he was undermined by the government and the Football Association, saying: 'Even Jesus Christ only had one Pontius Pilate – I had a whole team of them.'

So many people have been involved in this national embarrassment, that to blame one man would be wrong. We should blame them all. And the time and money it took to pay for this stadium will affect English football for years to come. It is money that could be better spent elsewhere.

Don't even mention the legal battles arising from this stadium. Lawyers are the clear winners from the whole fiasco.

Let's clear up this nonsense about where the stadium is situated. It has to be in London, and it had to be on the site of the old Wembley Stadium. Only if you've travelled the world watching football and talking to football fans, players and coaches do you realise how revered Wembley is globally. There is an undeniable and unbreakable connection between Wembley and football, and nobody should try to break that connection. So when a new national stadium was being planned, it was the correct thing to do when they dismissed bids from Bradford, Sheffield, Manchester and Birmingham and chose London.

I can hear Brummie accents wailing on about how they are at the heart of England. Wrong. Visitors to this country come to London. And if they are visiting the national stadium they want to be in the capital city.

Those same Brummies are now droning on about the advantage of the brilliant motorway network around Birmingham. Excuse me? Am I the only one who has been caught in a jam on the M6? I don't think so. Wherever you put a big stadium, nearly 100,000 people trying to get out of it at the same time will cause a traffic problem. Anyone who thinks it would be plain sailing anywhere else but Wembley is either stupid or very stupid.

Wembley has a one-way system leading straight onto the North Circular, and then on to the M40, M4, M1 and A1 very close by. It isn't quick, it isn't easy – there are 100,000 people all trying to do the same thing.

They got the location right, and the stadium – if you ignore the cost for a second – is decent enough.

There were tears when the towers were lost. And understandably so because they were iconic. The decision to demolish the twin towers was taken very early on but after his appointment as FA chief executive in 2000 Adam Crozier still had the chance to reverse the decision. He didn't, and the towers went.

Crozier is from Scotland, a Celtic fan, and as Scottish as a haggis in a kilt playing bagpipes. I cannot say that his nationality affected his decision, and I don't know if Crozier had the same emotional attachment as most England fans did. What I do know is that the iconic feature of the new stadium is a giant arch, illuminated at night, over the stadium. It is impressive for sure, but the Football Association have missed a trick.

During the World Cup 2010, we saw an arch rising above the Moses Mabhida Stadium in Durban, where Spain beat Germany 1–0 in the semi-final. But they cash in on the Durban Arch. You can walk up the arch, take the Skycar up the arch and even enjoy the swing from the arch which is like a bungee jump, only more terrifying. They charge for all of these attractions and make a lot of money. None of this fun stuff happens at the Wembley Arch, otherwise it may have paid for itself by now.

New Wembley could have been the best stadium the world has ever seen; but sadly it isn't.

How good was . . . Sir Alf Ramsey?

Nobody can ever take away the fact that Sir Alf Ramsey was England manager when we won the World Cup in 1966. So of course Sir Alf was, at the very least, a bit special. The doubters point to his sacking – more on that later – and the 1970 World Cup as evidence that he wasn't all that.

One decision in 1970 cost him global recognition as the undisputed No.1 manager of all time.

On the morning of 14 June in Leon, Mexico, the England team bus was about to leave for that day's quarter-final against West Germany. A late head count showed there was one player missing. The best goalkeeper in the world wasn't there. According to the doctor, Gordon Banks 'couldn't get off the loo'. After going to see Banks, Ramsey got back on the bus, told Chelsea's Peter Bonetti he was playing and then told Sid the driver to set off. In his autobiography Alan Mullery, who played and scored that day, said Bonetti 'looked shocked'. Mullery also said it was a mistake: 'I would have picked [Alex] Stepney . . . ahead of Bonetti. Alex was a very strong character, nothing fazed him, He had won the European Cup with Manchester United two years before and his big-match temperament was excellent. . . . Bonetti was a first-class keeper, but I don't think he was the right choice on the day.'

Of course we'll never know if Stepney's selection would have changed things. Mullery thinks it would have, and so do I.

One mistake should not undo the reputation earned from winning a World Cup. But that mistake denied Sir Alf the chance to enhance his reputation to staggering levels.

So we come to qualification for the 1974 World Cup. England were in a group with Wales and Poland, kicking off with a win in Cardiff thanks to a goal from Manchester City's Colin Bell. Being held by the Welsh at Wembley and beaten by Poland in Chorzow were not disastrous results after the Poles beat Dave Bowen's side 3–0 in the penultimate group game. It meant England had to beat Poland at Wembley to make it to West Germany for the finals.

The England team back then included Leeds players who, although club legends, were not great individual talents. The likes of Norman Hunter, Allan Clarke and Paul Madeley contributed massively to the team that Don Revie had cleverly put together at Elland Road. But taken out of that team, and asked to function in the England team, they struggled.

Witness Hunter's mistake on the halfway line to allow Poland to score in the crucial Wembley match. Same applies to some of the Derby players who had won the title under Brian Clough. McFarland and Hector just couldn't do for their country what they did for their club. Add in the undeniable but unpredictable talents of Tony Currie, and the sometimes negative effect of a maverick like my former talkSPORT *Drive* colleague Rodney Marsh and you have a group of players nowhere near the quality of those Ramsey had called upon in 1966. (Marsh infamously got on the wrong side of Ramsey when on England duty. Ramsey told Marsh that if his performance was not up to standard, he would be 'pulled off' at half-time. Marsh replied with a cheeky grin, 'At Manchester City all we get is an orange and a cup of tea.' He never played for England again.)

Perhaps the saddest part was the decline of the great Bobby Moore. Just at the crucial moment Moore lost his greatness. In Chorzow he had deflected in the first goal, and then been robbed for the second. An incredibly tough decision loomed for Ramsey – when is it right to drop your World Cup winning captain? The manager did it for the Wembley game against the Poles, but apparently told Moore he would need him to captain the team at the World Cup the following year.

The plan failed, Hunter came in to the team, made the same mistake Moore had made in Chorzow, and England drew the game and failed to qualify for the World Cup.

Bobby Moore told a story from that 1–1 draw with Poland which highlights why some people criticised Ramsey. Late in the game, with England desperate for victory, and with the score tied, Moore was sitting alongside Ramsey on the bench and kept suggesting he make a substitution. But Ramsey left it too late. In the 88th minute he told Derby striker Kevin Hector to get ready. Moore was so impatient he actually stripped Hector's tracksuit bottoms off on the touchline. Moore was quoted as saying afterwards: '. . . you could feel the minutes escaping. I said to Alf we need someone to go through the middle. He just nodded. We couldn't get Kevin out there quick enough. We almost threw him onto the pitch.'

England's run under Ramsey from 1966 proved their decline:

1966 – World Cup winners
1968 – European Championship semi-finalists
1970 – World Cup quarter-finalists
1972 – failed to qualify for the European Championships
1974 – failed to qualify for the World Cup.

Ramsey's sacking was down to a chemistry professor. Sir Harold Thompson, a leading director at the Football Association, and chairman from 1976, played a major part in the sacking of Alf Ramsey. Sir Harold was 'a bastard' according to one former FA official, and as reported by Leo McKinstry in an article for the *Guardian* in May 2009. According to McKinstry one of the key incidents which led to Ramsey's downfall revolved around a cigar. Thompson had already taken a dislike to Ramsey, but in the early 1970s with the England squad on a trip to Eastern Europe, Thompson sat at the breakfast table smoking a huge cigar. The England players objected and complained to Ramsey who then asked Thompson to put it out. Seemingly from that moment, Ramsey was a dead man walking. Wasn't the Football Association great?

Let's put this whole thing into perspective. Alf Ramsey's

salary when he was sacked was £7,200 a year (the average UK annual salary in 1974 was just over £3,000). Don Revie came in from Leeds United to replace Ramsey on a salary of £25,000. Revie failed to qualify for the 1976 European Championships and the 1978 World Cup, and then left to take up a big money contract in the Middle East (£85,000 a year). Sir Alf Ramsey may have made mistakes, but he was a great man, and a great manager, treated appallingly by the FA.

There is a lot of talk about Ramsey's inability to get England qualified for two tournaments, his tactical deficiencies, and poor selections and substitutions. But he is a legend because he won the World Cup and that is surely the end of the debate.

Stanley Matthews: 'He put thousands on the gate . . .'

He scored on his England debut. He scored a hat-trick for England against Czechoslovakia. He had an FA Cup final named after him. He was the first winner of the European Footballer of the Year award. Lev Yashin, Di Stefano and Puskas all turned up for his testimonial. He retired aged 50.

But was he as good as all that?

He was just a winger after all, an old-fashioned outside-right. And despite playing for over 30 years he only ever won one trophy – the FA Cup.

Now I never saw him play, and the footage shows a

right-winger getting to the by-line and crossing the ball. How can I judge someone on that?

What I do know is that Matthews played over 50 times for England, and he was a mainstay of the team when our fall from world grace took place. Matthews played in the 6–3 defeat at home to Hungary, England's first-ever defeat at Wembley. Now I'm obviously not saying the defeat was his fault but in that game England were tactically out-thought by the Hungarians. Yet Matthews didn't believe in tactics; in fact he was annoyed with England manager Walter Winterbottom for getting too tactical.

'You get enough Stoke and Blackpool fans telling you Matthews was the greatest the world has ever seen, then at some point you start to believe it.'

'You cannot tell star players how they must play and what they must do on the field in an international match. You must let them play their natural game. I have noticed in the past these pre-match instructions have become more and more longwinded while the playing ability of the players on the field has dwindled. So I say scrap the talks and instruct the players to play their natural game.'

Yeah, good one. Don't bother with tactics, go and get hammered by Hungary.

I do know that Stanley Matthews put thousands on the gate when he went back to Stoke City in the 1960s. Reports suggested he completely ran certain games, so much so that certain players were not always fulsome in their praise for Matthews. Sunderland and Hull legend Raich Carter played with him for England. Matthews said of Carter:

'[He] was the ideal partner for me . . . Carter was a supreme entertainer who dodged, dribbled, twisted and turned, sending bewildered left-halves madly along false trails. Inside the penalty box with the ball at his feet and two or three defenders snapping at his ankles, he'd find the space to get a shot in at goal . . . Bewilderingly clever, constructive, lethal in front of goal, yet unselfish. Time and again he'd play the ball out wide to me and with such service I was in my element.'

But the feeling wasn't mutual – this is what Carter said about Matthews: 'He was so much of the star individualist that, though he was one of the best players of all time, he was not really a good footballer. When Stan gets the ball on the wing you don't know when it's coming back. He's an extraordinarily difficult winger to play alongside.'

Tommy Lawton scored 22 goals in 23 games for England and also played alongside Matthews: 'We all had moments when we've been exasperated with Stan because he's taken the ball off down the wing as if he was playing on his own . . . [but sometimes] he'd produce a moment of sheer genius that nobody else could hope to match.'

I really need to have seen Stanley Matthews play to properly judge, but from all the reports I've read, and the footage I've seen, it's hard to criticise. I just think sometimes it's so easy to build a player up on hearsay alone. You get enough Stoke and Blackpool fans telling you Matthews was the greatest the world has ever seen, then at some point you start to believe it.

There are other things which can't be ignored when assessing whether Stanley Matthews was all that. Matthews was in the England team which gave the Nazi salute in Berlin ahead of a game with Germany in 1938. It's seen as one of English sport's darkest days, and Hitler wasn't even there.

To be fair to the players, they protested when they were told about it just before they left the dressing room, and they were not only under orders from the Football Association, they were also told they had to do it by the Foreign Office and the British Ambassador to Berlin. It was all in the name of Prime Minister Neville Chamberlain's policy of appeasement towards Nazi Germany. He felt that if Germany was not treated as an outcast, they would cease their aggression. Following the game the PM went to see Hitler for his 'peace in our time' talks, and the infamous 'I have in my hands a piece of paper' speech on the steps of the plane. He slightly misjudged that one.

I'd like to think in that position I would refuse to give the salute or refuse to play, but then I have the full knowledge of the evil history of Nazism, which those players did not have. I cannot take the moral high ground above footballers placed in an outrageous position. In his autobiography Matthews claims the players' guilt while making the salute was eased by focusing on a Union Jack flag held up by fans in the crowd.

Matthews was arrested for selling coffee on the black market during the Second World War, whilst on England duty in Belgium. His England and Blackpool colleague Stan Mortensen was also arrested. They claimed the cash they made was spent on presents for their wives. Both were formally reprimanded.

That doesn't mean he wasn't a brilliant footballer. But if a tabloid reported a story of an England footballer giving a Nazi salute and trying to make money out of people living under the threat of war, you wouldn't be impressed.

Matthews also lost his FA Cup winners' medal. He made a public appeal for it to be returned when he realised it was missing in 1965, claiming he lent it out for displays and functions regularly, but the last time it was borrowed it hadn't been returned. Matthews never saw the medal again. It was found after his death, in a box of momentoes found at the home of his first wife Betty, who hadn't realised it was important.

Stanley Matthews also left his wife and children and eloped to Malta with a Communist spy who had been married four times previously. He was so desperate not to be caught that even in Malta he sometimes insisted they walked on opposite sides of the street.

It's worth mentioning the work he did in Soweto at the height of apartheid in South Africa. He created 'Stan's Men', a team of young black men from the townships who were coached by Matthews and played games. He even took them on tour to Brazil in 1975 where Matthews thought it would be a good idea to meet up with convicted train robber and subsequent prison escapee Ronnie Biggs.

The Soweto adventure, though heavily sponsored by Coca-Cola, was a positive according to Archbishop Desmond Tutu. He said this about Matthews' work in Soweto: 'It had a significance: a white man who had been at the top of his trade coming into the townships at a time when racial discrimination was at its most intense; it was something that had all kinds of ramifications in the way it also helped to strengthen our hope for the future. So, it wasn't just, as it were, maybe a sporting gesture or a gesture of magnanimity; it had a very, very profound significance in that although you might not have thought that might be the case, it did make a dent in the apartheid armoury.'

Last word on Sir Stanley Matthews from another knight, Sir Bobby Charlton, who said: 'He was the best player in the world.'

Should have been an England regular? Michael Carrick

It is a truth universally acknowledged among talkSPORT listeners that I am a *huge* fan of Michael Carrick.

In reality I am deeply saddened that England have missed a massive chance to rule supreme with this sublime but brilliant footballer at the heart of their midfield.

He's not a chest-beating workhorse like Scott Parker, he doesn't score wonder goals like Steven Gerrard, and he won't get 20 goals a season like Frank Lampard, but Michael Carrick is the player who England should have had in the team as a regular in central midfield for years and years.

Putting it simply, England's biggest problem at major tournaments has been a complete inability to keep possession, to pass the ball to a team-mate. That has actually been Michael Carrick's main job for Manchester United. Not just any old club, but Manchester United, who under Sir Alex Ferguson won everything.

In April 2013 I went to United's training ground to interview Carrick. I asked him what his job is: 'I'm just there to help the defence and act as extra cover for them really, to stop the supply into opposition front players. At the same time to service our attackers and wide men; it's my job to keep the flow of service as much as possible to them and let them create and score goals.'

His former team-mate Gary Neville sums it up: 'The players that play with him love him, and the manager has picked him in probably 95 per cent of games during the most successful period of Manchester United's history. What he does isn't "wow", it's largely unseen stuff, but a lot of midfielders don't do it.'

So nothing spectacular but vital to any successful team.

At West Ham he made his name as a passing midfielder, Martin Jol said he was the best midfielder at Tottenham, and Manchester United paid £18.6 million for him in 2006.

At United he won five titles in his first seven years, played in three Champions League finals and won one of them.

At club level, managers trusted him – including the very best of them all, Sir Alex Ferguson.

Yet his international career never took off. He made his England debut in May 2001 in a 4–0 friendly win over Mexico at Derby County's Pride Park. But from that game, all the way through to the end of the World Cup in South Africa in 2010, Carrick has never been an established regular in the England team. Between his debut and England's 4–1 thrashing at the hands of Germany in 2010, Carrick played 22 times for England, 16 of those in friendlies, and in only ten of his games did he complete a full 90 minutes.

The best moment Carrick had in an England shirt

was controlling the midfield in a man of the match display in Berlin in November 2008. England beat Germany 2–1 that night. It was Carrick's first international for over a year.

He won the Premier League and the Champions League with United in 2007–08; also in that season he played just once for England, in a friendly. He was overlooked for crucial qualifiers in Russia and at home to Croatia – England lost both and didn't make it to Euro 2008.

The most remarkable fact about Carrick's international career is that he didn't play a competitive game for England from October 2006 through to September 2012 (apart from a game in Ukraine which was a dead rubber because England had already won their qualifying group. Keeper Robert Green was sent off after 14 minutes of that game, which England lost 1–0). This was a period when Carrick was in his mid to late twenties – prime time for a footballer. It was also a time when England were dreadful.

So while successive managers struggled with the tricky Lampard and Gerrard dilemma, and Gareth Barry and Scott Parker were golden boys for a while – even Jermaine Jenas played 21 times for England – the man trusted by Sir Alex Ferguson in Manchester United's central midfield was repeatedly overlooked.

Heads gone for the England managers there, and in particular Fabio Capello. A month after Carrick's son Jacey was born, Capello took the midfielder to South Africa for the World Cup. England were an embarrassing shambles, couldn't pass the ball to each other, yet Carrick spent no time on the field at all. Worse than that, Capello didn't even take him to one side to explain why.

Here are three examples of Carrick's brilliance: at West Bromwich Albion in Sir Alex Ferguson's last-ever game for Manchester United, Carrick tracked a runner into the box and intercepted a pass. Something he does regularly every single game. But instead of blasting it out of play, he found himself on the by-line, boxed in by West Brom players. He didn't panic, instead he turned towards his own keeper Anders Lindegaard, lofted the ball over his head, across his own goal, and out to Antonio Valencia in the right-back position. United then went forward.

In one Premier League game, Carrick was the last defender, but still brave enough to call for and receive the ball, inside his own half. Three opposition players, cutting off the route to the left, the right and forward, immediately surrounded him. Average players would knock it back to the keeper to launch it upfield, but Carrick steadied himself and curled the ball between two players and found a team-mate in the opposition half. I rewound it and freeze-framed the whole move. The pass simply wasn't on. But he found a way to do it.

Then in the FA Cup against Chelsea in the 2012–13 season, a square ball from Cleverley found Carrick just ahead of the centre circle. In one movement he let the ball roll across him and controlled it, shaping as if to lay a pass off to Nani on the right flank. Instead, he hooked his right foot around the ball and sent a 35-yard ball floating into the box, landing on the head of Javier Hernandez, who scored. As the TV commentator Andy Townsend said: 'What a fantastic ball from Michael Carrick. Credit the goalscorer . . . but what a sensational pass, it bamboozles Gary Cahill and Petr Cech is just marooned.' It was a brilliant pass.

And on the subject of passing, Carrick critics say he only plays the ball sideways or backwards – but statistics from April 2013 showed that nobody passed the ball forward more than Carrick across the whole of Europe. Not Pirlo, Busquets, Xavi, Schweinsteiger, Gotze or Yaya Toure.

At the end of the 2012–13 season, Carrick won the Manchester United Player of the Year award from his Old Trafford team-mates. Arsene Wenger – an expert observer of the game even if he has forgotten how to be successful as a manager – said Carrick was his Premier League Player of the Year: 'He is a quality passer. He could play for Barcelona, he would be perfectly suited to their game. He has good vision and is an intelligent player, and it is for what he has achieved in his whole career as well. I think Carrick is an underrated player in England and sometimes not only should the goalscorer be rewarded but the real players at the heart of the game.' We will never know if Carrick could have played a part in any kind of glory for England. But I do know this: Sir Alex Ferguson makes mistakes, but he doesn't keep making the same mistake for seven seasons running. Michael Carrick is the real deal. And while the doubters will still refuse to believe it, he'll keep on shining his medals.

Was Pele really the greatest?

Growing up in the 1970s there was a general acceptance that Pele was the ultimate footballer, the greatest. I've never been totally convinced. He was one of the greats certainly, but out there on his own as number one? Not for me.

Sometimes, if enough people tell you someone is the best then you start believing that there is no need to even check the evidence. Let me give you a quote:

'Football is like music . . . in music, there is Beethoven and the rest. In football, there is Pele and the rest.'

That's the kind of nonsense I'm talking about. It's a great quote but they're just words. What makes it worse is that it was Pele himself who said it. If he really was that good would he need to tell us?

The reasons why we love Pele (and he loves himself clearly) are obvious. As a 17-year-old he cried after winning the World Cup in Sweden. At that point he won everyone's heart. He didn't even have to kick a ball. But check out his first goal in that final, the one where he controls the ball on edge of the box, loops it over a defender's head and volleys it into the back of the net. Excuse me? Does that shot go straight through the goalkeeper? Yes it does and he should have saved it, but we all know that goalkeepers back then were useless. They wore flat caps and refused to dive. In fact, they point blank refused to save anything heading towards them. It's like there was a permanent goalkeeper's strike before Gordon Banks came along and showed other number ones that movement and the use of hands might help them stop goals going in.

In the 1962 World Cup Pele got injured in the second game and missed the rest of the tournament, which Brazil went on to win. (A little side story from that World Cup – Brazil's outside-right Garrincha was voted player of the tournament. Remarkably, he was allowed to play in the final, despite being sent off in the semi-final. Can you imagine the outcry if that happened today?)

In 1964 England went to Rio and with Maurice Norman at the back and Tony Waiters in goal we lost 5–1. Pele scored a couple and again impressed the English. But this was a shadow of the England side who would win the World Cup two years later.

So to 1966 and the Brazil squad were everyone's favourites, especially Pele. Their training ground at Lymm in Cheshire was open house and Pele was the star attraction, giving interviews, talking to football fans, and having fun with his team-mates. They played their first-round games at Goodison Park, home of the FA Cup holders Everton. Across Stanley Park, Liverpool had just won the league title. So football fever was running higher than normal on Merseyside, and as a result interest in Pele and the Brazilians boomed. But once the World Cup started, Pele couldn't handle the physical stuff, got injured again, and found himself outclassed by the European Footballer of the Year, Eusebio. Brazil didn't make it out of the group stage.

Now I'm not saying Pele was rubbish but public perception that he was a football superstar was at an all-time high. Next thing, this superstar declared he would never play at another World Cup.

His strop had ended by the time Mexico 1970 started, and Pele played his part in a truly magnificent Brazil team that won the World Cup in fine style. Their football was breathtaking at times, and some of the games they played in were classics (the second group game v England and the final v Italy in particular). I was always told Pele was the king of that tournament – 'El Rey Pele'. But when I was old enough to buy my own DVDs I realised that the real star was Jairzinho. His speed and skill were phenomenal, he terrorised the opposition, and of course, he scored in every game of the tournament. Pele played his part but Jairzinho was No.1 in 1970.

In fact Pele's highlights of the 1970 World Cup were as follows: a header, which produced a great save from Gordon Banks in the group stages; a shot from inside his own half that was off target (Beckham scored, so did Maynor Figueroa for Wigan – it's not that amazing); missing a completely open goal against Peru; a snap shot from a poor clearance by the Uruguayan keeper in the semi-final, which the keeper saved; an outrageous dummy in that semi when Brazil were 3–1 up (Pele completely fooled the keeper but managed to put the ball wide of an empty net); a goal in the final – a header past Dino Zoff; and a simple pass to Carlos Alberto for Brazil's fourth, arguably the greatest goal of all time.

Brazil were brilliant and Pele played his part. But he was by no means the best player of the tournament.

So why do we think he was the greatest? Could it be that he scored over 1,000 goals? Or did he? For a start Arthur Friedenreich, another Brazilian, is reported to have scored more goals than Pele. Secondly, around half of Pele's goals were scored in exhibition matches and friendlies. This undermines the statistic completely. Does he include goals in training? Does he include goals he dreams of in his sleep? Crazy.

Most of us think Pele is the best because so many so-called experts – including Pele himself – have told us he's the best. He stayed at Santos in Brazil for the whole of his career, never testing himself in Europe (think about Di Stefano at Real Madrid). He went to New York Cosmos in 1975 and lived the superstar life. He mixed with Brigitte Bardot, starred in the film *Escape to Victory* with Michael Caine and Sylvester Stallone, and before playing in his last game for Cosmos – a friendly against Santos (he played 45 minutes for each side) Muhammad Ali went into the dressing room, hugged Pele, and said: 'My friend, my friend. Now there are two of the greatest.'

Ali is the classic case of a self-proclaimed great. Even now some of you will be thinking it's absurd to think otherwise, but just stop and actually ask the question: 'Was he really the greatest? Really?'

Mick Quinn and I asked that question on a *Drive* show on talkSPORT in January 2005 and the phone lines went crazy. The truth is we only decided to ask that question five minutes before the show started! Neither of us were excited about whatever subject we had agreed to talk about, so we ripped up the running order minutes before the show started. I spotted that it was Ali's birthday and we went for it.

Quinny was adamant Ali was the No.1: 'Of course he was. Punch of a heavyweight, reflexes, footwork, he was clever and brilliant.'

'But Rocky Marciano went unbeaten!' I hit back.

'So what? Look at Ali's knockout ratio.'

Callers were at first indignant at my questioning the great man. Then the realisation crept in that actually it was Ali who kept declaring himself the greatest. And then the undeniable truth emerged that a number of boxers could easily have a greater claim than Ali to be called the greatest.

There's a nice story told about Ali, and it concludes with him being left speechless which is a rarity in itself. He was on a plane waiting for take-off when the stewardess came over and told him to buckle up. Ali replied: 'Lady, I ain't wearing that. Superman don't need no seatbelt.'

To which the stewardess replied: 'Sir, Superman don't need no plane.'

The moral of the story being that Ali wasn't as brilliant as he said he was.

Muhammad Ali was a great fighter, a great man and will always be a sporting icon. But was he the greatest boxer of all time?

In a similar way to Ali, Pele used his talents to try to do some good in the world. He's a tireless worker for UNICEF, he has won an International Peace Award, and when he retired Brazil's ambassador to the United Nations, JB Pinheiro, said Pele had done 'more for goodwill and friendship than any ambassador ever appointed'. He even advertised Viagra.

Pele – was he all that? Yes, he was in a way. Pele was a superstar, and a true talent, but not the greatest footballer of all time.

When someone mentions Maradona, what do you think of?

On 21 June 2006, when Lionel Messi started his first World Cup match for Argentina against the Netherlands in Frankfurt, stitched into his boots was the message: 'Hand of God 22 June 1986'.

When I found that out, Messi went way down in my estimation. But it's not his fault. The whole Argentine nation thought Maradona's handball goal against England was revenge for the Falklands War. Of course. I'm sorry, but punching a ball into the net does not bring back hundreds of soldiers killed because Galtieri and Thatcher decided to have a testosterone competition.

'Maradona was brilliant in the semi-final against Belgium ... but his cheating changed the course of the World Cup.'

In a purely sporting context, the Hand of God was unforgivable – remember this is an England fan writing this. The Hand of God is also the reason why Argentineans love Maradona. Yes, he was a terrific footballer. But he was also a bloody cheat.

Watching that World Cup quarter-final from 1986 again, it's a disappointing game. But England are doing what they need to do. Keep it tight, stifle Maradona, kill the threat, see out the first 60–70 minutes at 0–0. Then bring on John Barnes to tear Argentina apart. That was the game-plan. And it was working until Maradona tried to spark his team into action; drifting past one man, he tried to play a one-two on the edge of the box, but England midfielder Steve Hodge inexplicably looped the ball high in the air – a miscued back-pass to Peter Shilton. It was still straightforward for the England goalkeeper, he would easily get to the ball ahead of the diminutive Maradona, who had continued his run in search of the return ball. Maradona's arm went up, he beat Shilton to the ball and wheeled off to celebrate.

England were shell-shocked. So much so that the likes of Butcher, Fenwick and Reid forgot how to tackle in allowing

Maradona to waltz through for the second. Barnes came on and England got back into it, but the damage was done.

Maradona was brilliant in the semi-final against Belgium, and went on to help the team to victory in the final, but his cheating changed the course of the World Cup.

He cheated again in 1994 at the USA World Cup, but this time he didn't get away with it. After scoring against Greece, Maradona raced to a camera, eyeballs bulging, and we all thought he was truly pumped up with adrenaline. We were almost right. He was truly pumped up with ephedrine. Five different variants of it, to be precise. Maradona was a drugs cheat. The Argentine FA took him out of the tournament. Even then he had the front to stay on as a TV commentator.

My point about Maradona is this: I can accept depression at Barcelona and stories of cocaine and prostitutes at Napoli. I can accept his flaws. I can also recognise the amazing talents he had. It was like the ball was glued to his feet. But let's judge him on his World Cup appearances:

1982 – sent off against Brazil.

1986 – cheated England out of the tournament.

1990 – was part of the despicable Argentina side that tried to murder football with their cheating and diving.

1994 – a drugs cheat.

It's not the greatest CV, is it? I haven't even mentioned the 15-month cocaine ban, have I?

Great footballer, yes. That makes it worse – he didn't need to cheat. But he did cheat, and the glory of his cheating lives on. Still not having it? Try this then. Ask someone what they immediately think of when you say the name Maradona. Nine times out of ten the answer will be the Hand of God. Try it.

Take a look at Messi's boots.

George Best – even the ref applauded him!

It is common belief that Best wasted his talent, but he played 470 games for Manchester United and scored 179 goals. He was the club's top scorer for six successive seasons, and the country's top scorer in the 1967–68 season, when he helped United become European Champions. He won two championships, he was PFA Player of the Year and European Footballer of the Year in 1968. He was at United for 11 years. It was only when he left in 1974 that his career became fragmented and he underachieved.

Best claims his time at Fulham, where he earned £500 per game, was the most enjoyable of his career. It was fun at Craven Cottage – he once tackled his own team-mate Rodney Marsh in a game against Hereford, and he scored a goal away to Peterborough in a Cup tie that was so good even the referee applauded. Bobby Moore passed to Marsh, who passed to Best who, 25 yards out (the local paper in Peterborough claimed that was the distance, whereas Marsh claims it was the halfway line), stood on the ball, then flicked it up with his left foot and volleyed it with his right past goalkeeper Eric Steele, who would later become Sir Alex Ferguson's goalkeeping coach at Manchester United. The local paper called it 'a slice of genius' and the referee Jack Taylor, two years after refereeing the World Cup final, ran back to the centre circle applauding the strike. (Incidentally the only other time I have heard of a referee applauding a goal was also at London Road. Peterborough United's Mark Heeley scored it, at home to Lincoln in the 1976–77 season, a strike from 30 yards that ripped into the back of the net. The referee was Alf Grey, who would later go on to become a highly respected UEFA delegate.)

Great times at Fulham then, but Best was a loyal servant at Old Trafford, and deserves his legend status at Manchester United.

When United visited the County Ground, Northampton for an FA Cup tie in 1970, 27,771 fans packed into the ground to see Brian Kidd score two and Best bag six, still a United record despite their years of Premiership domination. His first was a header at the far post. The second was a lovely flick past the onrushing goalkeeper Kim Book (brother of Tony, who was playing for Manchester City at the time), and a finish into an empty net. Then, with Book stranded, Best controlled the ball in front of goal but his shot was blocked by two defenders scrambling back. So Best blasted home the rebound for his third, but celebrated by standing with his hands on his hips seemingly disgusted with himself that he hadn't scored at the first attempt. The fourth was a flying glancing header. His fifth saw him racing away from flailing defenders and firing past the keeper. His sixth was pure genius: he received the ball on the edge of the box, skipped past John Clarke, and headed towards goal. By now Book was in a daze, and desperate not to concede another goal. So he made the fatal error of trying to predict what Best would do. He dived to his left, but Best held onto the ball and with Book lying helpless on the ground, he walked past him and slammed the ball home. As Best slowly made his way back to his own half, Book shouted to him: 'Haven't you had enough yet?'

The truth is that Northampton's scout had watched Manchester United while Best was serving a month-long suspension imposed by the Football Association for knocking the ball out of the referee's hand during a game. So the players were told to focus on Bobby Charlton. The rest was just George Best making history. As Book admitted years later: 'He was just too good for me.'

George Best was too good, full stop.

Jimmy Greaves missed the biggest game in England's football history . . .

'I don't consciously scheme goals, nor take up pre-determined positions, I don't have a thunderous shot, nor have I spent hours working out shooting angles.'

Sounds pretty rubbish, doesn't he? Jimmy Greaves said that. In fact the only goals he scored were close range, and almost all with his left foot.

I say 'the only goals'. Jimmy Greaves got 357 in 514 league games. He scored six hat-tricks for England, and totalled 44 in 57 internationals. Even his short-lived adventure in Italy was successful – Greaves scored nine in 12 for AC Milan.

'He left his shadow standing,' said the Man City manager Joe Mercer.

Now Jimmy Greaves scored an astonishing number of goals, so you might be wondering what the problem is. Why is he even included in this book?

Well, it may sound harsh but Greaves' most significant contribution to World Cup history is that a dog once urinated all over his England shirt during a game.

At the 1962 World Cup in Chile, England lost to Hungary, were held goalless by Bulgaria, and beat Argentina to get through the group and into a quarter-final tie with Brazil. So to Vina del Mar, and England, with just three players who would start the World Cup final four years later (Bobby Charlton, Ray Wilson and Bobby Moore), were beaten 3–1 by a side that would go on to lift the trophy.

Play stopped during the game when a stray dog ran onto the pitch. Keeper Springett tried to catch it, but the mongrel charged upfield. And then Greaves took over. On his haunches, and making eye contact with the pup, they came together close to the halfway line. Greaves sank on all fours and the dog fell for it, paddling innocently towards the trap. When he was close enough, Greaves struck, grabbing the dog. But as he held the animal close to his chest, it urinated all over the England shirt. Brazil did much the same that day.

Legend has it that Garrincha – who had been the star of the game – was so amused that he took the dog home. Other stories suggest he won it in a raffle.

Greaves scored once in the tournament – the third against Argentina – and in his book *The Story of the World Cup*, Brian Glanville wrote of Greaves' performance in 1962: 'He was one of the most exciting talents England had thrown up since the war; yet now, when the chips were truly down, he would be . . . disappointing.'

This, by contrast, was off the back of an amazing season at club level. Nine goals for Milan, and then after moving back to England (for £99,999), he scored 21 in 22 league games for Spurs, and then the opening goal in their FA Cup final win over Burnley. Yet, by all accounts, he flopped at the 1962 World Cup.

So to 1966 and Greaves was still the most prolific goal-scorer in English football. He was top scorer in England in 1963, 1964, and 1965. Unsurprisingly he was a definite starter for the national team, although at times Greaves' character had wound up the very straight, almost humour-less, Alf Ramsey.

Greaves started up front with Liverpool's Roger Hunt, but neither impressed, and England drew their opening game of the World Cup 0–0.

A blistering long-ranger from Bobby Charlton broke the deadlock in the second game against Mexico, and Roger Hunt tapped in a rebound after Greaves had failed to convert when sent through by Charlton.

In the final group game against France, Greaves suffered a gash on his shin that needed stitches, and Hunt scored both goals in a 2–0 win.

The injury ruled Greaves out of the quarter-final against Argentina, so Geoff Hurst came in, and he scored the winner in an ill-tempered game. More significantly Hurst scored with a header. As team-mate Ray Wilson observed: 'Jimmy Greaves was bloody useless in the air.' Indeed, Ramsey, whether he was trying to be smart after the event, seemed to suggest that he would have dropped Greaves for Hurst even without the injury (this was not implausible; Ramsey had dropped Greaves once before in 1965).

The goal saw Hurst retained for the semi-final against Portugal which England won 2–1 thanks to a double from Bobby Charlton.

So to the final and Greaves was fit again, but it was more likely to be Hunt who made way, rather than Hurst. Ramsey chose to leave Greaves out. Greaves maintains to this day he does not bear a grudge.

Hurst scored a hat-trick and England beat West Germany 4–2. Bobby Moore lifted the World Cup.

During the World Cup, Ramsey had changed the system, changed the personnel, and at times England had been far from convincing, and on more than one occasion relied on the individual genius of Bobby Charlton, rather than any great tactical acumen from the manager.

At two World Cups, Jimmy Greaves had played in seven games, and scored just one goal. His club statistics are phenomenal, and his international stats are equally breathtaking. But his World Cup statistics are not special, during a period when England became world champions. Perhaps most significantly, Jimmy Greaves wasn't considered so special and indispensable that Ramsey had no choice but to play him in the final. Indeed, England coped just fine without him.

After the World Cup Greaves played only three more times for England, scoring just once. He was 27, and still scoring goals for Spurs.

History shows that Jimmy Greaves scored a lot of goals, but never proved himself on the highest stage of all – the World Cup.

Shock of the century?
USA 1 England 0

You remember your schooldays, and you're playing football in the playground and someone scores but the keeper starts crying, saying he wasn't ready for it? Well, this is what happened at the World Cup in Brazil in 1950 – England literally were not ready for it. And the Americans cheated. And they were lucky.

The US were 500–1 with the bookies, and their Edinburgh-born coach Bill Jeffrey said his players were 'sheep ready to be slaughtered'. In his book *The Anatomy of England*, Jonathan Wilson says England were beaten by a 'mongrel team of no-hopers'. But for me England were beaten by themselves and the circumstances of the defeat render it meaningless in my eyes. In no way should USA 1 England 0 in the World Cup in 1950 be seen as some sort of watershed for the game.

This was the first World Cup England had bothered to enter – before that the tournament was seen as beneath them. England regarded itself as the king of world football and so the idea of lowering themselves to play against other countries was a whole bowl of wrong. Indeed, some high-power figures in English football were of the opinion that England should not help 'lesser' nations improve their skills, the assumption being that a match against the English would obviously help the 'minnows' improve.

The most incredible example of England's pomposity in the midst of their 'splendid isolation' was ahead of the 1938 World Cup. Austria were a decent side back then – they had been semi-finalists in 1934, thanks largely to the

'Mozart of football' Matthias Sindelar. He was the captain, the centre-forward, and the main man of that Austrian side. In the semi against Italy, Sindelar was battered by Luis Monti. (Monti was a tough defender who played in the 1930 World Cup final for Argentina, and would then play for Italy in the 1934 World Cup final. His nickname was 'the one who walks' probably because he left everyone he marked, unable to walk. He was a beast.)

By 1938 Austria, having beaten England and Italy, were among the favourites for the World Cup in France. But weeks before the tournament started, Hitler's Germany announced the Anschluss, the German occupation of Austria that saw the country annexed. It basically wiped Austria from existence. The Austrian national football team also ceased to exist, and so withdrew from the World Cup. Latvia finished runners-up to Austria in qualifying, but they were not offered a place at the finals (even though minnow nations like Cuba and the Dutch East Indies were there only because every other nation in their qualifying groups had withdrawn; DEI were thrashed 6–0 by Brazil, and Cuba somehow beat Romania in a first-round replay, before being battered 8–0 by Sweden). FIFA begged England to join the World Cup. England still thought they were above all of this World Cup stuff, so they declined. FIFA decided against inviting any other country, and so Sweden received a bye in the first round.

One tragic story from that whole episode with the Anschluss was that Sindelar refused to play for the new Germany team, which had swallowed up some of the Austrian players. In fact, in a match organised by Hitler before the World Cup to celebrate the Anschluss, Sindelar had ordered that Austria wear a new kit in the colours of the national flag, and he celebrated the 2–0 win in Vienna energetically in front of the Nazi officials in the stands.

> 'The USA result should not have stood. And in modern times it wouldn't have stood.'

Less than a year later Sindelar was dead, aged 35. Officially the death was recorded as carbon monoxide poisoning, but there is a theory that he committed suicide because he could not come to terms with the Anschluss and everything it meant. There is also a theory that he was murdered. A Gestapo file on Sindelar highlighted that he was pro-Jewish. The death was recorded as an accident by a local official who it is believed was bribed by friends of Sindelar, thus ensuring he received a proper funeral. (Nazi rules said that anyone who committed suicide or who was murdered could not receive a grave of honour.) I know there is no doubt among right-thinking people, but this kind of story proves what a total bastard Hitler was.

England refused to accept the late offer from FIFA in 1938, but they finally entered the next World Cup in 1950, which was seen as a major moment in football history.

Two years previously, England had gone to Turin and thrashed Italy 4–0, a game where Stanley Matthews was accused of taking the ball into the corner to waste time, wiping his hands on his shirt and then combing his hair.

So on to Brazil for the World Cup, where opinion was divided. England would either assert their authority and run out easy winners, or their pompous attitude would be shown up for what it was – a load of old rubbish. Of course, it was England, so we proceeded to prove the critics right and embarrass ourselves beyond belief.

We beat Chile and then lost 1–0 to the USA, the biggest shock in world football at that moment in history.

But the result was meaningless. And here's why. First of all, the USA goalkeeper Frank Borghi had a mad day. He made save after save, some miraculous. This was a goalkeeper who never ever kicked the ball because by his own admission he didn't have any skills with his feet. He never took goal-kicks and always threw the ball out, never kicked out of his hands. He wasn't a proper goalkeeper. But fair play to Borghi, he made those saves.

The USA goal came from their only attack in the whole game, and rebounded into the net off the back of Joe Gaetjens' head – he knew nothing about it. Alf Ramsey was playing in the game and said: 'He ducked to avoid the ball.' The USA press (only one American reporter was at the game) called it: 'The Goal That Shook The World'.

One of England's top players at the time was Stanley Matthews. He didn't play in the game because of what now seems like a spectacularly bad decision by the Football Association. Astonishingly the FA had chosen to send Matthews to play on an England exhibition tour in Canada at the end of the regular English domestic season, and it was only out there during this PR stunt that Matthews was called up for the World Cup squad. One newspaper headline read: 'The FA have had to send a soccer SOS to Old Man Matthews.' Matthews was 35 and would be the oldest player at the 1950 World Cup (he was also the oldest player at the 1954 World Cup and after going out 4–2 to Uruguay, the winning side's best player, Pepe Schiaffino, suggested England needed to find some younger players).

So having sailed to Canada and played in several games, Matthews then took a train to New York for a game against the USA (Matthews was injured and didn't play – the FA XI, unlike the 'proper' England team, won 1–0). Apparently one FA official told the New York audience at a post-match dinner: 'Wait until you meet the real England team in Brazil.' The arrogance was painful.

Matthews and three others – Fulham's Jim Taylor as well as Manchester United's John Aston and Harry Cockburn – then flew to Brazil via Trinidad. He missed the first game; England beat Chile 2–0 but according to skipper Billy Wright: 'There was no elation in our dressing room . . . we were determined to show the United States just how well we could play.' England never changed a winning side so Matthews then sat in the stands watching the USA game. Matthews said the game was 'agony to watch', according to his biography. The England team wasn't picked by the manager Walter Winterbottom, whose main job it seemed was to teach staff at the Luxor Hotel on the Copacabana in Rio de Janeiro to cook (he actually put an apron on and showed them what to do after they served fried eggs drowned in black oil for breakfast one morning). Instead an FA selector, Arthur Drewry, made the trip. This fishmonger from Grimsby – later a FIFA president – named the side at that World Cup.

The USA result should not have stood. And in modern times it wouldn't have stood.

Three American players did not have US citizenship, including their goalscorer, Gaetjens (more on him in a moment). FIFA allowed the result to stand because all three said they planned to get citizenship. However, one of them, the captain Ed McIlvenny, who was Scottish (could it get more painful?), never ever became a US citizen. McIlvenny wasn't even the regular captain – that was Walter

Bahr. McIlvenny took up the role for this game only, simply because he was Scottish.

Shortly before the World Cup got underway, the USA realised their team was no good (at the 1948 Olympics they had lost 9–0 to Italy), so they drafted in some ringers. Gaetjens was washing pots at a café in Harlem, New York, and studying at university. He was also earning money playing for a local team Brookhattan, and that's how the American football authorities knew about him. Two days before they left for Brazil, the squad met Joe Gaetjens.

By the way, in those days of limited telecommunications, when word got back to English newspapers and sub-editors on Fleet Street that we had lost 1–0, they thought it was a mistake and printed that we'd actually *won* 1–0 (which would excuse the irony of American newspapers claiming Landon Donovan and co. had beaten England at the 2010 World Cup, when actually their match finished 1–1.)

Compared with today's saturation coverage, there was little reporting of the game back then when England went abroad. The English FA had a low opinion of the World Cup, and bigger news that day was that the England cricket team had lost to the West Indies for the first time ever.

Walter Bahr, whose shot was deflected in for the only goal, said he flew home to be greeted at the airport by his wife and nobody else.

The life of Joe Gaetjens, who scored the goal that day, would take an amazing turn. Three and a half years after seeing off England, he played in a World Cup qualifier for his country of birth, Haiti. He was from Haitian aristocracy, and this is where the story becomes sinister. In 1957,

'Papa Doc' Duvalier won the Haiti presidential election. This was a man so in love with himself that he commissioned a portrait of himself with Jesus Christ, whose hand on Papa Doc's shoulder proved he was the 'chosen one'. A subsequent attempted coup failed, and Papa Doc tightened his grip and ruled like a dictator, declaring himself President for Life (his son, Baby Doc took over when he died in 1971).

Among those who wanted him out was the Gaetjens family, and while most of his opponents fled the country, the Gaetjens family stayed and went into hiding. Joe wasn't involved in the political work of his family, but instead chose to quietly go about running his own dry-cleaning business in Haiti. But his connections meant he was arrested by Papa Doc's ruthless and vicious secret police, the Tonton Macoutes, on 8 July 1964 – fourteen years and nine days after scoring that famous goal in Belo Horizonte.

He was taken to Fort Dimanche, the notorious prison on Haiti where people were not only incarcerated but were tortured – sometimes sexually – and murdered. It is widely believed that 'men were sent there to die.' Up to forty prisoners were crowded into rooms measuring just a few square feet. They ate gruel off the floor, and drank only the water they were hosed down with. According to one American journalist: 'Most men do not leave Fort Dimanche; if they are not beaten to death they die of tuberculosis, dysentery, or having the blood sucked from them by scores of vermin.'

Gaetjens' relatives never heard from him again. Six years after he went missing, the Haitian government admitted he had died, but wouldn't say how. It is widely believed Joe

Gaetjens, a World Cup hero, was one of the 30,000 or more murdered by Papa Doc in Haiti.

Gaetjens' life ended in horrific tragedy. But his place in football history is secure. As Bahr said: 'David brought down Goliath.'

PART 2

'Ron Saunders bore a striking resemblance to Victor Meldrew, and to many he was a very dour man. But he came up with one of my favourite ever football quotes. He said: "Allegations are all very well but I would like to know who these alligators are." Genius that.'

Who needs penalties?

Now I know I'm English, and I may have had some bad experience of them in the past, but penalties are so unfair, aren't they? I don't just mean shoot-outs. I mean the spot-kick itself.

It's 2 July 2010 at Johannesburg's Soccer City Stadium. The whole of Africa is supporting Ghana as the last hope for the African continent at the World Cup. They face Uruguay.

Ghana's Inter Milan midfielder Sulley Muntari, having made little or no impact at the tournament up to this point, fires in a free-kick to open the scoring right on half-time. Ten minutes into the second half Uruguay equalise through Diego Forlan's free-kick. Deep into extra-time Dominic Adiyiah's effort is heading in for the winner for Ghana. But Uruguay striker Luis Suarez pushes the ball out with his hand. Suarez is sent off, Ghana awarded a penalty. Asamoah Gyan fires the penalty against the crossbar, Fernando Muslera the Uruguay keeper leaps up having thrown himself the wrong way to slap the crossbar in gratitude, Suarez stops crying like a baby and suddenly celebrates on the sidelines. Uruguay win the shoot-out to go through, while Ghana go on an open-top bus tour of Soweto.

People have said to me that situation is a one-off, and indeed it is a highly unusual set of circumstances. But doesn't it prove the inadequacy of a penalty kick as a form of punishment for a team that has done wrong?

For years the laws of football stated that the goalkeeper could not move his feet before a penalty was taken. Of course keepers regularly got away with this by darting off their line to narrow the angle. At times you wondered if the keeper would get to the ball before the penalty-taker.

In 1997 that law changed and goalkeepers were allowed to move as much as they wanted, provided they stayed behind the goal-line. It seems so unfair that the team that committed the offence leading to the penalty are then allowed to break penalty rules, and have them altered in their favour.

Keepers rarely get punished for infringing rules at a penalty kick. In fact the only time I can remember it happening when I was at a game was when Peterborough United got completely done by the officials at Millwall in 2008–09. Posh keeper Joe Lewis saved the first penalty, but it had to be re-taken because he was judged to be off his line. He saved the second penalty, but that also had to be re-taken after he was again judged to be off his line. The third time, Millwall changed the penalty-taker, and scored. Check out what Joe Lewis had to say straight after the game: 'It's a sickener that I saved two penalties and neither counted. The ref wouldn't even tell me why. The linesman told me it was because I had come off the line. I got the feeling they wouldn't be happy until Millwall had scored. I wondered if it was worth diving for the third. Had I saved that, they probably would have made them take it again. It's the first time I've ever been pulled up at a penalty; and that includes youth football. I don't think I did anything wrong.'

Watching the penalties played back (and I couldn't sleep that night so watched the game twice – it finished 2–0, Millwall deserved to win), Lewis was slightly off his line for the first penalty, but was not guilty for the second.

Joe Lewis' misfortune was the exception that proves the rule that keepers are rarely punished. Lewis made national news after that incident. When a keeper jumps off his line early and saves a penalty, it rarely registers on the news-ometer.

What exactly do penalties prove? Diego Maradona missed a penalty in the World Cup in 1990 ('I think God made me miss that penalty for superstitious reasons,' Maradona explained afterwards). Michel Platini and Zico have missed them. At Arsenal, Dennis Bergkamp missed one in the 1999 FA Cup semi-final against Manchester United which helped United win the treble. One of the most talented players I have ever seen in the flesh, Chris Waddle, blasted a penalty into orbit in the 1990 World Cup semi-final. Apparently on his gigantic run-up, Waddle claimed to be telling himself to at least 'hit the target'. One wonders whether an enterprising German had painted a target on the moon that night. Perhaps most (in)famously, Roberto Baggio missed one to lose the World Cup final in 1994; this, after he had been the star of the tournament. Even Diana Ross has missed a penalty at the World Cup. Does it prove they lacked technique? I guess in Diana Ross' case it does. Does it mean you lack bottle if you miss a penalty? Does anyone want to ask Stuart Pearce that question?

Take the 1986 European Cup final. Barcelona, under Terry Venables, and with Steve Archibald up front, were kept at bay for 120 minutes by a dogged, determined and defensive Steaua Bucharest side. In other words, Steaua completely killed the game because they knew the only way they would stand any chance of winning was through penalties. It didn't guarantee them victory, but it did give them a 50/50 chance. In fact they were favourites when the final whistle went because Barcelona couldn't believe they hadn't won the game. In other words, Barça bottled it. They missed all their penalties, the Romanians (who missed their first two), won it with the wonderfully named Gavril Pele Balint (manager of the Moldova national team until 2011) scoring the crucial penalty.

So does that prove that Steaua were the better team? No. Yet they took the European Cup back to Nicolae Ceausescu's Romania. A trophy won with football as austere and cold as 1980s' Romania itself. The ruthless leader's son Valentin was on the staff at Steaua. Three and a half years after Steaua's win, Nicolae and his wife were shot by firing squad after the uprising against the Communist regime and Valentin never attended a football match again. He's now a nuclear physicist.

In short, penalties are a dramatic way to end a football match. But they offer little measure of ability, technique or courage.

One in the ear
– for semi-final winner

This might sound like the stuff schoolboys' dreams are made of, but it could lead to a nasty and violent conclusion. Big striker George Reilly had been Cambridge United's record signing of £165,000 when he joined from

Northampton in the early 1980s. He then moved on to Graham Taylor's Watford, exactly the kind of target man Taylor loved up front.

Reilly would later play in an FA Cup final for Watford in 1984, but that cup run led to an extraordinary incident in 2003. In the semi-final, Watford met Plymouth, Reilly scoring the only goal to send Watford to Wembley.

In 2003, while working on a building site in Corby in Northamptonshire, Reilly was attacked by another worker, who bit part of his ear off, and then whispered into the other ear: 'Plymouth.' Reilly was fixed up in hospital but later told the press: 'I can't believe someone held a grudge for that long. I know people have strong loyalties but this is taking it a bit far.'

Thierry Henry . . . and *that* handball

Having a World Cup winner's medal hanging around your neck and getting your hands on that gleaming golden trophy might seem like a dream come true to most football lovers, but it didn't quite go to plan for one of the most decorated players in the game, the Arsenal legend Thierry Henry.

Back in 1998 Henry's career was flourishing: he was named French Young Player of the Year as a teenager, he helped Monaco win the title in France in 1997, and in 1998, with Henry scoring seven goals in the competition, Monaco reached the semi-finals of the Champions League.

'To miss the World Cup final after playing in every game at the tournament is like not having sex on your wedding night.'

His stunning form meant a call-up to Aime Jacquet's squad for the World Cup held in France in 1998. Some questioned the selection, others were calling for Jacquet to be sacked (the France fans chanted 'Sackez Jacquet!' with loud regularity during the build-up to the tournament).

The tournament got underway and France faced South Africa in their opening game. Dugarry and Djorkaeff scored, and then came Henry's moment in injury-time. A corner was fired over, the ball landing on Henry's chest 35 yards out; he controlled it, weaved his way towards the box, and nutmegged a defender before dinking over the keeper. A defender helped it in, but FIFA gave the goal to Henry. According to Philippe Auclair's biography of Henry, his father Tony celebrated so wildly in the stands he gashed his leg open, telling reporters he had fractured his leg but 'didn't feel a thing'.

Henry scored twice in the next game against Saudi Arabia – the first when he swept home a Lizarazu centre from eight yards out. That was with his left foot. His second, and France's third, was with his right after a long ball forward from Barthez and a mistake from a Saudi defender. Henry had three goals in two games but would not add to his tally during the tournament. Three was enough to make him France's top scorer of the 1998 World Cup though.

France were through, so Jacquet rested players for the final group game against Denmark, including Henry. He appeared as a substitute after 71 minutes, and France won 2–1.

Onto the knockout games and Henry was back in the starting line-up for the clash with Paraguay in Lens. His pace gave him a fantastic chance to open the scoring, bursting through the static backline from halfway, but he hit the post when he should have hit the target. He was replaced by future Arsenal team-mate Robert Pires after 65 minutes. France won it with a 'golden goal' from Laurent Blanc.

Henry had not played well, possibly because he missed Zidane who was suspended after a rash red card against Saudi Arabia.

Italy were next in the quarter-finals back in Paris: neither side could make the breakthrough. So the stage was set for a hero when the two young friends at Monaco, Henry and Trezeguet, replaced Guivarc'h and Karembeu after 65 minutes. But the young stars couldn't seize the moment. Henry played on the right wing, and nothing seemed to work for him that day.

So to penalties and while some leaders like Desailly, Thuram, Djorkaeff, Petit and even the captain Deschamps sat out the shoot-out, the 20-year-old rookies Trezeguet and Henry stepped up to the plate and scored their spot-kicks. Henry sent his penalty to Pagliuca's left, the keeper guessed correctly but Henry's strike was true and hit the back of the net. He approached the kick with focus, and he walked back to the halfway line to rejoin his team-mates with measured celebration and clenched fist. He then hid behind Trezeguet, unable to watch the rest of the shoot-out. Di Biagio hit the bar, and France went through.

In the semi-final against Croatia, Henry joined the action just past the half-hour mark when Karembeu had to come off injured. Thuram's defensive error played Suker onside and Croatia took the lead two minutes into the second half. But Thuram more than made up for his mistake by striking both goals to seal the win for France. Henry was first in with the goal celebrations.

It had been an excellent World Cup so far for the young kid at Monaco, the boy from Les Ulis, 14 miles south-west of Paris, where Manchester United's Patrice Evra was also brought up. He could not have dreamed that by the age of 20 he would be playing and scoring at the World Cup on home soil.

The final on 12 July 1998 in the Stade de France, Saint-Denis, Paris loomed large. Having started or played a part in all six games so far, Henry was told he would not be starting. Tactically what he offered did not fit in with what Jacquet wanted to do. There was no room for Henry in a system designed to stop Brazil, and in particular, the threat of their full-backs.

Henry accepted it, feeling certain he would get the chance to come on as a substitute at some point in the game. And it almost happened. Years later, ahead of Arsenal's 2006 Champions League final in the Stade de France, Henry revealed what actually happened that day.

'I have never told this story but I was warming up and I was supposed to come on 10 minutes after the beginning of the second half, but Marcel Desailly got sent off and the plan changed. I respected it. On the spur of the moment I was disappointed, obviously, that I didn't come on. But once you know you are going to lift that cup you can't be that upset. I was 20, I played six games at the end of the day.'

Henry's words may be sincere, but I would feel robbed in that position, and although he would have come to terms with it as time went on, it must surely have hurt. A lot. To miss the World Cup final after playing in every game at the tournament is like not having sex on your wedding night. He was denied something he'd worked so hard to achieve.

Sure enough it ended with divorce – or at least a trial separation. Henry played a couple more games for France, but was then out in the international wilderness for eighteen months before a recall in time to make a truly outstanding impact at Euro 2000, not least when he was awarded man of the match in the final.

But Henry's World Cup pain continued.

In 2002, as holders, France arrived in South Korea tipped by many to retain their title. They lost the opening match 1–0 to Senegal. The next game finished goalless but Henry was sent off after just 26 minutes for a wild, studs-high lunge on Marcelo Romero after he had lost control of the ball. Some put it down to injuries leading up to the tournament, others said Henry was frustrated at not being allowed to play up front with his friend Trezeguet. Whatever the reason, it was madness from Henry and he, more than any of the others, was held to blame by the French media. Without him, France lost to Denmark and went home without having even scored a goal.

Germany 2006 was better from a personal point of view, Henry was seen as one of the better players at the tournament. It didn't start well, France making it four successive World Cup games without a goal with a 0–0 draw against Switzerland, and Henry missing two decent chances in the first half.

He struck after nine minutes of the next group game against South Korea; Wiltord played it through to Henry who fired home. But Ji-Sung Park struck the equaliser in a 1–1 draw.

Against Togo, Henry controlled a long ball in an instant, turned and fired across the keeper into the back of the net to make it 2–0 and send France through.

After a 3–1 win over Spain, Henry was left unmarked to volley home Zidane's free-kick from close range to seal a 1–0 win over Brazil.

Henry was fouled for the penalty that decided the semi-final against Portugal. But then the final.

It finished France 1 Italy 1, Zidane was sent off for head-butting Marco Materazzi in the chest, and Henry had to be subbed because he had cramp. He didn't even get to take a penalty in the shoot-out. Trezeguet did, and was the only player to miss.

This is news that will shock England fans – we actually were not the worst team at World Cup 2010 in South Africa. That honour belonged to France. They were a shambles. The leadership of the coach Raymond Domenech was laughable. Nicolas Anelka had been sent home after launching into a foul-mouthed tirade against Domenech at half-time during the game against Mexico. Then the players had refused to train after the Anelka expulsion. On the pitch they went home after finishing bottom of the group. Everyone involved with the France squad at 2010 let the nation down in an embarrassing way.

Henry had been told by Domenech before the tournament that he would only be used as an impact sub. The coach was half-right; Henry was a sub but had no impact.

He sat back and watched his colleagues – coaching staff and players – implode in South Africa. When the players refused to get off the bus and train, Henry sat at the back and did nothing. People reading this may rightly point out Henry was no longer the captain of the national team, and not even in the first team. But he could have had an impact. And he still had power within the squad to influence things, hence his one-to-one meeting with French President Nicolas Sarkozy upon his return from South Africa. The French football magazine *So Foot* called Henry 'teacher's pet'.

At the end of his international career which featured a World Cup win, another World Cup final, and a European Championship win, Thierry Henry had few friends in France.

So what is Henry's place in World Cup history? Sadly for him, his biggest moment was not glorious, it was shameful. And it came not during a tournament, but during a qualification campaign. In fact it came during a World Cup play-off second leg in the Stade de France when even the French nation turned against Thierry Henry.

Thirteen minutes into extra-time, with the score at 1–1 and with the Republic of Ireland probably the better side on the night, the ball reached Henry in the penalty area to the left of Shay Given's goal. He clearly controls the football with his hand, not once, but twice. Shameless cheating. Fellow pros called it instinctive, others said they would have done the same, France coach Raymond Domenech said he didn't see it, David Ginola said Henry is 'a very honest player who was just doing his best for his team'.

The Hand of Gaul, the Hand of God (part 2), or, as talkSPORT called it, the Hand of Frog.

Henry admitted what he had done. He issued this statement: 'I have said at the time and I will say again that, yes, I handled the ball. I am not a cheat and never have been. As a footballer you do not have the luxury of the television to slow the pace of the ball down 100 times to be able to make a conscious decision.

'People are viewing a slow-motion version of what happened and not what I or any other footballer faces in the game. If people look at it in full speed, you will see that it was an instinctive reaction. It is impossible to be anything other than that. I have never denied the ball was controlled with my hand. I told the Irish players, the referee and the media this after the game.

'Naturally I feel embarrassed at the way that we won and feel extremely sorry for the Irish, who definitely deserve to be in South Africa. Of course the fairest solution would be to replay the game, but it is not in my control.

'There is little more I can do apart from admit that the ball had contact with my hand leading up to our equalising goal and I feel very sorry for the Irish.'

It didn't stop Henry celebrating the goal wildly. The free-kick from Malouda travelled a very long way and whilst I can accept it hit his arm for the first handball, the second time he clearly puts the palm of his hand out to control the ball and stop it going out of play before squaring it for Gallas to head home the goal that sent France to the World Cup.

The Ireland defender Sean St Ledger said: 'As a boy I used to dream of playing in the World Cup, and now I'm not.'

World Cup winner Bixente Lizarazu watched the game for French media, and said afterwards: 'We're going to go the World Cup, but we go to the locker-room with our heads bowed. It was not something to be proud of. I'm not going to party.'

Thierry Henry is one of the few footballers to play at four World Cups. He has scored, he has been sent off, he has a winner's medal and a loser's medal. He has known failure and success. But his most memorable moment in World Cup history is a blatant handball that robbed the Republic of Ireland of a chance to play at the tournament in South Africa in 2010. In an instant, his raw, exciting performances from the 1998 tournament were forgotten. His inclusion in the FIFA FIFPro World XI after the 2006 World Cup meant nothing. His selection for the World Cup All-Star Team the same year seemed inappropriate somehow.

When you think of Thierry Henry in a France shirt, you think only of that handball against Ireland.

To paraphrase Brian Clough: 'Chuck all your medals into the biggest dustbin you can find . . . you've done it all by bloody cheating!'

Aston Villa 1980–82
– the forgotten champions

Do you know where Aston Villa won the European Cup in 1982? Not many with hands up, I'm guessing. That says it all really.

Aston Villa won the league title in 1981, and then won the European Cup the following year, yet this great side rarely gets a mention when most football lovers get nostalgic about that great era of domination across the continent for English clubs. Villa 1980–82 have been lost down the back of the settee possibly because Liverpool won four European Cups and dominated the domestic league at that time. And Nottingham Forest will always get more credit because Brian Clough was such a remarkable character.

I'm not here to take anything away from the achievements of either Liverpool or Forest, but Aston Villa are long overdue a standing ovation for what they did. For a start, Villa's two major trophies may have been won in consecutive seasons but they were under different managers. Ron Saunders took them to the title, but he quit after a row with the board and Tony Barton took Villa to European glory.

Saunders bore a striking resemblance to Victor Meldrew, and to many he was a very dour man. But he came up with one of my favourite ever football quotes. He said: 'Allegations are all very well but I would like to know who these alligators are.' Genius that.

It was a remarkable success in Rotterdam – opponents Bayern Munich had blown their opponents away en route to the final. They had scored goals for fun including eight in the two legs of the semi-final, Dieter Hoeness and Karl-Heinz Rummenigge doing most of the damage up front. Saunders had walked out before the quarter-final against Dynamo Kiev. Villa had taken the lead against Manchester United in a Division One game, but then collapsed and were hammered 4–1. Saunders was in dispute over his contract and decided the time was right to go.

Despite no managerial experience, Saunders' assistant Tony Barton took over and led them to victory against Bayern. Again it seemed fate was conspiring against Villa when goalkeeper Jimmy Rimmer had to go off injured after just ten minutes. But young keeper Nigel Spink came on and was in brilliant form, keeping a clean sheet. The Germans dominated the game, but Peter Withe scored the only goal halfway through the second half. ITV's brilliant commentator Brian Moore described it: 'Shaw, Williams, prepared to venture down the left. There's a good ball in for Tony Morley. Oh, it must be! It is! Peter Withe!' Those words are on display on a banner on the North Stand at Villa Park. I'm not sure there are many football fans (other than Villa supporters) who could tell you much about that final, or where it was played, or even who it was against. Yet most neutrals remember Trevor Francis's header for Forest in 1979 against Malmo, Bruce Grobbelaar's spaghetti legs in 1984 in Rome, and Kenny Dalglish's little chip at Wembley in 1978. Villa seem to have been forgotten, almost swept under the carpet by English football history.

The astonishing thing about that Villa side is that they won so few England caps. Cultured midfielder Gordon Cowans played ten times for his country, Peter Withe made 11 appearances and Tony Morley six. But Gary Shaw, Kenny Swain, Gary Williams, and perhaps most incredibly captain Dennis Mortimer were never capped. Having won the league title in 1981 and the European Cup in 1982, no Aston Villa players played for England at the World Cup that summer. Peter Withe went to Spain, but didn't play. Can you believe that? Not one of them pulled on an England shirt at the World Cup, yet they were European champions.

And a word on the title Villa won in 1980–81. Only 14 players were used by Ron Saunders that season and four of those came through the youth system at Villa. The rest cost £1.8 million – yet £3 million had been raised from selling players the season before. Forest broke the transfer record to pay £1 million for Francis (and they paid the same for Justin Fashanu at a later date), while Liverpool regularly spent more than they recouped. At a time when Liverpool were dominating, and Forest were a major force, Villa's title and subsequent European Cup victory must go down as one of the most remarkable achievements ever in English club football. Were Aston Villa 1980–82 all that? You bet they were. And they deserve more credit.

Video technology – bin it!

I'm getting sick and tired of people saying video technology *must* come into football.

Football has been brilliant for years and years without cameras and replays making decisions for referees, so why is there this seemingly unstoppable need to fundamentally change our game forever? Tweaking the laws of the game is one thing, but video technology will change the game beyond recognition, and will do it great harm.

It seems simple on the face of it – the ref has a tight decision to make, he calls for the video ref, various angles are analysed and the right decision is relayed back to the ref out on the pitch. What could possibly be wrong with that?

Loads.

In fact there is nothing *right* with it. Football is a fast-moving game. We love it when the ref lets the game flow, and we urge refs not to keep blowing up for slight fouls. As entertainment, football is hard to beat when it comes to spectator sports – look at the size of crowds at games, and TV viewing figures will back that up. So why would anyone want to throw in a video ref, checking four or five different replays before coming up with a decision? It may only be by a matter of seconds, but it will slow the game down. I've seen video decisions in rugby league take over *four minutes*. I love rugby league and it's a very fast sport, but with play-the-balls every few seconds there are natural breaks in play that fans are accustomed to. Similarly in cricket, they stop for long periods sometimes between each ball, never mind between each over. But in football, the delays would drastically alter the way our game is played and I think fans would get fed up with it.

And are we always guaranteed the correct decision? Anyone who saw the Super League Grand Final in 2009 knows that the video ref actually got a crucial decision wrong. Leeds' Danny McGuire, kicked through, Lee Smith looked offside, but collected and scored a try. Match ref Steve Ganson went to the video ref Phil Bentham, who somehow seemed to ignore all the angles we saw on TV, and gave the try. Leeds went on to beat St Helens.

At Super League's 'Magic Weekend' in Manchester in 2013, the Hull derby was decided by a truly horrendous decision from the video ref, who this time was Steve Ganson. With the scores level late in the game, Hull FC's Danny Houghton kicked through, and Chris Green touched down for a try. The ref on the pitch asked Ganson to look at the video. Ganson looked five times, each time it was clear that Green was offside, and yet he gave the try and Hull beat their enemies Hull Kingston Rovers. The sport of rugby league went into meltdown. Ganson apologised and explained that he had been 'tracking the wrong man'. That means on each of the five occasions he replayed it, he was following the wrong player. The Rovers' coach Craig Sanderock called it a tragedy, and the Rovers' chairman Neil Hudgell called it 'the single worst decision in the last ten years of rugby league'.

So the video ref is actually human as well, and he can make mistakes. And a lot of decisions are open to interpretation. Handball in the penalty area for example: was it ball to hand, or does the arm move towards the ball? Is there intent? Does intent matter? Sometimes it's not so black and white and one referee will give a penalty, while another won't. And they'll both have justifiable reasons for each decision. The referee interprets the rules and most of the time when a manager complains about a decision it is because he has a different interpretation. That doesn't mean the ref's interpretation was wrong though.

I was never a fan of goal-line technology, but that has been forced through. Hawk-Eye is widely accepted in sport and claims to be 'millimetre accurate, ensuring no broadcast replays could disprove the decision'. That is a bold claim and I hope it proves to be correct, assuming it has been 100 per cent efficient at the time you read this.

One of the greatest players tennis has ever seen, Roger Federer, has a history of questioning the use of Hawk-Eye, asking how the system was developed and whether it took into account conditions, speed and bounce of the ball and 3D. It is fair to say Federer is not a fan. In the fourth set of the Wimbledon final of 2007, Rafael Nadal was using up his challenges towards the end of the set and on one particular call a shot to Federer's baseline looked totally out. Hawk-Eye called it in, Nadal won the point, and Federer complained to the umpire saying Hawk-Eye was 'killing' him. I have sympathy with Federer here: with his naked eye he has seen the ball land out, only for a cartoon to tell him it's in. It just doesn't feel right.

Others advocating goal-line technology have suggested a

chip in the ball. Are they absolutely sure about that one? What exactly does the chip read? And when a ball is being smacked full force and then travelling at high speed towards the goal before crunching against a crossbar, are we really sure that this super-strength chip in the ball will work for 90 minutes? What if the ball goes out of the ground, do we have to wait a long time for the chip in the next ball to be activated? So then they'll tell you we can have a laser sitting in a little box next to the goal with a flashing light if the ball crosses the line. Excuse me? Are we at the funfair now? How does this laser distinguish between legs, boots and balls? And is this laser really going to work in all weathers? Cricket and tennis can handle such technology because they don't play outside in cold, wet conditions. Football is very different.

Sometimes decisions go against you and it's the mark of a good manager if his team shows the character to come back from those decisions. On a decision like Thierry Henry's handball in the 2009 World Cup play-off against the Republic of Ireland the whole situation could have been dealt with by the referee asking Henry if he had actually handled the ball. If he says yes, the referee takes appropriate action. If he says no, then the player is a cheat and a liar, and his card will be marked accordingly.

The main reason why video technology won't work in football is because of managers. If, for example, FIFA declare we can use the video referee up in the stands for all penalty decisions, do you think a manager under threat of the sack will let it rest there? No way! Picture the scene: final day of the season and Team A need a point to stay up, but are losing 1–0. They attack and a shot comes in and a finger-tip save sends it wide. The ref doesn't spot the save

'But video technology, or a video referee, is not the way forward. It will seriously detract from the beautiful game of football . . .'

and awards a goal-kick. Do you honestly think the manager of Team A will let it lie? Can you hand-on-heart picture that manager standing there saying: 'Well, you're quite right ref, the video evidence may well be there and it may well take just a few seconds to confirm that it should have been a corner, but I defend your right to uphold the laws of the game and give completely the wrong decision even though it will effectively relegate my team and may well get me the sack'? Oh no! He will rant and rave and demand that the same video used to check the penalty decisions is used to give Team A a corner. Now you might think that's justice and it's right that the correct decision is made. But you're then looking at hundreds of decisions being referred to the video throughout the course of the game.

As Everton manager, David Moyes took the time to make up a DVD and send it out to referees to prove that his striker Andy Johnson didn't dive. He will push for everything he can get, and he's not the only manager made that way. They are all rightly competitive and willing to fight for their club. And if the video technology is available they will campaign tirelessly to ensure all decisions are subject to the video. You know as well as I do a manager can complain that a throw-in being given the wrong way was the reason a goal was conceded five minutes later. Soon all sorts of decisions in all sorts of areas of the pitch will be referred to the video ref. Games will kick off at 3pm on a Saturday afternoon, and some won't finish until nearly 6pm. The full-time classified check at around 5pm will be a thing of the past – another of football's wonderful traditions dispensed with. We could go on until midnight with extra-time and penalties in midweek cup-ties.

The suggestion that a manager is given three chances to challenge decisions during a game has been made as well. Think this one through: if he's challenged three decisions and been unsuccessful with all three, and then a last-minute blatant penalty shout is turned down, do you think that manager will hold his hands up calmly and say: 'Well, fair enough, I used up my three challenges so I no longer have the right to challenge any more decisions, no matter how bad and no matter how much those decisions may cost my team the game or cost me my job. Carry on, referee.'? No way! He will rant and rave and probably burst into tears screaming that the technology is there so why not use it. I can see managers campaigning endlessly until all decisions are made by video, and refs are done away with. Games will take two or three hours and the lack of controversy will render the game boring and so staccato that it becomes difficult to watch, except for the odd flash of brilliance now and then.

Incidentally, one decision from an official doesn't decide a manager's future or a team's fate. Of course a decision made in the final game of the season never relegates a team. A team is relegated because they were one of the worst three teams in the Premier League over the course of 38 games. Can you think of any teams that were relegated only because a ref made a bad decision against them? No, me neither. Can you think of any teams relegated from the Premier League who didn't deserve to go down? No, me neither.

Yes, refs make bad decisions. But as an example let's take

one of the worst decisions in recent memory – the Stuart Attwell ghost goal in the Watford v Reading game in 2008. That was so blatantly down to total incompetence that it should not be used as an example of why football must have video technology. Nobody needed a replay (apart from the incompetent ref) to see that it wasn't a goal. In that instance the Reading players should have been more sporting, but no! They actually had the audacity to celebrate a goal. What a bunch of cheats! What a disgrace to the word 'sport'! I can still see Stephen Hunt wheeling away, arm in the air, when the ref confirmed he'd given a goal. Outrageous. There was something sweet about seeing Hunt crying like a baby after the Republic of Ireland had been victim of Thierry Henry's handball in the World Cup play-off game in 2009.

How about Manchester United goalkeeper Roy Carroll clawing the ball back after he's spooned it two miles over the goal-line? He pretended it hadn't gone in! He's got some front! Spurs didn't get their goal but I don't blame the officials for that one. It was a monster long-range effort from Pedro Mendes which was never going in. It was an easy save for Carroll, but he cocked it up big-style (and a few months later was given a free transfer out of Old Trafford). The linesman couldn't possibly stay in line with it, the ref would've been in his correct position halfway up the pitch. It looked obvious on TV but there is no way the officials could have seen that it was over the line. No video replay should have been needed for this one, just honesty from a professional footballer.

The same goes for Frank Lampard's strike against Germany in World Cup 2010. Better officials would have seen that (and on talkSPORT we had expressed concerns about Uruguayan referee Jorge Larrionda before the game, and after it, when he was shown the video, he simply said, 'Oh my God' and retired a year later aged only 43), but Manny Neuer, the German keeper, could have come clean. My own suggestion was that the Germans should have done the decent thing and allowed England to walk a goal in. I got laughed at for that one, but it can happen in professional football. Gary Johnson's Yeovil were involved in such an incident during a cup-tie against Plymouth in August 2004. The Plymouth keeper kicked the ball out of play, and an injured player was treated. Yeovil's Lee Johnson (son of the manager) then kicked the ball back towards the Plymouth keeper. However, he put too much behind it and the ball sailed into the net. Plymouth went crazy, their manager Bobby Williamson – a rugged-faced, tough no-nonsense Scot – was purple on the sidelines. Manager Johnson told his players to let Plymouth walk a goal in and they did. As he explained afterwards: 'I thought, "Let them have a goal back and we're back where we started."' Germany could have done this, but I recall a conversation with my colleague Mark Saggers on air in which Saggers barked: 'You don't let teams walk goals in at the World Cup!'

Well, I wonder if that's true. There was almost a similar incident in the 2010 World Cup final itself. Holland were giving the ball back to Spain after a player received treatment for an injury. But as the ball was fired towards Iker Casillas it nearly deceived the Spain keeper and he was forced to tip it wide for a corner. Now had he not been able to get to that ball, and it had gone in, would Holland have allowed Spain to walk a goal in? I'd like to think so. And indeed Holland passed the resulting corner back to Casillas. Before every match at the 2010 World Cup banners were carried on to the pitch expressing FIFA's desire for fair play. Germany obviously weren't too keen to play their part. If we start a culture of more sportsmanship in the game and try to stick to it, giving the players the chance to change their mentality, then maybe that might be a better way than slowing up the game and taking sometimes two minutes, or even more, to make a decision when people want to see the game being played. If you watch Super League you'll know decisions are not all straightforward; different angles are looked at and different phases of play are checked too.

Has your laptop ever gone wrong? Of course it has. Well, the day that expensive technology goes wrong, or a video referee gets it wrong, and that mistake decides a game, there will be uproar. All those who are so desperate to change the wonderful game of football so dramatically will wonder why they bothered. I'll be sitting there shaking my head wondering why people were so daft. Some rule changes are fine – I'm not against change in football if it's for the right reasons, my head isn't in the sand on this one. But video technology, or a video referee, is not the way forward. It will seriously detract from the beautiful game of football that we've all been in love with for so long. It will completely change the game, but all those who support it won't realise that until it's too late. Did George Best need video technology to show us football perfection? Did Robin van Persie need Hawk-Eye to score his beautiful volley against Aston Villa in the 2012–13 season? Of course not. I sometimes think people have forgotten what makes this game so great.

FOOTNOTE – IT'S NOT CRICKET

I have heard ex-cricketers tell me that the use of video replays in their game has made it more exciting for the spectators. Remember this is cricket, where they decide not to play if the clouds are a bit dark. A cricket crowd is desperate for entertainment if they can get excited about a video screen displaying 'OUT' or 'NOT OUT'.

However, I totally accept such a screen display can make cricket more interesting. But if you're telling me introducing something similar will increase the excitement levels at football matches, then you obviously need to go to more games. Football isn't boring, and it's not crying out for big-screen verdicts to pimp it up and get crowds in.

Story of a substitute

In his first management job at Peterborough United, John Barnwell, a life Vice President of the League Managers' Association, and the man who led Wolves to League Cup glory in 1980 against Brian Clough's Nottingham Forest, once grabbed a 17-year-old youth team star by his shirt collar, dragged him down some stairs, and literally threw him out of the London Road stadium. Witnesses said Barnwell 'kicked him out of the ground'.

It was the opening day of the 1977–78 Division Three season and Barnwell was angry that the player, local lad Mark Heeley, had stormed up to his office to say that he didn't want to sit on the subs' bench, he wanted to be in the starting line-up. 'I'm not going to play, I'm not in the right frame of mind,' the teenager said.

Heeley went to a mate's house near the ground to have a cup of tea, and told him: 'I just couldn't be bothered any more.' He was suspended by the club, declared he might do a business studies course, and told the local newspaper: 'I don't feel all that happy at the moment but if I get the ITV Seven on Saturday that will cheer me up.' The ITV Seven, for younger readers, were seven horse races shown on ITV's flagship Saturday afternoon sports show *World of Sport* in the seventies and eighties.

In the end Heeley refused a loan move to Arsenal (set up by Barnwell – a former Arsenal player) but then changed his mind, went on loan and eventually joined the Gunners for £100,000, a huge amount at that time for a teenager with very few first-team games behind him. Bob Wilson described him as 'one of the best prospects I have seen in a long time'.

Two months after refusing to sit on the Peterborough bench, he made his debut – as a substitute – for Arsenal in a 1–1 draw at home to Birmingham. In the end Heeley's attitude got in the way and after some flashes of brilliance – in particular a UEFA Cup tie against Red Star Belgrade at Highbury – he left the club after three years, went to Northampton in Division Four, and although brilliant on occasion, he sometimes went missing, failed to turn up to training and games and eventually ended up playing part-time at the age of 22, five years after a record-breaking move to one of the biggest clubs in the country.

His hometown club Peterborough gave him a chance to resurrect his career with the offer of a pre-season trial in 1985. He turned up several days late and told the manager he didn't want to have a trial and was starting a job elsewhere.

Imagine if he had quietly sat on the bench that day in August 1977. The game actually finished goalless, but if he had come on with half an hour left, created or scored the winner, then he would have sealed his place in the first team, and somewhere down the line got his big move and had a better career.

So why do players hate being a substitute so much?

David Fairclough became a Liverpool legend with the nickname 'supersub'. With Kevin Keegan and John Toshack leading the line so well, chances to start games were limited. David Johnson was also in the first-team picture, so Fairclough only had substitute appearances to really make a mark. His most famous goal was against St Etienne in the third round of the European Cup in 1976–77. Bob Paisley sent him on with 17 minutes left and with Liverpool needing to score. Fairclough obliged. Ray Kennedy won the ball in midfield, and played the ball in behind the French defence. Fairclough challenged for it, won it and in a moment of calm composure belying his 20 years, pushed it past the advancing goalkeeper. The story goes that the roar from The Kop could be heard three miles away. There were just six minutes remaining. Liverpool went on to win the European Cup final in Rome 3–1 against Borussia Moenchengladbach. Fairclough stayed on the bench that night.

There were other big moments for Fairclough: scoring in each leg against Kevin Keegan's Hamburg in the European Super Cup, and a hat-trick against Norwich in a 5–3 win away from home in February 1980, but even that was overshadowed. Fairclough had already scored his three goals at Carrow Road when Justin Fashanu received the ball on the edge of the Liverpool box with his back to goal.

He flicked it up to his right, turned and smashed in a left-foot volley for one of the goals of the season.

Fairclough has always hated the nickname supersub. In his words, he felt he 'had a lot more to offer'. He may be right but he has plenty to be proud of.

The reality is David Fairclough is a true Liverpool legend. In 2006 Liverpool Football Club's official website surveyed 110,000 Liverpool fans worldwide, asking them for their top ten Liverpool players of all time to form a list of '100 Players Who Shook The Kop'. When all the votes were added up Fairclough came in a very creditable 18th, higher than other strikers who kept him out of the first team during his nine years at the club. (Incidentally Kenny Dalglish came first, Steven Gerrard second, Jamie Carragher seventh.)

For Fairclough, coming on as a substitute and scoring a goal to send Liverpool through their European Cup tie with St Etienne was a moment of history. It's why we still talk about 'those great European nights at Anfield'; that night set the standard and it was because of the situation – Fairclough coming on as a sub and scoring the crucial goal.

Twice in three years substitutes made a massive impact for their clubs on the biggest occasion of them all – the Champions League final. Their names have gone down in club and Champions League history. The first name is Lars Ricken. He scored one of my favourite goals of all time. Let me set the scene: Champions League holders Juventus have reached a second successive final, Borussia Dortmund were there for the first time. In the final, Juventus were favourites, as Dortmund coach Ottmar Hitzfeld acknowledged: 'Nobody thought we had a chance, since Juventus had won the previous year and had beaten all the great teams in Europe. We were the underdogs.'

Andi Moller joined Juventus from Dortmund, scored against his old club to help the Italian side win the UEFA Cup in 1993, and then returned to Dortmund in 1994. He was the main man in the 1997 Champions League final in Munich. He had set up a goal for Ricken in the semi-final at Old Trafford as Dortmund beat Manchester United home and away.

'United players celebrated wildly. Sir Alex said they were all "blissfully demented".'

Moller had a hand in the two goals in five first-half minutes for Karl-Heinz Riedle that put the Germans 2–0 in front. Alessandro Del Piero's clever flick on 64 minutes pulled a goal back for Juve and that's when most expected the Italians to march on to victory.

Hitzfeld had other ideas, and at 2–1 he made a change: 'As a coach you depend on a little bit of luck. When you see your players are tired you think of who you might bring on, and Lars Ricken was a player who would usually explode when you put him on as a sub.' Sixteen seconds after coming on the pitch as a substitute for the Swiss international Stephane Chapuisat, Ricken scored a wonder goal to seal Dortmund's victory.

Moller, who else, picked the ball up in his own half and Ricken started running. Moller's pass was perfect, Ricken hit it first time over Angelo Peruzzi, and into the back of the net. It was his first touch of the ball. Watching from his role as Zinedine Zidane's man-marker was Paul Lambert: 'Andi's pass was defence splitting, it was wonderful and Lars didn't even have to break his stride. It was his first touch, and given the magnitude of the game it's one of the best goals ever scored. As soon as it went in I knew we'd done it, I knew we would go on to win.' Lambert went on: 'I knew Lars was capable of that because he was always a goal threat. He had great potential, he was a good guy and the goal was fantastic.' Ricken, like Fairclough, was a local boy, born in Dortmund who never left his hometown club. He went on to play for Germany but injuries were a major problem in his career.

Lambert found a major difference in the role of substitutes when he left the UK for the Bundesliga: 'Only when I went to Germany did my attitude change – over there being on the bench is just as important as starting the game. It's all about team unity and the subs know that they may have a major part to play. That was different to what I had experienced at home.'

Former Republic of Ireland midfielder Matt Holland told me: 'Players sometimes switch off when they're on the bench, they don't focus on the game. A load of subs chatting away, having a laugh and then all of a sudden someone is injured and you've got to come on. But you're not ready. It's always disappointing to be left out knowing that you might not get on, but you have to be ready. I sat on a bench at Charlton once next to Dennis Rommedahl and he was wearing Ugg boots to keep his feet warm. That's not ideal preparation, is it? If you're cold you should go and warm up.'

Two years after Lars Ricken's Champions League final goal, two more substitutes made their mark in Champions League history.

Manchester United were playing Bayern Munich in the final in Barcelona. The Germans led thanks to a sixth minute free-kick from Mario Basler, and Bayern hit the woodwork twice in the second half. Sir Alex Ferguson had started with Dwight Yorke and Andy Cole up front but it just didn't click. As Fergie said: 'The most prolific scoring partnership in the Premier League was subdued on the night, and our superior possession went unrewarded for ninety minutes.'

With time ticking by, substitutions were made – Teddy Sheringham on for Jesper Blomqvist halfway through the second half, and then Andy Cole was replaced by Ole Gunnar Solskjaer with nine minutes of normal time remaining. Still Bayern were leading. 'When ninety minutes had been played I had to start practising to be a good loser,' Fergie said. 'I was out on the touchline when the fourth official displayed his electronic board signalling there would be three minutes of stoppage time and I was still out there when we won a corner on the left.'

As David Beckham prepared to take the corner, Peter Schmeichel went charging upfield. Fergie turned to his assistant Steve McClaren and said: 'What the hell is he doing?'

The ball came over, bobbled about the box before Ryan Giggs swung a right foot at the ball, and the first sub Sheringham steered it into the corner of Oliver Kahn's net. In the 93rd minute, the other sub Solskjaer chased down a long ball from Denis Irwin and won a corner. Beckham took it again. He aimed it towards the near post, Sheringham flicked it on and Solskjaer stuck out a leg and diverted it into the net.

Bayern players fell to the ground in shattered despair. United players celebrated wildly. Sir Alex said they were all 'blissfully demented'.

Two subs, two heroes. But Solskjaer's reaction, despite scoring the winning goal, sums up how it feels to be left on the bench for such a huge game. 'It's a strange feeling because I didn't really get to play that much of the final. I came on about ten or twelve minutes before the end. I don't even think I realised I scored the winning goal. I scored *a* goal. I was so focused on playing a football game. I wasn't focused on winning the cup or anything. I was just going out there and performing and trying to score.'

Ricken, Sheringham and Solskjaer all prove that it isn't such a bad thing to be a substitute. Unless you're John Kosmina.

Peterborough United's stroppy sub from the start of this chapter, Mark Heeley, had been running a UEFA Cup tie against Red Star Belgrade for the Gunners at Highbury on 6 December 1978. A goal down from the first leg, Arsenal dominated the return match but couldn't find the net until the 70th minute when Alan Sunderland headed in an equaliser from Heeley's superb turn and cross on the right. A minute later Arsenal had a goal ruled out for a dubious offside. Then Heeley crossed into the box and Ivan Jurisic clearly handled, but 'no penalty' said the referee. It was just a matter of time before the Gunners got the winner. But then Red Star worked out how to deal with Heeley, midfielder Ned Milosavljevic smashing into him, crunching his ankle. In the words of team-mate Frank Stapleton: 'He got clattered, got taken out, well and truly crocked.'

This is where the story gets ridiculous. The *Sun* reported it like this: 'There were just five minutes left when young Mark Heeley, who had an outstanding game, was cruelly chopped down. The Arsenal youngster was hurt so badly that skipper Pat Rice immediately signalled frantically to the bench to get a substitute on. Heeley went off and was carried around the ground but still no substitute appeared.'

The official story was that Arsenal manager Terry Neill was waiting for extra-time to see if Heeley could be strapped up to get back out onto the pitch. But in his book *Rebels for the Cause – The Alternative History of Arsenal Football Club*, Jon Spurling offers a different version: '. . . when [Kosmina] was supposed to be on the pitch as a substitute against Red Star Belgrade, he went to the toilet instead and ten-man Arsenal lost a goal, and a UEFA Cup tie, because of it.' The *Daily Express* headline the next day seemed to back that version up: 'RED FACED GUNNERS – SUB SHAMBLES KILLS ARSENAL.' Later in the season skipper Rice reflected on the game in the club programme: 'All the boys were sick. We fancied ourselves to win that competition.'

So Arsenal were knocked out of Europe, because the substitute needed a pee.

Supporters singing songs

It's Christmas time at The Hawthorns and West Bromwich Albion players leave the field at half-time to rapturous applause after midfielder Robert Koren's low shot gave them a 2–0 lead against a Scunthorpe side reduced to ten men.

Up in the stands, Adrian Morris, the grandson of West Brom legend Len Millard (he won the FA Cup with the club in 1954), was enjoying the game after being given complimentary tickets by the club for him and his girl-friend Lydia. Adrian told Lydia they would be meeting some of the players at half-time, so they left their seats and headed down towards the pitch. But as soon as they walked onto the grass she knew something wasn't quite right. In a flash, Adrian sunk to one knee, produced a ring, and proposed. She said yes, and he lifted her up. From all four sides of the ground, the 25,000 fans sang out loud and clear: *'You don't know what you're doing!'* Adrian obviously didn't hear the song because he said afterwards: 'It couldn't have gone better.' He also said he suggested Scunthorpe for a honeymoon but they chose Thailand in the end.

West Brom won the game 5–0. All Nigel Adkins, the Scunthorpe manager, said afterwards was that the first goal was clearly offside.

The humour of football fans is legendary, and topping the bill are Scotland fans. They sang: *'We're gonna deep fry your pizzas'* during one trip to Italy. And at a qualifier in Tallinn against Estonia in 1996, they saw the funny side when the game was abandoned after just three seconds. Estonia were in dispute with UEFA over the game, and their team failed to turn up. So at kickoff time, the Scotland eleven were the only players on the pitch. The fans sang: *'One team in Tallinn, there's only one team in Tallinn.'*

When your team needs a goal, and you want to urge them forward, the cry from the fans sometimes goes up: *'Attack! Attack! Attack, attack, attack!'* But they did it with a difference at Brighton. Right in the middle of a game at the club's old home, the Withdean Stadium, the pitch was invaded by a cat. Play stopped to let the moggy run rings round the players. The fans took their chance and sang: *'A cat! A cat! A cat, a cat, a cat!'*

Sometimes, thinking up a song for a player can be a headache and that's exactly what faced Arsenal fans when midfielder Emmanuel Petit was starring in the Gunners' midfield. But they did it: *'He's blond, he's quick. His name's a porno flick. Emmanuel, Emmanuel.'*

But the very best song was created by Liverpool fans. In January 2005, Rafa Benitez took his team to Burnley for an FA Cup third round tie. Six minutes into the second half, Burnley midfielder Richard Chaplow crossed into the box. It was a routine clearance for Liverpool full-back Djimi Traore, but somehow he threw shapes and dragged the ball back into his own goal, and the Reds went out of the Cup. Benitez said: 'In the six yard box, you need to clear the ball.' Good advice.

Liverpool fans have a sense of humour, but this time they excelled themselves. Taking a selection of names from the Liverpool squad at the time, and to the tune of the Jacksons' 'Blame It On The Boogie', they sang:

'Don't blame it on the Biscan,
don't blame it on the Finnan,
don't blame it on the Hamann,
blame it on Traore – he just can't, he just can't, he just
*   can't control his feet!'*

Outstanding lyrical work. Four months later Traore won the Champions League with Liverpool.

Old Wembley –
ten of the best

There were only two good things about the old Wembley Stadium: its towers, and its history.

The reality is well known to football fans who visited the place. I went for the first time for the play-off final in 1992, when Peterborough United beat Stockport County 2–1 to get promotion to what is now the Championship. As I drove towards the official Wembley car park, I remember feeling proud that my team was playing at what I, and many others, considered to be the home of football. I also felt awestruck by its magnificence as we got closer. The towers, the sheer size of the place, and the astonishing price of the car park all left me thinking I was visiting somewhere very special, a place of global importance. I was right of course.

But inside it was a concrete horror show. Grey blocks everywhere, pillars spoiling the view. You just couldn't warm to the place.

The towers were made from concrete, but they were white, and they were special. You can wipe away the towers, but you cannot wipe away that history. So as I doff my cap to that history, here are my top ten old Wembley moments.

10) Liverpool 1 Leeds 1, Liverpool won 6–5 on penalties. This was the 1974 Charity Shield, an amazing game for so many reasons. First of all, Bill Shankly led Liverpool out, even though he had retired and made way for Bob Paisley. Brian Clough led Leeds out for his first game in charge. Clough had asked former manager Don Revie to lead the team but he refused. Clough had already done his 'put all your medals in the bin because you won them by cheating' speech by the time the Wembley show-piece came around. The Leeds players hated him and made life impossible for him at Elland Road. At Wembley, Leeds were dirty and Keegan was being targeted that day. Johnny Giles took a swipe at Keegan after the England man had pushed him in the back. And then Bremner got involved, and according to Clough, in his autobiography, Bremner 'kicked him just about everywhere – up the arse, in the balls'. It ended with ref Bob Matthewson sending both Keegan and Bremner off, both players stripping their shirts off as they left the pitch. Leeds lost when keeper David Harvey blazed his penalty in the shoot-out over the bar, before Ian Callaghan stepped up to score the winner.

9) Sunderland 4 Charlton 4, May 1998. Paul Scholes, Alan Shearer, Geoff Hurst, Gary Lineker and Clive Mendonca. They all scored Wembley hat-tricks. Mendonca's was against the team he supported, Sunderland, in a play-off final, with a place in the Premier League the prize for the winner.

John Aldridge, Gary Lineker, Ronaldinho and Michael Gray have all missed penalties at Wembley. Gray's penalty was almost as bad as Diana Ross's spot-kick at the opening ceremony for World Cup 1994. Charlton won the shoot-out and were promoted. Gray had taken one before, at Liverpool, and missed that too.

The following season Gray was brilliant as Sunderland marched to the title and back to the Premier League. Gray was so good he made his England debut while playing outside the top flight.

8) England 4 Netherlands 1, 1996. Euro 96 created a brilliant atmosphere and passion, and it was probably because of this game. Going into the tournament Alan Shearer had gone nearly two years without an international goal. But not even his strike in a 1–1 draw against the Swiss could stop the country feeling deflated after the opening game. Then came the Scots, and a 2–0 win thanks to a penalty miss from Gary McAllister when the ball mysteriously moved off the spot (why, oh why, did he still take it? I'll never understand that), and a wonder goal from Paul Gascoigne. And Gazza was the key to the Holland game for me. I've watched it over and over again. People talk about Christmas trees – I'm sorry, you don't get them in the middle of June. In my opinion we played 4–2–4 because Anderton and McManaman out wide were both very attacking players, who pressed and closed down when the Dutch had the ball, but no more than our front two did.

The big difference was that our playmaker Gazza turned up, while the Dutch magician Dennis Bergkamp did nothing. Gazza had his critics but England manager Terry Venables knew how to get the best out of him – just tell him to go and play, while others did the running for him.

Two goals for Shearer and two for Sheringham in a performance which was pure quality had us all thinking we could go on and win it. We even won a penalty shoot-out against the Spanish. And then they let Gareth Southgate take one against the Germans.

It's worth mentioning the shambles the Dutch were in. Edgar Davids had been sent home after telling coach Gus Hiddink to 'get his head out of the arses' of the senior squad members. They were there for the taking, and England took them apart.

7) **England 3 Hungary 6, 1953.** Described as the Match of the Century. The self-proclaimed kings of world football were dethroned. This defeat may have come three years after England put in a pitiful showing at the 1950 World Cup, but it was far more significant in the history of the England team and English football generally. In drawing

2–2 with a Sweden side who played a lot like England did, Hungary had been dismissed as 'an over-rated bunch' by the English press. The Hungarian full back Jeno Buzansky described Wembley as 'a holy place for footballers', and England didn't have a prayer that night in front of 105,000. England were undone by numbers: Hidegkuti wore the No.9 shirt but played deep, and England were bemused by this. He opened the scoring after 45 seconds and went on to score a hat-trick. Puskas and Kocsis were more advanced and caused havoc. England had five shots, Hungary had 35. We were battered.

Bobby Robson was at the game – he called the Hungary team 'men from Mars'. Captain Billy Wright said they had 'completely underestimated' the Hungarians. Not least their boots. Wright noticed before the game that the Hungarians were all wearing modern-style boots, while the English still had boots which rose up above the ankle. Wright turned to Stan Mortensen in the tunnel and said: 'We should be all right here, they haven't got the proper kit.' Wright looked bewildered as he trudged off the pitch.

England were so annoyed they organised a re-match, in Budapest the following May. Hungary won 7–1, and Puskas said: 'England just played the same; it was the only way they knew how to play, and they stuck to it. Naturally we knew what to do to take them apart.'

Amazingly English football continued to be inexplicably arrogant for many many years. And probably most of us still think England are the kings of football.

6) Benfica 1 Manchester United 4, European Cup final 1968. Yes, Best scored a terrific goal, and Bobby Charlton scored two. United were awesome that night at Wembley as they became the first English side to win the European Cup. Two things struck me when I was researching the game. The first was that in those days you were allowed only one substitute. Matt Busby chose to put a goalkeeper on the bench, Jimmy Rimmer. Only one sub was allowed, and Busby used a goalkeeper! The chances of one keeper getting injured are minimal. The chances of one of the ten outfield players getting injured are far, far greater.

The thing about substitutions in those days was that they were frowned upon. The modern game has substitutions for a laugh. Back in the day it was totally different. Substitutions were happening in the 1950s, but only arrived in English football in the 1965–66 season. Keith Peacock was the first ever substitute, coming on for the injured Charlton keeper at Bolton in the first game of the campaign. For that season, and the following one, subs could only come on for injured players. But managers got wise to this, and instructed players to pretend to be injured, so they could make a change. So at the beginning of the 1967–68 season, subs for tactical reasons could be made.

A letter published in the Arsenal matchday programme for a game against Wolves in February 1979 made me smile when I stumbled across it recently. Anthony Miller of Stanmore was the sender, and he started by complaining about tactical subs. The letter continued:

> . . . a manager can defeat the whole object of having a substitute, and the use of substitutes can completely change the result of a match and enable a manager, who may have fielded the wrong side, to make amends for selecting a wrong player.

So Manchester United would never have won the 1999 Champions League final had tactical substitutions never been allowed. Neither Sheringham nor Solskjaer would have got on the pitch at the Nou Camp.

The letter goes on:

> . . . it is all very well for a manager to change a defender for a forward when his team are winning, and vice versa when his team are losing, and thereby perhaps win a game because of this. I feel this defeats the object of football, where two teams of 11 are playing each other and not two teams of 11 out of a choice of 12 are playing. It is up to a manager to choose a team that he thinks is right, before the match and not during it.

Hasn't football changed?

The other thing that struck me about the 1968 European Cup final is that I'm pretty certain not many people, other than hard-boiled Manchester United fans, know that John Aston was man of the match. Not Best, not Charlton, not Stepney, not Crerand. But John Aston. The winger followed in the footsteps of his dad by playing for United (his dad was in the England team that lost to the USA at the 1950 World Cup). A broken leg ended his United career, and after spells with Luton, Mansfield and Blackburn he ended up running a pet shop with his dad in Stalybridge.

5) Barcelona 1 Sampdoria 0, May 1992. The European Cup final at Wembley is still goalless and they're into the second period of extra-time. Ronald Koeman then fires a free-kick into the back of Gianluca Pagliuca's goal and

Barcelona, under Johan Cruyff, win their first ever European Cup.

I had watched many European Cup finals, but this was the first one I had thoroughly enjoyed from start to finish. Mancini, Lombardo and Vialli always a threat for the Italians – I loved watching Vierchowod, imperious and majestic on the ball. And then you get to that Barcelona side – Michael Laudrup so graceful, Hristo Stoichkov an artist, Ronald Koeman always commanding, and Pep Guardiola so calm on the ball. It was a great final, decided by a great goal.

Incidentally Barcelona's three unused subs that day were tennis God Rafael Nadal's uncle Miguel Angel Nadal, Carles Busquets, the father of Barcelona star and Spanish World Cup winner Sergio Busquets, and Txiki Begiristain, who was Director of Football at Barcelona when Pep Guardiola made them the best club side the world has ever seen, and then moved on to take up the same role at Manchester City.

4) Coventry 3 Tottenham 2, FA Cup final 1987. Spurs were amazing that year but won nothing. They were beaten by a Coventry side who weren't filled with superstars, but who simply played very well on the day. Hoddle, Waddle, Ardiles, Mabbutt, Gough and Hodge were undone by the hard work of midfield general Lloyd McGrath, the endless dribbling of Micky Gynn, the solid defending and ugliness of Brian Kilcline, the towering presence of Steve Ogrizovic, the quality of winger Dave Bennett, and how about Cyrille Regis? A brilliant goalscorer at West Brom, he then led the line at Coventry as well as any striker I have ever seen. Regis should have won far more than his paltry five international caps. He didn't even play the full 90 minutes for

England – he was subbed twice, and came on as sub three times.

At Coventry, Regis was up front with Keith Houchen, a journeyman striker plucked from lower league obscurity just 12 months previously. His story is a lesson to all footballers who think they're never going to make it.

Houchen was released as a schoolboy by Middlesbrough, went to Chesterfield, but ended up being released without signing a professional contract. He went back home to Middlesbrough, and got a trial at Hartlepool, who were next to bottom of the football league. He averaged better than one goal every three games at Hartlepool as a target-man striker, with a touch of quality in front of goal. A move south to Orient saw him get the nickname Hovis, then back up north to York City where he scored a late penalty to beat Arsenal in the FA Cup in January 1985. Incidentally, according to the book *A Tenner and a Box of Kippers*, Houchen's biography by Jonathan Strange, he lost the video of that goal against the Gunners when one of his children vomited on the tape.

In March 1986 he moved to Scunthorpe for £40,000. Nine games and three goals for Houchen later, and it was the end of the season. But Scunny boss Frank Barlow had to go begging to his first-team squad, asking them to play in reserve games which had to be completed before the summer. Houchen's hand went up, he volunteered to play against Coventry who had already won the reserve league. He scored two goals in a 3–1 win and returned home to Middlesbrough, watching Liverpool beat Everton 3–1 in the FA Cup final.

But Houchen's two goals against Coventry reserves had been spotted by the Sky Blues' management team of John

Sillett and George Curtis. They signed him for £60,000 and took him into the top flight. Less than a year later, Houchen would score arguably the best ever goal in an FA Cup final, a brilliant diving header from a superb Bennett cross. It pulled Coventry back to 2–2, and they went on to win in extra-time.

It would never have happened had he not volunteered for that reserve game.

3) Peterborough 1 Darlington 0, League Two play-off final, 2000. I did say they were *my* top ten old Wembley moments, so I make no apology for self-indulgence. I'd be lying if I didn't put Posh in here. This was a ridiculous game. It was played on a Friday night because England were playing at Wembley on the Saturday. It rained all day, I got drenched waiting outside the stadium for my mate Mick to bring my ticket, and there were pools of water on the pitch as the game kicked off. Marco Gabbiadini ran rings round us and only two outstanding saves from keeper Mark Tyler kept it goalless at half-time. The water dried up a bit and Andy Clarke fired home the winner with 16 minutes left.

Two years later Clarke would be banned from the game for a month after testing positive for cannabis. He failed a random drugs test after a goalless draw at Cambridge (he came on as a last-minute substitute). A friend of Clarke told the local newspaper in Peterborough, the *Evening Telegraph*, that he had eaten a slice of cake someone brought back from Amsterdam, not knowing it was laced with cannabis. That's right, he said he didn't know a cake from Amsterdam might be laced with cannabis.

I'll also include the other Posh visit to Wembley, and my first visit too. PETERBOROUGH 2 STOCKPORT 1, DIVISION

THREE PLAY-OFF FINAL 1992. I watch football at all levels, and sometimes when I'm watching lower division football I feel sorry for the football snobs who miss out on some amazing action. Yes, yes, yes, Messi . . . . Of course, Ronaldo. But those of you who never saw Dave Farrell's breathtaking hat-trick for Posh against Barnet, or Robert Taylor's truly stunning hat-trick for Gillingham against Bristol City in 1999, are really missing out. That's just two examples from years gone by. Every week something special happens in the lower leagues.

This game, Posh's first ever visit to Wembley, wasn't a great spectacle but provided two moments of pure quality. King Kenny Charlery had put us in front with a Geoff Hurst-type bounce down off the crossbar. The main difference was that unlike Roger Hunt, Tony Adcock threw himself at the ball to make sure it went in, and took a boot in the face for his trouble. Stockport levelled on 89 minutes through half-man, half-lighthouse Kevin Francis (now a policeman in Canada). And then they had a chance to win it. Jim Gannon (who would later manage both Stockport and Peterborough) was a yard from goal with the ball in front of him. Out of nowhere Posh sub Lee Howarth, a centre-half, flipped his body upside down to wrap his foot around Gannon and hook the ball away. It was the best goal-line clearance I have ever seen. I still don't understand how he did it. Incidentally many people think the Nevilles were the first brothers to captain opposing teams, but they weren't. Lee skippered Barnet against Macclesfield, led by his brother Neil, in the 1997–98 season.

A few seconds later came the other special moment: midfielder Marcus Ebdon looked up, saw Charlery making a run, and delivered a long ball which bounced once, spun back into Charlery's chest, and the striker buried the winner past keeper Neil Edwards. I went crazy.

2) England 6 Luxembourg 0, 1999. My first ever England game at Wembley, and I covered it for talkSPORT (then Talk Radio). Kieron Dyer was superb. I saw Shearer's only England hat-trick and Michael Owen's first Wembley goal for England – an absolute beauty curled in from 25 yards. I thought all England Wembley games would be this good, but on my next visit we lost to Scotland.

1) England 4 West Germany 2, World Cup final 1966. Yes, it was over the line; we don't need technology for that one.

Brian Clough was one of a kind

Did you know Brian Clough actually turned his back on England? More of that later. So much has been said and written about Brian Clough over the years. Winning the title with Derby County was a huge achievement, then doing it with Nottingham Forest, and then winning back-to-back European Cups was stunning. One of my favourite players when growing up was John Robertson, an orthodox left-winger who was brilliant in that Forest side.

Brian Clough achieved some remarkable things in the game. He also didn't bother with diplomacy. Sometimes that blunt-speaking abrasiveness worked against him, especially at Leeds United. At his first meeting with the Leeds players – who were the reigning champions of England at the time – Clough launched into them. According to Roger Hermiston's book *Clough and Revie* he told Peter Lorimer he was a 'diver', he accused Billy Bremner of having 'a fiery temper' that 'would be quickly curbed'. He said to Norman Hunter that he had 'a terrible reputation in the game'. And that Johnny Giles was 'another with a bad reputation'.

His most ill-advised comments though, were aimed at Eddie Gray, a player who had suffered with injuries, but on his day was a brilliant winger capable of the spectacular and undeniably one of the greatest Leeds United players of all time. Clough told him: 'If you'd have been a racehorse, you'd have been put down years ago. You're never fit.'

This was the meeting at which Clough launched his now legendary 'pots and pans' rant. Can anyone quote it word for word? Probably not. But I love the version from David Peace's 'fiction-based-on-fact' book *The Damned United*. In it Clough tells the players:

> As far as I'm concerned, the first thing you can do for me is to chuck all your medals, and all your caps and all your pots and pans into the biggest fucking dustbin you can find because you've never won any of them fairly. You've done it all by bloody cheating.

In Lorimer's words: 'Brian committed professional suicide at that meeting . . . he went through the team being basically as nasty as he could be about each and every one of us.'

Clough's 44 days at Leeds were a disaster, after the success at Derby. But to bounce back and do what he did at Forest was astonishing. He was exactly what England

> 'After the game Clough wouldn't speak to the Turin-based local press, saying: "I will not speak to cheating bastards."'

needed and in my opinion the time was right for him to take the job in 1990. The FA chose Graham Taylor instead. Clough said: 'I'm sure the England selectors thought if they took me on and gave me the job, I'd want to run the show. They were shrewd because that's exactly what I would have done.' Clough was invited into the England set-up under Ron Greenwood in 1978. He was asked to combine his role at Forest with the job of looking after the England Youth team. Along with his Forest assistant Peter Taylor, he was enthusiastic about the job: 'I've always wanted to be national manager and I'm very happy that Peter and I are at last helping England in some way. I'm looking forward to working with Ron Greenwood. England will be back at the top soon, believe me!' He didn't quite get that prediction right, and in fact the whole idea of Cloughie working within the England set-up went horribly wrong.

On the eve of England's participation in the European Youth Tournament in Monaco in 1978, Clough and Taylor dropped out of the trip, saying they 'felt unable to leave Nottingham Forest's affairs at what [they] considered to be a crucial time for the club.' England went out in the first round, the Football Association were far from impressed, and from then on Clough's commitment to the England cause was always questioned. Clough had already had a disagreement which had seen another coach, Ken Burton, leave the FA.

I will give you one more quote from Clough that sums him up for me. In the 1972–73 season Derby County had made it to the semi-finals of the European Cup. They were all but out after losing the first leg in Turin 3–1. Derby were highly suspicious of the German referee Gerhard Schulenberg who had booked Roy McFarland and Archie Gemmill, and that meant they couldn't play in the second leg at the Baseball Ground, which finished goalless.

At half-time of that first leg Schulenberg had been seen going into the referee's dressing room with Juventus substitute and veteran of West Germany's World Cup final defeat at Wembley in 1966, Helmut Haller. The pair were seen apparently laughing and joking. Peter Taylor, Clough's assistant, had a confrontation with Haller and was detained by police.

After the game Clough wouldn't speak to the Turin-based local press, saying: 'I will not speak to cheating bastards.' He also made sure it was translated in case they didn't understand.

That to me sums up the character of the man – he didn't suffer fools gladly and wasn't afraid to speak his mind. And he not only wanted to play the game in the right way, he wanted to do it fairly as well.

Hillsborough shouldn't mean no safe standing

I went along with my good friends Alistair and Jon to watch Aston Villa v Man City in April 2004. It was an end-of-season 1–1 draw, nothing spectacular. But as Jon is a

City fan we were in the away section at Villa Park that Sunday afternoon. I clearly remember standing up for most of the game, despite having an allocated seat. Most of the other City fans at the game were also standing. A few rows back a woman was shouting at all of us to sit down. One lad shouted back to her: 'It's not the opera, love.'

Jon and I used to go to a lot of games at City's old ground Maine Road, and we would stand on the Kippax, one whole side of the ground completely for standing. For us and for many of our generation (born in the 1960s), watching football standing on the terraces is how it should be done.

Away fans visiting London Road, the home of my club Peterborough United, have tweeted me countless times saying they thoroughly enjoyed the chance to watch a game from terracing.

All-seater stadia became the rule after the Taylor Report into the Hillsborough disaster. On 15 April 1989, 96 Liverpool fans were crushed to death and hundreds more injured at the Hillsborough stadium in Sheffield. The details of the day are well documented, but in short, loads of Liverpool fans were trying to get into Hillsborough in time for kick-off, but couldn't. The police decided to stop the crush outside by opening a gate and letting those fans in. That decision to open a gate had disastrous consequences. Once inside they went straight into the fullest pens, when they should have been directed into empty pens either side. Within the pens the crush was horrific, but police didn't open the gates at the front to allow the fans onto the pitch.

The Taylor Report said the match commander Chief Superintendent David Duckenfield froze. While he froze the crush happened and 96 people died.

The police got it wrong. They shouldn't have opened the gate in the first place – they should have dispersed the fans back onto the streets. But even after opening the gate, they should have directed fans away from the crowded pens. And after that didn't happen, they should have opened gates at the front to allow fans to spill out onto the pitch. The police fed stories of fans misbehaving to the newspapers. Journalists didn't do their jobs properly and just printed those lies as facts without checking them. Shoddy journalism. But those words are still repeated by people who should actually find out exactly what happened.

It's sickening that Liverpool fans were blamed by some for Hillsborough. I haven't seen any evidence of ticketless fans or drunken behaviour among Liverpool fans. But even if some of those fans had drunk alcohol before the game, even if they had turned up without a ticket, even if there was some pushing and shoving, nobody deserved to be sent to their deaths inside a football stadium. My memories of Liverpool fans are only positive: they carried the dead and injured on makeshift stretchers. The Liverpool fans in the top tier above the crowded pens were hauling their friends up and away from the carnage below. For families of the dead, the pain will never go away.

In December 2012 the original inquests were quashed, a new police inquiry set up and new inquests were ordered. Evidence came to light that more than 160 police statements had been altered; 116 were changed to remove negative comments about the then policing of the match. There was evidence that 58 of the dead 'definitely' or 'probably' could have survived beyond the 3.15pm cutoff point made by the original inquest.

In his excellent book *Hillsborough: The Truth*, Phil

Scraton describes how the man who should have been match commander at that semi-final, Chief Superintendent Brian Mole, was relieved of his duties 21 days before the disaster happened. This was an officer who knew how to handle big games at Hillsborough: he had done it before, including the semi-final in 1988 between the same teams, Forest and Liverpool. Indeed, his operational abilities had led to Hillsborough regaining its status as a semi-final venue, after suspension in 1981 because of safety and crowd management issues. But with just three weeks to go before the semi-final in 1989, Chief Superintendent Mole had been moved from Hammerton Road Police Station in Sheffield to Barnsley.

Why was Mole moved? Some believe it was down to the resignation of four police officers from Hammerton Road over an alleged initiation ceremony for a young officer who was handcuffed, forced face down in mud, had his trousers pulled down and had a gun put to his head. A group of his police colleagues were behind the 'prank'. As well as the four resignations, two sergeants were demoted, and two constables were reprimanded and fined following the incident.

The official reason for Mole's move was 'changes in the rank structure'. Whether the 'prank' had anything to do with it remains speculation, but the net result was that Chief Superintendent David Duckenfield was left in charge, and he was a novice when it came to policing big games at Hillsborough. Lord Justice Taylor singled Duckenfield out for criticism. We will never know if Chief Superintendent Brian Mole would have handled things differently.

I understand the sensitivity around Hillsborough. I also understand the passion for the truth that led the families of those who died to pursue justice for years and years.

The tragedy didn't happen because of fans standing on terraces. The tragedy happened for many reasons, but not because of terracing.

It happened because there was no cordon set up a quarter of a mile away from the stadium to check tickets and therefore slow down the flow of fans heading to the game.

It happened because the police opened a gate to allow huge numbers of fans into Hillsborough at the same time. It was an incredibly dangerous decision that had tragic consequences.

'If standing areas at football grounds are properly policed, and clubs and fans adhere to strict safety rules . . . then I see no reason why they shouldn't be reintroduced.'

It happened because those fans allowed in were not properly directed once they were inside, and they all rushed to the same area and that caused a crush. It happened because there were not enough crush barriers on the terracing, and the barriers that were in place were inadequate. It happened because, inexplicably, police officers saw fit to refuse to open the gates in the fences at the front of the terracing, to allow fans to spill onto the pitch rather than be crushed.

It happened because Duckenfield froze.

It happened because the police made bad decisions.

It happened because Duckenfield didn't have the experience to deal with such an event.

It happened because police failed to look at what was actually going on. They simply assumed it was crowd disorder.

It did not happen because people were standing on terracing.

If standing areas at football grounds are properly policed, and clubs and fans adhere to strict safety rules, and fences at the front are not put up, then I see no reason why they shouldn't be reintroduced.

There was anger after Hillsborough and a need to change things, to do something, to be seen to be doing something. While evidence was covered up and withheld, inquest verdicts and investigations into the tragedy proved to be inadequate.

The Taylor Report provided something substantial for people to grab hold of. So I understand the reasoning behind the move to all-seater stadia. But for me that reasoning was blurred, and it's time to bring back some safe standing at football matches, whilst never forgetting the 96 who died at Hillsborough.

The last words of this chapter are devoted to the family of one of the Hillsborough victims. Put yourself in their shoes for a moment, and imagine, if you can, the pain they went through. The tragedy should never have happened, and neither should the inhumane treatment of those who suffered because of it.

Doreen and Leslie Jones lost their son Richard at Hillsborough. They had to identify him and his girlfriend Tracey when their bodies were wheeled into the gymnasium next to the stadium on trolleys. Doreen said this: 'I wanted to touch my son, I wanted to hold him and I wasn't allowed to. We were told he was the property of the coroner and I couldn't touch him.'

PART 3

'I went up to him, shook hands with him, and told him he had been an inspiration to me. He told me football was in the past, it was another life that he had left behind, and he just wasn't interested in talking about it. He produced from his pocket one of the letters I'd written, and apologised for not replying. We shook hands again and he got on a bus and disappeared. I was shell-shocked, and felt truly deflated. My boyhood football hero, the kid from Peterborough who had gone on to play for Arsenal, didn't even want to talk about football . . .'

The Champions League

A tournament for champions, which consists mainly of teams who are not champions. Only in the crazy world of football could that happen.

The arrogance of the English is to blame. And it's all the fault of the England national team.

When England lost 6–3 to Hungary in November 1953 it was the first defeat the English had suffered at home. Before the game one of the England players looked at the great Ferenc Puskas and said: 'Look at that little fat chap. We'll murder this lot.'

The Magnificent Magyars proved it was no fluke when they thrashed England 7–1 in Budapest the following summer. English football was in a deep dark depression. Lofthouse, Finney, Wright and Matthews were shell-shocked.

Meantime the Hungarians went to Switzerland for the World Cup in 1954 unbeaten in 28 games. They scored nine against the Korean Republic, eight against West Germany, four against Brazil and four against Uruguay. Then they were in the final. Puskas got the first, and Hungary were 2–0 up in the first eight minutes. But West Germany had fielded a weakened side when they were thrashed by the Magyars earlier in the tournament. This time the Germans came back to win 3–2, although English referee Bill Ling controversially disallowed a Puskas equaliser late in the game, and the German players were accused of taking illegal performance-enhancing drugs at half-time, something that was never proven. The Hungarians' unbeaten run was over, but their reputation as masters of football was intact. Small consolation was that the morale-boosting World Cup triumph for the Germans led to their political and economic recovery after the war.

Incidentally, Bill Ling was a ref from the village of Stapleford near Cambridge. He sent off a player for swearing in a Sunday League game in 1951. Not long after that he was chosen to be the man in the middle at the FA Cup final when Newcastle won 2–0 against Blackpool. Ling was walking down Wembley Way before the final and saw a policeman who by spectacular coincidence happened to be the player he'd sent off for swearing. Ling, keen to show the copper how well respected he was as a referee, said to him: 'Now what do you think?' The bobby replied: 'I still think you're no f***ing good.'

Domestically at that time, Wolves were top dogs. They had won the FA Cup in 1949, were runners-up in the league in 1950, and then champions in 1954, but without any sort of European tournament they couldn't test themselves against the best of the rest. In 1953 Wolves spent £10,000 to install floodlights and went on to play a series of big midweek friendlies. They beat a South Africa national team, Maccabi Tel Aviv, Spartak Moscow, Celtic and Racing Club of Buenos Aires. First Vienna drew 0–0 at Molineux.

The big test was Honved of Hungary. This side contained six players from the national team who had swept almost all before them before and during the 1954 World Cup. Almost 55,000 fans packed into Molineux on a chilly

December night in 1954. Honved led 2–0 at half-time, and the Wolves manager Stan Cullis told his players they were too nervous. Wolves settled those nerves and went on to win the game 3–2, the second half was screened live on BBC TV, and pride in English football had been restored. After the game Cullis paraded his players before the press and declared them as 'champions of the world'. That was the headline in the *Daily Mail* the next day.

It was that comment which led to the development of the tournament that became known as the European Cup. The editor of the French sports newspaper *L'Equipe*, Gabriel Hanot, wasn't impressed that Wolves had declared themselves champions of the world, or that the English media had hyped that up even more. Hanot wrote: 'Before we declare that Wolverhampton Wanderers are invincible, let them go to Moscow and Budapest. And there are other internationally renowned clubs: AC Milan and Real Madrid to name but two. A club world championship, or at least a European one – larger, more meaningful and more prestigious than the Mitropa Cup and more original than a competition for national teams – should be launched.'

The Mitropa Cup was a central European club competition developed in Austria in 1926 that originally included two sides from each of Austria, Czechoslovakia, Yugoslavia and Hungary. In time, Italy became involved, as did Romania and Switzerland. Countries taking part could send champions and runners-up, or cup winners – there was no strict ruling on which clubs specifically qualified to take part. So effectively the Mitropa Cup was the original European Cup, and it did not involve only champions. The Mitropa Cup's growth and inclusiveness suffered hugely because of World War Two.

'I've got no problem with the modern Champions League. The top clubs are usually involved in the latter stages, and they usually contain the best players. What's wrong with that?'

In the 1950s, Hanot wanted to devise a better competition – a way of determining the best team – so he drew up a blueprint for the competition and managed to persuade UEFA to put it into practice. He did this by telling them that if they didn't do it, his publication *L'Equipe* certainly would.

When the tournament was first conceived, the idea was that it would include all those teams with huge fan appeal, not necessarily champions. However, as the structure was developed, only the champions of each country were invited to take part.

So Hibs were the first British team to enter the European Cup, reaching the semi-finals of the first tournament, before losing to Real Madrid.

In England, the Football League refused to allow champions Chelsea to enter, secretary Alan Hardaker saying it was in football's best interests if Chelsea stayed at home. Hardaker, who died in 1980 aged 67, has sometimes been described as a 'little Englander' and indeed he told the esteemed football writer Brian Glanville that he didn't like dealing with Europe because there were 'too many wops and dagoes'.

Eventually, after Wolves defeated European Cup holders Real Madrid 3–2 in one of their midweek friendlies in 1957, English clubs joined in with the foreigners and the competition was strictly for the holders and the champions of each league. Wolves won the title, and were duly knocked out by Schalke in the first round.

It didn't really get much better the following season. Wolves were champions of England again, but were hammered 9–2 on aggregate by Barcelona – including a 5–2 defeat at Molineux. Rangers made it to the semi-finals that year but probably wished they hadn't – they were destroyed by Eintracht Frankfurt 12–4 on aggregate.

Burnley made the quarter-finals in the 1960–61 season before losing 5–4 to Hamburg, who had a young Uwe Seeler scoring freely up front. After winning 3–1 at Turf Moor, Burnley found themselves 4–1 down in Germany. They hit the post twice but couldn't find the net for the goal that could have sent them through to the semi-finals.

Spurs reached the semis, where they lost to Benfica – going out despite a second-leg victory on a Thursday night. (Spurs then beat Sheffield Wednesday on the Saturday, before a 3–3 draw with Sheffield United on the Monday; three games in five days and it wasn't even part of the Easter programme of fixtures.) Then Ipswich, under Alf Ramsey, were dumped out by AC Milan in the first round. Everton failed to make it past the preliminary stage in 1963–64, Liverpool got through a quarter-final with Cologne in 1965 after two goalless draws and then calling right on the toss of a coin, before going out to Inter Milan, despite winning the first leg 3–1 at Anfield. The following season, Manchester United were also knocked out at the semi-final stage. In 1966–67 Liverpool were dumped out by Ajax in the second round, but Celtic went on to win the European Cup. The following year Manchester United took it.

The champions-only rule was in place in the European Cup: only those who won their league title, as well as the holders of the European Cup, could take part. This led to a massive difference in quality – let me throw a few examples at you from the period of English domination of the European Cup between 1977 and 1982.

Oulun Palloseura were Finnish champions in 1979 and 1980; both times they were knocked out by Liverpool in their subsequent European Cup campaigns. First time Liverpool beat them 11–2 on aggregate, the following season 8–0.

Who remembers Red Boys Differdange? The Luxembourg champions were beaten 7–3 by the Cypriot champs Omonia in the first round of the 1979–80 European Cup. In the same round Finnish champions HJK were beaten 8–1 home and away by Ajax (that's 16–2 on aggregate for the mathematically challenged). The Dutch masters then went on to face Omonia in the second round. The first leg in Amsterdam finished 10–0. Tie over.

Results like that led people to believe that the champions of England, Germany, Holland, Italy and Spain were always so much better than the champions of the smaller countries. And although Swedish side Malmo and FC Bruges of Belgium made it to finals, the champions of countries like Cyprus, Finland and Luxembourg never competed properly.

So the European Cup was changed to the Champions League in 1992, and the champions of the smaller footballing countries have to get through a series of qualifying rounds before they can actually get into the tournament proper (Artmedia Bratislava of Slovakia are the only 'minor' champions to achieve this, highlighting how difficult it is: they did it in 2005, among their victories a 5–0 win over Celtic, and then in the tournament proper they actually won 3–2 at 2004 European Champions Porto).

Meantime the top three or four clubs from the big countries like Italy, Spain and England all get into the Champions League.

The European Cup was an idea conceived to determine who are the best club on the whole continent. It was not originally an idea to specifically decide who were the best champions. And so for that reason I've got no problem with the modern Champions League. The top clubs are usually involved in the latter stages, and they usually contain the best players. What's wrong with that?

In 2010 Bayern Munich and Inter Milan met in the final. Two sides full of internationals and two managers – Louis van Gaal and Jose Mourinho – who had both won Europe's top prize before.

In 2009 Lionel Messi, Xavi, Andres Iniesta, Carles Puyol, Thierry Henry and Samuel Eto'o all featured in the Barcelona side that beat Manchester United 2–0.

The year before, Chelsea and Manchester United slugged it out in the final. AC Milan won it in 2007. Barcelona in 2006 and Liverpool beat Milan on penalties in 2005. Great clubs with great players and that surely makes it a great competition. And it still retains the fundamental requirement of any competition – the potential for a shock. Witness European Champions Barcelona, arguably the greatest club side the world has ever seen, losing 2–1 at home to Russian champions Rubin Kazan in October 2009. The seeding system in the early stages makes it easier for the top sides to get through but it doesn't guarantee it.

Great clubs and great players – in my opinion, the Champions League is a great competition.

Scoring the decisive goal
. . . in a European final

On 17 May 1972, Alan Mullery was stuck in traffic at Henley's Corner on the North Circular so he decided to weave through the north London side streets to make his way to Tottenham's White Hart Lane ground. He was the Spurs captain, and he was very late for the second leg of the UEFA Cup final against Wolves, their biggest night in Europe for nearly a decade.

He made it, but he was flustered. Mullery had suffered a season blighted by a groin injury, and wanted to end it on a high note. He scored a cracking goal to seal a semi-final victory over AC Milan, and for this final most of the hard work had been done two weeks previously when Spurs had gone to Molineux and won the first leg 2–1.

At White Hart Lane, 29 minutes had gone, when Martin Peters floated in a free-kick and Mullery headed in the opening goal, getting wiped out by the goalkeeper in the process. Wolves pulled one back but Spurs held on and having skippered the side, and scored the goal that ultimately separated the two sides, Mullery lifted the trophy and was held aloft by the Spurs fans who had invaded the pitch at the final whistle. Back in the dressing room Martin Chivers filled the cup with champagne and they all took a drink – Joe Kinnear, Pat Jennings, Alan Gilzean, Mullery, and the rest of the team. The celebrations continued until Bill Nicholson, Spurs greatest manager ever, and a double winner in 1961 with the club, walked in. He told his jubilant players: 'I've just been in the Wolves' dressing room. I told them they were the better team. You lot were lucky.

The best team lost tonight.' And he walked out. To quote Michael Caine in the film *Alfie,* 'Now there's a morale raiser!'

That was Alan Mullery's last game for Spurs. His reward for captaining the club to European success and scoring the crucial goal in the final was to be told in Bill Nicholson's office that he wasn't wanted and that he could use the phone on the manager's desk to ring around clubs to see who wanted him. Mullery said: 'What hurt most was how I'd been treated by Bill Nicholson.'

Mullery's last call was to Alec Stock, manager of Fulham, and that's where he headed. During one game, Mullery had an argument on the pitch with team-mate Jimmy Dunne. 'The next thing I knew, I'd punched him in the face.' At half-time Dunne waited for Mullery in the tunnel, but Mullery punched him again and this time they had to carry Dunne into the dressing room. Final score Fulham 5 Brighton 2. Mullery said: 'I was sorry I'd hit him . . . but I expected every player to try his best in every game.' Seems reasonable to me.

When Mullery was later appointed manager of Brighton the chairman Mike Bamber, who had been at that apparently one-sided Craven Cottage boxing match between Mullery and Dunne, said he got the job because he'd had a dream the night before about the incident and 'anyone who wants to win that much, I want as our next manager.'

Meeting your football hero

They say you should never meet your heroes, because it will only end in disappointment when you realise that actually, they're not heroes after all.

Let me start by saying that the term 'hero' is a little dubious in this context. The dictionary definition is as follows: 'a man of distinguished courage or ability, admired for his brave deeds and noble qualities'.

So anyone who puts his life on the line to help others is a hero. Yet generally we use the term more loosely and describe sportsmen as heroes. So if my 'heroes' do not display genuine dictionary-definition hero qualities, then please forgive me and don't blame them.

I've met two men who I would consider to be my football 'heroes' and received mixed responses.

The first was David Beckham. I had been sent to La Manga, a sports complex in Spain, in summer 2001. The England squad were there for a training camp ahead of a qualifier in Greece (which we won 2–0 thanks to goals from Scholes and Beckham). I was there on my own (in those early days of talkSPORT I had the roles of engineer, producer and presenter all in one) to interview players and host radio shows.

To get the chance to meet Beckham was fantastic for me. At that time he was England captain so I had the chance of a one-to-one three-minute interview. David Beckham walked into the room, shook hands with me, we chatted a little bit about children (we had kids around the same age) and then got on with the interview. This was a man questioned and photographed all the time, and yet he conducted himself in a way that said this was the most important interview he had ever done. He was a true gent and a proper professional. Meeting my hero on that occasion was awesome.

'... somehow that sub appearance from Heeley gave me the confidence to go on and achieve goals I set myself.'

The only other time wasn't so great. Elsewhere in this book you will have seen me make reference to a footballer called Mark Heeley. After being told he could leave Arsenal he dropped to the deepest depths of the Football League with absolute no-hopers Northampton Town. He was described by team-mates as the 'George Best of Division Four'. A gifted footballer, he regularly missed training, sometimes didn't turn up for games, and, according to team-mates I have spoken to, was a big drinker and heavy gambler.

Despite failing to take his chance at Arsenal, and being completely unprofessional at Northampton, Heeley was still a hero to me, after he had wowed the crowd on his debut, which was also the first game I ever attended.

Having had a bad start in life, I had no father figure, no role model, and no concept of what I could achieve. I just thought it would be one big struggle and then you die.

But at the match, Peterborough v Shrewsbury at London Road, Posh brought on this substitute – 16-year-old local lad Mark Heeley. His bright blond hair made him unmissable, as did his brilliant skills.

As soon as he came on the crowd lifted. When he nutmegged Shrewsbury's record signing Graham Turner there was another roar. Then when his shot clipped the outside of the post and went wide there were 'ooooohhs' and 'aaaahhhs'. Peterborough's David Gregory had made it into the PFA Team of the Year that season, yet Heeley ordered him out to the wing while he took control. It was a stunning 20-minute cameo in the final game of the season and the crowd went home wanting to see more from this kid.

For me it was a big moment. I had seen the impression a boy from Peterborough could actually make. If he could do it, what was stopping me doing what I wanted to do? The memory stayed with me, and somehow that sub appearance from Heeley gave me the confidence to go on and achieve goals I had set myself.

I wanted to find him, if only to say thanks. And so in autumn 2008, after writing to him and getting no reply, I tracked Heeley down to an industrial estate in Peterborough. He was working the early shift in a warehouse and at lunchtime as he left, I went up to him, shook hands with him, and told him he had been an inspiration to me. He told me football was in the past, it was another life that he had left behind, and he just wasn't interested in talking about it. He produced from his pocket a letter I'd written, and apologised for not replying. We shook hands again and he got on a bus and disappeared. I was shell-shocked, and felt truly deflated. My boyhood football hero, the kid from Peterborough who had gone on to play for Arsenal, didn't even want to talk about football. Mark Heeley just wanted to be left alone. So I left him alone.

Meeting your hero might be brilliant, but it might also be a huge disappointment.

The underdog

The world loves an underdog, regardless of how they achieve victory.

Take Wimbledon's FA Cup win in 1988 for example. Apparently the Dons' victory that day over then mighty Liverpool was on the cards from the moment midfield hardman Vinnie Jones clattered into his direct opponent Steve McMahon early in the game. The two players went for a 50-50 ball in the middle of the pitch, Jones went high, McMahon escaped without injury. But even if the Liverpool hardman survived that one, the tone was set and Jones' intimidation had started. Liverpool were beaten 1–0. In short then, a bad foul at the start of the game helped Wimbledon win the Cup.

It would be mean-spirited to take away from the ultimate achievement, but I deal with facts.

New Zealand at the 2010 World Cup were one of the underdogs. And when they scored an equaliser deep into injury time against Slovakia, they celebrated like they'd won the World Cup. Next up for them was Italy, one of the classic David vs Goliath games of all time: Italy the world champions, and New Zealand playing in their first World Cup for 28 years. Of course New Zealand took the lead (Winston Reid pushed a defender in the back in the build-up, and Shane Smeltz was three yards offside, but it was a great goal). Italy got a penalty to scrape a draw.

But the story goes back way before the tournament in South Africa kicked off. New Zealand's qualification was virtually guaranteed as soon as Australia made the decision to leave the Oceania group and join up with Asia. That left the Kiwis as the dominant country on their continent, so off they went to the Confederations Cup in South Africa in 2009. They didn't score a goal, and couldn't even beat war-torn Iraq.

Qualification for the 2010 World Cup was a formality. The opponents in their group were Fiji (population 849,000), Vanuatu (243,000) and New Caledonia (249,000). New Zealand's population is 4.3 million. Ricki Herbert's side comfortably topped the group (although somehow they managed to lose to Fiji). That put them into a play-off with Bahrain, who had finished behind Australia and Japan in qualifying, and had already won a play-off (on away goals) against Saudi Arabia. Had Bahrain qualified, they would have become the smallest country ever to make it to the World Cup finals. But they missed a stack of chances in the first leg and lost out to Rory Fallon's goal in the return leg. So New Zealand made it to the finals.

New Zealand's qualification was, by anyone's standards, easy. At that time they had one Premier League player – Ryan Nelsen – but that's one more than any of the teams they faced in qualifying.

Compare New Zealand's route to South Africa with the Republic of Ireland. In their qualifying group the Irish faced world champions Italy, Bulgaria (World Cup semi-finalists in 1994, and with players featuring regularly in the top divisions in Holland, England and Germany), Cyprus (who beat Ireland 5–2, conceded three goals in the last 12 minutes to lose 3–2 in Italy, and had a host of players in the Greek premier league), Montenegro (newly formed but with a host of top players including Roma's Mirko Vucinic), and Georgia (again with a lot of players featuring at top-flight clubs around Europe). After the Irish finished second behind the Italians, they then had a play-off against France, World Cup finalists in 2006, and slightly better than Bahrain.

In short, FIFA made qualification easier for New Zealand than it was for the Republic of Ireland. That is unfair.

As soon as New Zealand became the top team in Oceania, players like Rory Fallon, who had previously signed up for England, realised he might be able to play at the World Cup so he switched to New Zealand. Even worse, as soon as qualification for South Africa had been achieved, two players suddenly became Kiwis. Tommy Smith, a young defender born in Cheshire and playing for Ipswich Town, had played for England at Under-17 and Under-18 level. He even represented England at the Under-17 World Cup in 2007, a FIFA-recognised tournament. Yet because his family moved to New Zealand when he was eight (he returned to England in his mid-teens to sign for Ipswich), he was eligible for them. No rules were broken of course. Smith, described by the New Zealand press as a 'mystery man' a month before the World Cup started, said when he was selected: 'It's every boy's dream to play at the World Cup.' Surely it is every boy's dream to play *for his country* at the World Cup?

Winston Reid was born in New Zealand, with a Maori mother. The real deal. The only problem is he moved to Denmark aged ten and pledged his international future to them, having played ten times at Under-21 level. So in March 2010 Reid played for Denmark Under-21s, but in May 2010 he made his New Zealand debut, two and a half weeks before the World Cup started. In March Reid was quoted as saying: 'I feel that it is in my best interests to continue to play for the Danish national team.' Apparently

> '**A World Cup should be competitive; we are surely past the days where we celebrate the achievements of the little nation?'**

a TV journalist contacted Reid through Facebook and persuaded him to change his mind.

Again no rules were broken, but FIFA have engineered qualification to ease New Zealand through, and subsequently players have switched allegiance because they see the prize of playing at the World Cup. It trivialises international football, doesn't it?

New Zealand were the only unbeaten side at the 2010 World Cup. But even a sad and sorry England side won more games than they did. It's easy to go unbeaten when you're not even trying to win games. A World Cup should be competitive; we are surely past the days where we celebrate the achievements of the little nation?

The same applies to Tahiti's pathetic contribution to the Confederations Cup in Brazil in 2013. They conceded 24 goals in three games. Fans rooted for the underdog, so much so that when a Tahiti player dived to try to win a penalty against Spain, the fans criticised the referee for not giving it! After Spain's reserves scored ten, most TV stations only chose to replay Fernando Torres' penalty, which struck the bar and flew off into the crowd. Bizarrely, the goalkeeper celebrated as if he had pulled off some miracle save.

It was a surreal experience watching Tahiti winning friends for being useless at FIFA's second most prestigious showpiece tournament. They didn't belong on the same stage as the African, European, South American and World Champions, and to me it seemed that in trying to do the right thing, FIFA hadn't got the changes to Asian and Australasian qualification right.

In the 2012–13 season in England, both domestic cup finals involved underdogs, with contrasting outcomes. In the League Cup Bradford City from the fourth tier beat Wigan, Arsenal and Aston Villa to make the final. It was an incredible achievement. Sadly they were thrashed 5–0 by Premier League Swansea in one of the most one-sided and embarrassing finals ever. The Bradford manager Phil Parkinson said afterwards: 'We would have liked to make more of a game of it.'

Many people thought two clubs which had experienced ups and downs coming together at Wembley, would make for a great final. But it didn't.

A few months later Manchester City were firm favourites to beat Wigan in the FA Cup final. But City were useless in what would turn out to be Mancini's last game in charge. The game was heading for extra-time until Pablo Zabaleta was sent off and Wigan seized the initiative. Ben Watson headed in an injury-time winner. Wigan didn't win it by superior tactics. They won it because Manchester City's prima donnas couldn't be bothered to play to their capabilities.

But there's no escaping the fact, Wigan won the FA Cup. And got relegated.

Maybe I'm unenthusiastic about underdogs, and unwilling to champion them because my team Peterborough have such a truly appalling FA Cup record. When we are underdogs we live up to the tag and get hammered regularly: losing 3–0 at home to Norwich in 2013, 2–0 at home to Sunderland in 2012, 6–2 at Fulham in 2011, 4–0 at Spurs in 2010, 2–0 at home to West Brom in 2009 and 3–0 at home to West Brom in 2008. Absolutely rubbish.

I don't mind underdogs having a go, but underdogs playing above themselves and winning can leave you with a poor team through to the next round. That devalues a whole cup competition.

Are Spurs a big club?

One of Tottenham's legends, Graham Roberts once tweeted that Spurs are 'the best club in the world'. It's fan bravado of course – hence the song even Huddersfield fans sing: *'We're by far the greatest team, the world has ever seen . . .'*

The sad thing is there are actually Tottenham fans who do think they're the best club in the world, and even more think they're bigger than Arsenal.

If Spurs are so huge, and so important, how come over 50 years has passed since they won the title? This is a club that has spent a lot of money and bought some stellar players – Paul Gascoigne, Ossie Ardiles, Ricky Villa, David Ginola, Gary Lineker and, er . . . Paul Stewart. They've nurtured some top talent, some signed as youngsters, others through their system – Glenn Hoddle, Gareth Bale, Darren Anderton and, er . . . Vinny Samways.

Not only have Spurs failed to win the title since 1961, they have had only one season in the Champions League since the new format was developed making it easier for losers to get into Europe's top club competition.

Of course, if you say any of this to a Spurs fan he will talk about having a small stadium, and limited resources and bore you senseless with all those empty excuses.

In the world of a Spurs fan, Tottenham are a massive club – until you get down to discussing the finer detail. They should have won more trophies, should have won the league title a few times since 1961, and they should be regulars in the Champions League.

They remain in Arsenal's shadow, and even if they sneak above them one season, it will not reverse a whole load of trophies the Gunners have stacked up while Spurs failed time and time again.

I don't mean to be harsh but for a club the size of Spurs to have won only two titles, and none since 1961, is a huge underachievement. And to have had only one season of Champions League football is woeful. They're a self-proclaimed cup team but only two League Cups in 40 years, and no FA Cups in over 20 years means that tag is fast-fading.

The Premier League needs a healthy Tottenham Hotspur. They should sort it out big time at White Hart Lane. Or maybe the fans are happy making excuses for mediocrity.

How good was . . .
Laurie Cunningham?

General Franco, Spain's military dictator between 1936 and 1975 when he died, had a massive house in an area of Madrid described as the Beverly Hills of Spain. From the sixth floor of Laurie Cunningham's castle you could see Franco's old place. Cunningham's home was amazing. Gated driveway, a swimming pool and it was full of sun-drenched balconies, yet he only used the lounge, the kitchen and the bedroom. None of the other rooms were furnished. That's just the way he lived his life: him, his girlfriend, and five dogs.

Not sure Franco would have approved of a rich black man with a white girlfriend on his doorstep but the kid from Archway, North London had done well.

Cunningham was a brilliant winger. Or was he? He was stunning on the clips we've seen from that amazing game at Old Trafford in December 1978, when West Brom went to Manchester United and won 5–3. He was explosive and dynamic – my kind of player. You can't base a judgement on one game (the exception being England keeper Robert Green after that howler against the USA in the World Cup 2010), but West Brom had won eight and drawn two before that United thriller, and went top of the table a few days later. Cunningham was one of the stars in a terrific team. He scored four in the first seven games of the season, two as Coventry capitulated 7–1, and he scored at Old Trafford in one of the best top-flight games ever.

Cunningham sets up West Brom's first, just as he's being booed by United fans for having brown skin. He then beats Steve Coppell and David McCreery before slipping a pass between two United players to Cyrille Regis, who back-heels for Len Cantello to smash the ball home. It's 3–3 at half-time. In the second period Cunningham runs onto a Regis flick-on to score the fourth for West Brom, finishing superbly into the corner. And then the goal of the game: deep in his own half the ball comes to Cunningham who lets it run past his body and Stewart Houston, the United full-back, is left for dead. It's clever thinking, perfectly executed – Cunningham didn't even have to touch the ball to beat his man. He runs half the length of the pitch with commentator Gerald Sinstadt saying: 'He's away again showing that pace and grace and control.' He slips a perfectly weighted ball to Ally Brown who feeds Regis for a magnificent finish. It's a wonderful goal and capped Albion's 5–3 win.

After the game, when West Brom boss Ron Atkinson was asked who was man of the match, he said: 'It's a toss-up between one of the coloured front people.' That was the kind of language deemed acceptable at the time. (In April 2004 Atkinson was caught describing Marcel Desailly as a 'lazy thick nigger', and rightly vilified for it.) But at West Brom it could be argued he pioneered the cause of black players, picking Regis and Cunningham (who were already at The Hawthorns when Atkinson arrived) as well as full-back Brendan Batson, who he brought with him from his old club Cambridge United.

Regis was one of nine black players picked by Atkinson for Aston Villa for a game at Everton in the 1991–92 season, and according to Regis' autobiography, a photo of that team was published by racists, who added the caption 'Aston Nigger'. Regis says this about Atkinson: 'I can say without the slightest hesitation that Ron was brilliant with us as black players. I feel the use of the word by anyone in any context is degrading and offensive and I was shocked . . . in all the years I had known Ron I had never heard him use that particular word. He slips up once. Am I supposed to lock away the memories of all those good times because of that? With the many mistakes I have made in my life, I am the last person to judge him. We had a lot of good times together that will far outweigh that foolish moment.'

In the 1978–79 UEFA Cup, Albion reached the

quarter-finals, but it was a tie in the third round which launched Cunningham's football career into orbit. The Baggies had drawn away at Valencia in the first leg, but back at The Hawthorns, three and a half weeks before that famous win at Old Trafford, Albion won 2–0. Cunningham was awesome, dancing past his full-back numerous times, setting up the second goal, crossing for Regis to head against the inside of the post, and another cross for Regis to head in, although Tony Brown (who scored both on the night) touched it across the line from an offside position so it was disallowed. Real Madrid representatives were at the game and decided to sign Cunningham. The deal was agreed at Atkinson's house, and according to the manager the English people there couldn't speak Spanish, and the Spanish couldn't speak English. Figures were written down on paper and crossed out until agreement was reached. Atkinson said: 'When they offered £250,000 my dog barked and I told them, "Look, even the dog knows that's not right."' Albion wanted £1.5 million but a fee of £950,000 was agreed. Cunningham earned £100,000 annual salary plus bonuses, and signed a five-year contract.

Cunningham's decision to move to Spain, freshly released from Franco's grip, was bold – especially as he took with him his girlfriend Nicki, who was white.

The English press constantly questioned Cunningham's contribution in Madrid. Here are just a few headlines from *Shoot!* after he moved to Spain: 6 October 1979 – 'CUNNINGHAM UNDER FIRE IN MADRID.' The article, written a few weeks after he had scored twice on his debut against Valencia, suggests his team-mates didn't like him because they didn't talk to him. As Cunningham says in the article: '. . . until I speak more Spanish I simply can't communicate very much with the rest of the lads. I'm a fairly quiet sort of person anyway.' The article also quotes the Madrid coach Vujadin Boskov: 'Laurie is an excellent footballer. What he's got to do is to make closer contact with the group and become part of the family.' Cunningham had been in Spain for just three months.

On 22 March 1980 – in an article titled 'SOCCER'S WASTED TALENT' – Cunningham was pictured in a Madrid shirt with a small piece saying: 'Cunningham has disappointed on his four outings for England, and it is to be hoped Real Madrid can impress upon him that greatness is not bestowed lightly – it has to be earned and worked for.' A month later, Cunningham won the double in Spain. The piece was also published a month after Madrid had gone to Barcelona and won 2–0 with Cunningham in stunning form. In 2005, the Spanish sports paper *AS* published a special 25th anniversary feature on the game titled 'THE MAN WHO RAN RIOT IN THE NOU CAMP.' A Barça fan said this about Cunningham: 'It was like seeing Cruyff but with black skin. That kid could do anything with a football.' And there was another article titled 'CUNNINGHAM: THE END FOR ENGLAND?' and another 'LAURIE'S REPUTATION IS SLIPPING.' And then another: 'CUNNINGHAM MUST TRY TO IMPROVE.'

And yet 18 months into his spell at Real Madrid, Spanish magazine *Don Balon* ran an article comparing Cunningham with Barcelona's Danish international Allan Simonsen, with the Englishman coming out way in front.

So who was right? Was he brilliant in his first season in Spain as all the evidence seems to suggest? Or were the English press providing some sort of insight from somewhere to show us he was no good? If there was an agenda against Cunningham, was it based on the fact that he was black? Prior to Cunningham, Regis and Batson all teaming up in that West Brom team, no top-flight English team had ever fielded three black players at the same time. Regis described it as 'radical', saying it destroyed the stereotype that black players didn't like cold weather and hard work.

In 1978, Jamaican-born centre-half Bob Hazell, who had been starring for Wolves (he was the first black player to ever score for the club), was selected for the England B-squad. The *Sun*'s headline was: 'ENGLAND ADD HAZELL TO BLACK EXPLOSION'. It was a new thing for black players to wear the white of England.

Ricky Hill, a black player who was part of a Luton side that achieved amazing success for a club its size in the 1980s, told me this: 'There is no doubt that colour played a part in Laurie only receiving six full caps. Unfortunately, instead of being hailed as the future for an exciting, attacking England national team, he was looked upon as somewhat of a risk at international level. A flair player who perhaps couldn't fit into a traditional system which at the time relied on a basic organized 4–4–2 (Cunningham played 4–3–3 at Madrid).'

By the time Hill was one of seven black players in Bobby Robson's first squad in September 1982, Cunningham was out of the England picture. But then Hill himself was dropped, and despite Robson telling him personally he was very much in the picture, it was three years before he was called up again. Hill acknowledges injuries and availability affected Cunningham's England career, but he also highlights the power of the press, who he says played 'a major part in the selection of favoured players'.

Hill remembers a world in the 1970s which would have

been difficult for Cunningham: 'It always seemed slightly strange to me; universally the greatest footballer on the earth was acclaimed to have been Pele, who just happened to be black. Yet in the European leagues, and in particular the English leagues, black players . . . were rejected and in most cases totally ignored.

'Along with the rejection came the stereotypical statements: "black players didn't like the cold weather" . . . "black players can't head the ball" . . . "black players are too volatile."'

Having black players as a fixture in the England team simply didn't happen in the 1970s – as a country we were still developing our attitudes. Hill told me that when Cunningham once played a game at Luton, the home fans booed him every time he touched the ball. Hill and Hatters' team-mate Brian Stein came out afterwards and told the fans if they were booing him because he was black, then they were booing them too. Hill says from that moment onwards, he heard no racism from the home fans at Kenilworth Road.

Despite some issues over turning up on time at Orient (the club once telephoned him to find out why he hadn't arrived for training but got no response. Cunningham told them the next day that he had heard the phone ring but he was resting upstairs and the phone was downstairs so there was no way he could answer the call), the club persisted with Cunningham because he was so talented. But aged 16, Arsenal had turned him away. Don Howe was with Arsenal as player, coach and manager in the 1960s, 1970s and 1980s, and he said: 'Discipline was the main thing at the club – that is what the Arsenal is all about. And players had to follow those rules. If there were players who hadn't

'Yet in the European leagues, and in particular the English leagues, black players... were rejected and in most cases totally ignored.'

prepared properly all week, and didn't have the discipline they would get found out, and they wouldn't last long.'

So Cunningham, whose passion besides football was dancing, usually until the early hours of the morning, was released by Arsenal, despite being 'as good as Cristiano Ronaldo', according to his former team-mate Vicente del Bosque, who won all sorts of silverware as head coach of Real Madrid and Spain.

Cyrille Regis felt Cunningham left England too early. Just before Cunningham left, Regis himself had turned down a lucrative move to St Etienne (he was eligible to play for France, but chose England, playing just five times and never completing 90 minutes). The pair had built up an amazing understanding, Cunningham saying: '[It] came about naturally – we don't have to work at it, and don't plan any particular moves in mid-week training. We each instinctively know where the other will be when he is needed.' But Regis knew those understandings, times when two players click so well together, don't come around too often in a career, and he felt that playing alongside each other a few more years might have helped Cunningham become a more rounded professional: 'Managers cherish consistency and reliability and Laurie, bless him, wasn't always like that. He had amazing skills and balance and was truly talented, but you never knew which Laurie you would get from week to week. He was exciting to watch and people wanted to see that all the time. If Laurie had been able to do these things on a consistent basis, he would have been an absolute superstar. He never really found a home. Perhaps if he had stayed at West Brom for another two years or so, he would have learned to be more consistent and disciplined and gone on to be the player he should have been – but we'll never know.'

There were issues over Real Madrid letting him join up with his national side – back then there was no FIFA ruling on clubs releasing players for internationals. Kevin Keegan insisted on a release clause when he moved abroad, Cunningham didn't. But the difference was Keegan was an established regular with the national team at that time. Without an agent, it may not have crossed Cunningham's mind to include it. He was desperate to play for England though; in one interview he said: 'I'm very worried about the situation, and I was even thinking of just slipping away from Madrid and turning up in London but Real have paid big money for me and they're paying me well, so it seemed fairer all round to play it straight with them. According to the contract they will only release me if the club hasn't any important matches near the [international] fixture date – and a team like Real always has important games. I hope there's some way of sorting this out.'

I can't help thinking that if England and the FA at the time had really wanted to sort the situation out with Madrid over Cunningham, they would have made efforts to do that. But they didn't, it was easier to ignore him.

Can you imagine a player winning the title with Real Madrid, but being overlooked by England? Well yes, it happened with Steve McClaren and David Beckham. We failed to qualify for Euro 2008, and McClaren was sacked. England didn't take Cunningham to the Euros in 1980 and went out in the group stage. If we had topped the group we would have automatically made it to the final in Rome. But we were beaten by Italy after drawing with Belgium (who lost 2–1 to West Germany in the final), so we came home.

Fair to say that in Cunningham's six England appearances, some of which were off the bench, he did nothing spectacular. But then not many players have been spectacular for England given only six caps to prove themselves. Graham Rix was preferred by Ron Greenwood ahead of Cunningham, and he went to the 1982 World Cup. Before that Greenwood operated with one winger, and that was usually Steve Coppell. While Cunningham played in the European Cup final in 1981, after winning the Spanish double the year before, he didn't get a look in at the World Cup in 1982. We went out because we couldn't break down West Germany and Spain. If injuries were the reason he wasn't picked, then why were Kevin Keegan and Trevor Brooking selected? They were both crocked, and didn't feature until appearing as late substitutes in the final game.

When I think of the reasons why Laurie Cunningham won only six caps, and take all the factors into consideration – attitudes towards black players, injuries, Real Madrid refusing to release him, and inconsistency – I'm left to conclude that he was far too skilful and talented to be overlooked so many times by England. In today's game, with better career advice, Cunningham could have been an international star.

Injury blighted his last two years at Real Madrid and he floated from club to club across Europe – Charleroi in Belgium, Leicester in England, Marseille in France (where he helped them stay in Ligue 1 after promotion the previous season), Gijon and Vallecano in Spain.

Having missed out on the FA Cup final whilst on loan at Manchester United in 1983 because of injury, Cunningham won the Cup when he appeared as a substitute for Wimbledon when they beat Liverpool in 1988. Sitting in the crowd at Wembley that day, 12 months after winning the FA Cup with Coventry, was Cyrille Regis. Cunningham had given him a ticket.

The final was dubbed 'The Crazy Gang versus the Culture Club' – Wimbledon players did daft things like go to the pub the night before a game, or set fire to the clothes that belonged to a new signing.

They also had a reputation for playing the long ball game. So how did a sophisticated talent like Cunningham end up there? An agent telephoned Dons chairman Sam Hammam and told him if he signed Cunningham it would take the 'Long Ball Club' into another league. Wimbledon manager Bobby Gould loved him: 'We took a gamble and everybody won. For Laurie Cunningham to join The Crazy Gang was sacrilege to football, but he revelled in it. A lovely soft person, to work with his talent was a pleasure for everyone at Wimbledon FC. A life that was taken too quickly but we had seen true pure footballing ability.'

With an FA Cup medal around his neck, Cunningham then returned to Madrid to play for Rayo Vallecano and scored the goal that got them promoted to La Liga. He was desperate to go back to the Bernabeu and show the Madridistas he was still a class act. But that summer Laurie Cunningham was killed in a car crash in Madrid. Cyrille Regis recalled how two years earlier he and Laurie had been out in bars in Madrid and as Laurie drove home, he fell asleep at the wheel. The car flipped over and landed upside down. The two friends were lucky to be alive and uninjured. They got out and hitchhiked back to Laurie's house.

Cunningham's luck had run out. He was just 33 years old when he died.

Last word to Cyrille Regis: 'Laurie was a truly great player whose contribution to the progress of black players in English football shouldn't be underestimated.'

4-4-2

'. . . yours is the Earth and everything that's in it,
And – which is more – you'll be a man my son.
Ladies and gentlemen, England will be playing 4–4–f***ing–2.'

The legendary words of Mike Bassett, England manager from the film of the same name, after he had just taken a pounding from journalists at a press conference.

Quoting Kipling, then going 4–4–2. I laughed out loud when I watched it.

English football is synonymous with 4–4–2. A keeper, a right-back and a left-back, two centre-halves, two central midfielders, a left and a right-sided midfielder, and two strikers.

After England played 4–4–2 and drew 1–1 with the Republic of Ireland at Wembley in a friendly in May 2013, manager Roy Hodgson was compared to Bassett. This seemed to be done without any real depth to the analysis of the comparison, and therefore seemed unfair. Had Theo Walcott and Alex Oxlade-Chamberlain taken easy one-on-one chances in the second half, England would have won the game comfortably. That, to me, suggests it was the lack of quality from players, rather than a tactical system, that was to blame.

To criticise 4–4–2 is absurd given the success some coaches have had with it in the past.

Arrigo Sacchi at AC Milan is a fantastic example of success with a 4–4–2. He not only produced a winning side, he put on a show as well. Milan were fantastic to watch. In successive years they won the Scudetto, and two European Cups with a solid back four of Tassotti, Baresi, Costacurta and Maldini; the brilliant Donadoni on the right, Evani on the left, Ancelotti and Rijkaard in the middle; with Gullit and Van Basten up front. They produced some of the most breathtaking football in history – all in a 4–4–2.

The key was the high line of the back four, the pressing game, and it may sound basic but one of the big factors was the ability of the players – they could all do pretty much anything asked of them on the field. Most of all, it was about teamwork.

The centre-halves defended and passed it with simplicity. The two full-backs had engines so they could go up and down all day. The two wingers had quality. The two central midfielders could do the defensive side of the game, but with the ball at their feet they were talented. Gullit and Van Basten were world class – that helped. But crucially, they also pressed.

In his book *Inverting The Pyramid* Jonathan Wilson quotes Sacchi: 'There was partial pressing, where it was more about jockeying; there was total pressing which was more about winning the ball; there was fake pressing, when we pretended to press, but, in fact, used the time to recuperate.'

That's the attention to detail that is needed to be truly successful.

Sacchi did all this at a time when Italian football was being heavily criticised for overloading defensively, whether by packing the midfield and sacrificing a striker, or by playing five at the back.

What he did was bold and successful.

Incidentally some argue that it was actually a 4–2–3–1, with Gullit dropping deeper. I disagree with this totally. At times the way the game developed may have led to the shape resembling a 4–2–3–1, but it was never by design, and if anything I would argue Sacchi's system at times was more 4–2–4 given the frequency of the advanced position of the wingers.

Things changed – coaches found ways past it, personnel changed, players got older – and for whatever reason a team playing a certain way can only last so long.

Does the fact that Sacchi stopped winning things mean 4–4–2 is outdated? Of course not.

In the 2012–13 Champions League semi-finals Bayern Munich went to Barcelona not just to defend a stunning 4–0 first-leg lead, but they went to the Nou Camp to add to it and create a special moment in history. They won the game 3–0 and to quote Sam Tighe's excellent online analysis of the game in the *Bleacher Report*: 'Bayern set out 4–2–3–1 on paper, but in reality it was a 4–4–2.' A high defensive line, Robben and Ribery working alongside Martinez and Schweinsteiger, Muller was Sacchi's Gullit and Mandzukic his Van Basten. That system kept Barcelona's main men quiet, with Robben and Martinez working especially hard to close down Iniesta.

Or is it much simpler than this? As Jimmy Greaves once said: 'Football tactics are rapidly becoming as complicated as the chemical formula for splitting the atom.' After Dagenham & Redbridge were relegated from League One in May 2010 following a 5–0 defeat at Peterborough United, I spoke to the Daggers' manager John Still and asked him for his tactical analysis of the game, and how Peterborough had won. His answer? 'They had better players.' And he wasn't wrong. It really was that simple.

'So tactics can win a game, but in my opinion it's the players, and how they perform within that tactical framework, that determines the result.'

Players need a shape and a plan, they need a way of playing. But if those players aren't very good they probably won't win, whatever system you play.

I love tactical analysis – it fascinates me. Every game is different, even if it's just down to the tiny detail.

There is no doubt that sometimes one coach outcoaches another – he gets his tactical plan right and his opponent has no answer. And that's how a game is sometimes won.

Innovative, sometimes revolutionary, tactical ideas are fascinating and sometimes create an era of their own. The 4–2–3–1 was the hallmark of the World Cup in South Africa in 2010 for example. But tactics can also be misleading: Barcelona under Pep Guardiola and Tito Vilanova played without a recognised striker, preferring to employ what they called a 'false No. 9'. It didn't mean they were negative, far from it. They scored plenty of goals.

A 4–5–1 is often interpreted as negative. A coach is

accused of packing the midfield. But if those five in midfield are mainly attacking players, how can it be seen as negative? Chelsea in 2012–13 won the Europa League and played some fantastic football at times with effectively a five-man midfield. They played without orthodox wingers, and the five in midfield would more often than not be made up of Hazard, Ramires, Mikel, Lampard and Mata. Of those only Mikel can be described as a defensive midfielder (although employed more offensively by his country Nigeria). Ramires covers so much ground in a game it would be wrong to label him defensive. His forward forays were noticeable particularly in Chelsea's back-to-back European triumphs.

So Chelsea played with one out-and-out striker – Torres or Ba – but the players in that five-man midfield were mainly attacking and creative players. That cannot be classed as a negative system in any way.

So tactics can win a game, but in my opinion it's the players, and how they perform within that tactical framework, that determines the result.

With the understandably much-maligned 4–4–2, adaptability is the key, as Jupp Heynckes showed with his Bayern Munich treble winners in 2012–13. But again it is down to the players – if they can change formations during a game, change again, then change back, then a team has more chance of winning, assuming the coach knows what he's doing when he makes those changes.

At Euro 2012 few sides played an orthodox, old-school 4–4–2 – in fact from what I saw only England and the Republic of Ireland used it. Both struggled to play well; Ireland were awful, although England did win their group.

The final of Euro 2012 saw Italy's 4–1–3–2 up against

Spain's striker-less 4–6–0. The team with no strikers won 4–0 although two of those goals came when they switched to 4–3–2–1 after bringing Torres on for Fabregas.

In my view 4–4–2 still has a place in football. But as a system to employ when starting a game against top-level opposition, I would say it will get found out more often than not. England fail with it because we struggle to keep possession. When we played Italy in Kiev in the quarter-finals of Euro 2012, both teams had four midfielders on the pitch, but Italy's were closer together and able to maintain possession more easily. England insisted on using out-and-out wide players, Young and Milner, leaving the two in central midfield, Parker and Gerrard, outnumbered. The wide players ended up being peripheral to the game. Italy dominated but couldn't score, but Roy Hodgson's only answer to the problem was to bring on Walcott for Milner, like-for-like, one winger for another, and he brought on Carroll for Welbeck – a striker for a striker. There was no tactical change, which was what was required if England were to have a chance of winning the game before a shoot-out.

As Glenn Hoddle once said: 'I often felt as a player in a 4–4–2, you end up being outnumbered in midfield and chasing the ball, so as a manager I liked wingbacks to push forward; it gives the midfield player on the ball three or four options.' Hoddle, and Venables, were two tactically innovative managers for England – they both left the job for non-football reasons, which is a shame.

Coaching in England

One of England's most successful youth coaches, John Cartwright, tells a story from his teenage playing days in the late 1950s at West Ham United. In a training game, the first team played the reserves, with Cartwright playing at 'inside forward' for the second string. He takes up the story: 'I received a throw-in near the halfway line; instead of playing the ball back to the thrower, I dummied and allowed the ball to roll on past me. From there I ran forward with the ball, beating another defender. Just outside the area I combined with a team-mate with a "wall-pass" and hit his return into the top of the goal from about 20 yards – GOAL! Yes, a real classic. As I walked back to the centre circle, Ted Fenton, the manager, who had been watching from the directors' box, stood up and, with the aid of an electric megaphone called out my name: "CARTWRIGHT, WHY DON'T YOU DO IT SIMPLE? EVERYONE ELSE CARRY ON AS NORMAL, CARTWRIGHT YOU PLAY TWO-TOUCH!" I was being told to be ordinary! For me the "music of the game" died that day.'

Let me go back to my boyhood hero, Mark Heeley, to reiterate the point. As a youngster growing up in Peterborough, Heeley had a huge reputation. These are some of the things coaches and newspaper reports said about him when he was a teenager. Peter Deakin, youth coach and Chelsea scout: 'He was a boy with special talent.' His school coach Terry Jones: 'It was the way he held and struck a ball at the age of 13, that's how I knew he was special.' Local sports reporter Russell Plummer: '[He] has control and skill way beyond his years.'

Yet by the age of 17 Heeley was saying: 'I enjoyed

playing in the youth team and I enjoy a kickabout in the local rec, but I wasn't enjoying the rest of it . . . I lost all my enthusiasm for football, I wasn't happy. I'm finished with football.'

Heeley's love of the game had died.

At school this boy had once been challenged by a teacher, who wanted to bring him down a peg or two, to prove how good he was by scoring from the halfway line. So he said, 'No problem,' and dribbled all the way back from the opposition penalty area, turned around inside his own half, looked up and smashed the ball in before running up to the teacher and saying to his face: 'I told you so!'

This is the kid whose coaches told the rest of the team to give it to Heeley because 'he will do something sensational'. He was full of tricks, pace and individual talent.

Then one day in training, Posh manager John Barnwell set up a drill for the players. He had a back four and a keeper, and then asked certain attacking players to take a ball from the centre circle towards a defensive player who would come to meet him, then play it out to the right winger before running into the penalty area to meet a cross. Several players obliged, and then it was Heeley's turn. He ran with the ball towards his opponent, nutmegged him before smashing in an unstoppable shot from 25 yards.

Barnwell sent him home.

Heeley wanted to quit football.

It's been a tradition in England to see flair players as at best a luxury, and at worst troublemakers. The likes of Rodney Marsh, Tony Currie and Stan Bowles won just 31 caps in total. Paul Gascoigne was one of the greatest individual talents English football has ever seen, yet as England manager Graham Taylor couldn't always accommodate him in the team. For a qualifier in Ireland, Taylor chose Gordon Cowans ahead of Gascoigne. I liked Cowans, he was a thoughtful passer of the ball, but didn't have the match-winning dynamism or flair of Gascoigne. Taylor defended his decision: 'I picked a midfield which I thought would cope better with the onslaught we knew we would face.' England drew 1–1 and were awful.

Later in the campaign for USA 94, Gascoigne was brilliant in a crucial qualifier against Poland but suspended for the next game in Holland, where England lost 2–0 and were dead.

Graham Taylor was a disaster as England manager: after a World Cup semi-final in 1990, we finished bottom of the group, and scored one goal at Euro 92, before failing to make it to the USA for the World Cup in 1994. We can laugh about it now, but Taylor's decision to let a film crew record every step of the way on that pathetic attempt to qualify for the World Cup was a masterstroke. The finished one-hour documentary featured Taylor saying the 'F' word 38 times. Taylor was the star of the show with lines like, 'Do I not like that,' and 'What sort of thing is happening here?' and his quip to the linesman, 'Referee's got me the sack. Thank him ever so much for that.' But my personal favourite was him constantly telling his players to, 'Hit Les! Hit Les over the top! F***ing hell!' as he instructed the team to smash the ball up to big Les Ferdinand. Five years later I was standing on the touchline of a football pitch at the Gosling Sports Centre in Welwyn Garden City watching a reserve game between Stevenage and Peterborough United. Phil Neal, who had been Taylor's coach with England and constantly repeated back to Taylor what the England boss had said, was now Barry

Fry's coach at Posh. He was shouting from the touchline, 'Hit Peter Shearer!' Shearer was a big striker who prompted a very excited local newspaper headline when he signed for Fry at Peterborough: 'POSH SIGN SHEARER!' He never played for the first team.

One other line in that documentary stands out. Carlton Palmer to Paul Gascoigne: 'You've got a f***ed-up knee, a f***ed-up brain and a f***ed-up belly.' Palmer was once described by his manager at Southampton, Dave Jones, like this: 'He covers every blade of grass out there, but that's only because his first touch is so crap.' Palmer won 18 England caps under Graham Taylor.

So, to recap, young players were being told not to show any individual talent, the England manager was relying on a tactic of smashing it up to the big striker, and flair players were not being accommodated in teams. Taylor's Technical Director at the FA in his time as England manager was Charles Hughes who believed that the shortest route to goal was the best way to score, and therefore win games. He believed in POMO, the Position of Maximum Opportunity. In other words, the quicker the ball gets near the opposition goal the better. It doesn't take a football genius to work out that the former schoolteacher was advocating a direct, long-ball game as the best route to success.

In an article in the *Independent* in 1994 Hughes audaciously claimed that Brazil had read his books and copied his philosophy to win the World Cup that year.

Hughes is blamed by none other than John Cartwright for England's failure to produce players to make the national team successful. He told the *Telegraph* in 2002: 'The Achilles heel of academy football is coach education. The coaches running the academies have come through the

Charles Hughes era and they really are grey in many ways. For me, football at the beginning of the coaching structure has to be about the individual, about making that player comfortable in possession of the ball. You encourage him or her to be clever on the ball. There's got to be a different approach to development that is about saying, "We want to take little Jimmy Smith from Bethnal Green and make him world class. And we want hundreds of kids like that." The only way we can do it is to place skill acquisition and skill development at the top of our requirements. Why can't our players be as skilful as the Brazilians? There's no reason why they shouldn't be.'

Cartwright says he was made to feel like an 'outcast' at the FA and resigned his post as Technical Director when he felt so opposed to Charles Hughes' views that he couldn't continue in that job. Hughes at that time was director of coaching and education, and Cartwright was shocked to find that the teenagers he worked with, the players who were supposed to be England's best in that age group, 'couldn't pass the ball, control it or run with it to the level they should have reached'.

Cartwright's point is proven when you consider the national team. Since 1966 the only times they have reached the semi-finals of a major tournament came when Paul Gascoigne, a flair player who emerged despite the system and not because of it, was allowed to express himself in an England shirt.

One of the most thought-provoking, fascinating books I've ever read on football was written by the late Dutch master Rinus Michels, who was successful at both Ajax and Barcelona, as well as taking Holland to a World Cup final in 1974 and victory in the European Championships in

1988. It's not even up for debate; he is one of the greatest coaches football has ever seen.

Michels developed the philosophy of 'Total Football'. If one player moves out of his position, he is replaced by a team-mate. The structure is maintained, but it is dependent on players who think, and who can quickly adapt to new roles many times during a game. In England we praise a midfielder for covering a marauding full-back, or we applaud the 'hard work' of a right-sided midfielder who tracks back. In total football, that is expected, and only noticeable if it is absent. It is why at youth level in Holland, players are regularly instructed to play 'out of position'.

'He covers every blade of grass out there, but that's only because his first touch is so crap.'

In his book *Teambuilding: The Road to Success,* Michels assessed lots of different styles of football and coaching. He wrote: 'In Great Britain . . . the long pass without a true build-up is the dominant style of play.' He praises 'circulation football', passing it repeatedly 'until the correct moment arises for the attacking phase'. This is fundamentally what Pep Guardiola's successful Barcelona were all about. Michels wrote: 'The counterpart of circulation football is the refined kick and rush football as seen mostly in England . . . as coaches though we cannot forget that the spectators in England enjoy watching these kick and run games. There is always something happening around the penalty box.'

Michels was no snob – he admits putting an emphasis on the long ball as he prepared Holland for their Euro 88 success. But with one vital difference to the way the long ball is sometimes used in England: 'Try to play the long ball . . . not at the expense of accuracy,' he wrote. 'Choose the correct moment to pass.' He also pointed out that when he put on coaching sessions of 'kick and run' the players couldn't last the pace for more than 20 minutes. And people wonder why England struggle at summer tournaments (although Michels does stress that England, under Glenn Hoddle, were one of the few teams at the World Cup in 1998 who showed an ability to play 'circulation football').

One fundamental underlies everything Michels says, and is a prerequisite to all his footballing philosophies: you need good players who have technical ability. He wrote: 'Total football . . . places great demands on individual excellence.' If English players don't have that excellence, they cannot play total football. John Cartwright has been telling us all for years that coaching in England does not place enough emphasis on individual excellence. The last word on this goes to Pep Guardiola, who after the death of his Barcelona predecessor Rinus Michels, created a team that the Dutchman would have admired. When he took the job at the Nou Camp, Guardiola said this: 'When we have the ball, we can't lose it.' It really is that simple. As Guillem Balague points out in his biography of Guardiola: 'The high technical quality of Barcelona's players enabled them to make passes that other teams simply could not even attempt. Xavi, Iniesta, Messi could receive the ball and pass or move out of the tightest of corners . . . everything depends on the ability, precision and concentration of the "artists".'

Or you could do it the traditional English way. As Barry Fry once said to me when I asked him how he planned to tackle the next opponent: 'We need to put the ball in the back of their net more times than they put it in our net.'

Does Dennis Bergkamp belong in the elite?

I look back at Dennis Bergkamp's career and I wonder to myself: 'Dennis Bergkamp . . . was he all that?' I've asked this before and you can barely get the question out before people are hammering you.

It was the same with Wenger in the mid-2000s. I used to get all sorts of verbal abuse for daring to question Arsene Wenger because people were only too happy to credit Wenger for being the saviour of English football, the man who invented pasta and warm-downs, the man who didn't see it. So to Bergkamp and it's important to put this into context. I enjoyed watching Bergkamp play – his goal for Holland against Argentina at World Cup 1998 is one of the best goals I've ever seen. His close control, touch, burst of speed with the ball, and vision were all special. And he could finish.

He was class, but does he belong in an elite on top of that? I know there are some fans who seem to think so.

Let's get the obvious negative out of the way. He flopped in Italy – he couldn't adapt, he didn't play well, and although he won the UEFA Cup there it wasn't a good time. One Italian newspaper renamed its 'Donkey of the Week' award, calling it the 'Bergkamp of the Week' award. I saw him play for Inter and he was a shadow of the player he looked at Arsenal.

At Ajax he scored a stack of goals, he was the top scorer in Holland three seasons running. At Arsenal he was more of a No.10, he scored goals, but created more. But if he was so good why did Arsene Wenger leave him on the bench for both the 2001 FA Cup final and the 2006 Champions League final, both of which Arsenal lost? How come he had zero impact in the 2000 UEFA Cup final? In fact he was replaced by Kanu with 15 minutes left.

It's okay to score a wonder goal at Leicester and bamboozle a lump like Matt Elliott (who also scored in that 3–3 draw), but on the big occasion Bergkamp was either ineffective or not good enough for the starting XI.

This brings me to that goal at Newcastle. Bergkamp starts the move, feeding the ball out to the left, then he sprints towards the box and gets the ball back. But it is pinged at him with pace and his momentum is taking him beyond the ball. He does well to steady himself and get something on it to try to control it. Now facing away from goal, the ball spins off the inside of his boot to his right while he spins away to his left. The defender, Nikos Dabizas, doesn't know which way to turn. Bergkamp's eyes are clearly searching for the ball, he finds it and from then on does brilliantly to compose himself and finish.

If you are prepared to believe he intended that turn, then it's spectacular. If, like me, you don't believe it then prepare to receive volleys of abuse from all Gooners and Bergkamp-lovers. Maybe they should listen to Bergkamp himself who told *FourFourTwo* magazine: 'The Leicester goal was pure, but there was luck with the Newcastle one. Against Leicester when the pass came I knew what I wanted to do.' In other words, the Newcastle goal was down to a huge slice of luck.

There seems to be a disproportionate amount of love for Bergkamp. I loved watching him play. I'm not saying he was rubbish. I just don't think he was as special as a lot of people seem to make out.

Take *Match of the Day*'s Goal of the Month competition in August 1997 for example. Bergkamp became the first player to come first, second and third. A brilliant run, acceleration and finish against Southampton, on top of two of his hat-trick goals at Leicester. All good goals, but if you look at the others in contention – including an unbelievable chest and overhead kick from Sheffield Wednesday's Benito Carbone, and a Yeboah-like finish from Newcastle United's John Beresford – it's hard to make a case for Bergkamp filling all three spots. The first of the two included on the shortlist from the Leicester game was good, but not extra special – certainly not in the same class as Carbone's overhead kick. It makes me wonder if a less fashionable player would have been given such an accolade. So bestowing the honour on Bergkamp adds to the aura of elite greatness that surrounds him. It possibly even takes his stock to a place where he doesn't actually belong. At the time he was at the peak of his powers with Arsenal, Real Madrid were signing up the galacticos – and Bergkamp was never mentioned. Madrid won three Champions League titles in five years. Bergkamp won none.

Bergkamp will go down as an Arsenal legend for sure, and one of Holland's finest ever players. But he doesn't quite cut it as a true great of football.

Ironically the transfer of Bergkamp to Arsenal came about thanks to one of the worst players ever to wear an Arsenal shirt. Fellow Dutchman Glenn Helder was George Graham's last signing and he was awful. Helder and Bergkamp shared the same agent; and the rest is history.

Playing in a World Cup

As a passionate football fan and a lover of international football and World Cups, it is hard for me to get my head around the fact that some players actually turned down the chance to play at the greatest global sporting tournament on the planet.

The World Cup is the pinnacle: you can question the quality of the football and the teams involved, but winning the World Cup should be the ultimate for any player. Some players retire from international duty, but there are a few who have actually turned down a specific call-up to a World Cup squad. Let me pick three examples.

Leeds United were dominant in England in the late 1960s and early 1970s, and five Elland Road players were called up to Alf Ramsey's squad who were on their way to Mexico to try to retain the trophy in 1970. (Les Cocker, the Leeds United trainer was also part of the England coaching staff. In fact Cocker coached the England team in 1966 when they won the World Cup, but he wasn't awarded a medal. Cocker, who died of a heart attack in the middle of a training session with Doncaster Rovers in October 1979, was finally awarded a posthumous medal in 2009, collected by his son David and grandson Lee.) Jack Charlton was the only Leeds player called up who was there in 1966. The others were striker Allan Clarke, full-back Terry Cooper, centre-half Norman 'Bite Yer Legs' Hunter and utility player Paul Madeley. But Madeley didn't go.

Madeley was a Leeds boy through and through, once signing a blank contract, giving it to then manager Jimmy Armfield, and telling him to fill in the numbers. When

Armfield asked if he wanted two or three years, Madeley said: 'I'll leave it to you, I just want to play for Leeds.' He could play anywhere. He won most of his England caps at right-back, but also played at centre-half alongside Bobby Moore. For Leeds United he wore seven different numbered shirts in nine finals (including the Charity Shield in 1969). At times he played left-wing, other times centre-forward. Paul Madeley was a true utility player. The fact that he was chosen three seasons running for the PFA Team of the Year tells you he was more than just an odd-job man.

England were World Champions heading to Mexico for the 1970 World Cup, and were many people's favourites to retain the trophy. In March, Alf Ramsey named a provisional 40-man pool of players which would be reduced to 28 and then 22 in time for the start of the tournament on 31 May. All 40 players had the required jabs to allow them to go to Mexico, and all of them received medical certificates. Madeley was surprisingly not in the 40, and he duly made plans to go on holiday with his wife.

Ramsey then reduced the squad down to 28. Among the 12 told they were not required was Arsenal full-back Bob McNab (whose daughter Mercedes would go on to star in the hit TV series *Buffy the Vampire Slayer* and the *Hatchet* movies). Then in April 1970, Madeley's Leeds United team-mate, full-back Paul Reaney (once described by George Best as his toughest opponent in English football), who was in the England squad, broke a leg in a Division One game at West Ham. McNab was expected to get the invite back into the 28, but Paul Madeley received the call, despite not being in the original pool of 40.

Madeley, however, declined the chance to represent the World Champions at the World Cup in Mexico in 1970.

Some said he was tired after a long season (Leeds had won the FA Cup final and reached the semi-finals of the European Cup that year), but Madeley was hurt after being snubbed for the original pool of 40. In Jeff Dawson's book *Back Home: England and the 1970 World Cup* Madeley said: 'If I had been in the original forty Alf had picked, I'd have been raring to go. But I was the forty-first choice for England and, by that time, I had already arranged my holidays with my wife.'

The holiday was in Cornwall. No Dubai, Vegas or Marbs for a proper Yorkshireman back in the day. With family and business concerns as well, Madeley said he wouldn't be 'mentally right'. The papers hammered the utility man for refusing his place in the squad: the *News of the World* portrayed an older Madeley speaking to his offspring, saying: 'I was too tired for Mexico, my son.' His Leeds team-mate Terry Cooper simply said: 'Paul's . . . very strong-minded. There's no point in going if you're not mentally right.'

So Madeley didn't go, Bob McNab was called up for the 28, but then, as if to justify Madeley's decision to turn down the invite, McNab was one of the six players cut from the final 22-man squad. Among the other five who missed out were a young Peter Shilton, European Cup winner Brian Kidd, and Peter Thompson of Liverpool – who had also been cut from bigger provisional squads, in 1962 and 1966. Later, after one-club man Madeley had completed a 17-year spell at Leeds, his family DIY business was sold for a whopping £27 million. He never again got the chance to represent England at a major tournament.

Madeley even had a 1970 England World Cup Esso Collection coin cut. I saw one available on eBay recently, starting bid £1.99. The description said it was the perfect size for use as a golf ball marker. The item remained unsold.

Madeley's wife was rather harshly blamed by some for his refusal and it wasn't the first time a wife had seemingly stood in the way of an England player going to a World Cup, only this one was even more heart-breaking.

Around Christmas 1965 somewhere on Merseyside, young lovers Brian and Patricia were planning their wedding. The excited couple set a date in July the following year, and booked the subsequent honeymoon. They had been 'courting' for several years and had decided to tie the knot after Brian's employers, Everton Football Club, had arranged a holiday for players and their wives, but had told Pat she couldn't go because she and Brian were not married.

Brian Labone was one of Everton's greatest ever players, and one of the finest centre-backs of his era. He played over 500 games for Everton, and like Madeley was a one-club man. He won the title twice and the FA Cup once at Goodison. Brian was so good, he was called up by Alf Ramsey for the 1966 World Cup on home soil. But he was in love, and without even discussing it with his fiancée, Brian turned down the opportunity to join up with the England squad.

Pat was shocked when she found out, but as you can imagine, such a gesture from a man made this young lady love him even more. They got married and went on honeymoon, and even on the day Geoff Hurst scored a hat-trick and England won the World Cup, Labone never mentioned a word about it.

Labone did play at the 1970 World Cup and was the man closest to Gerd Muller when the German volleyed home to cap his side's comeback from two down to win 3–2. Labone never played for England again after that game in Leon.

Everton Football Club have had many legends, but Labone is one of the very greatest. Kevin Ratcliffe, another Goodison great, said that if the club put together a team of former captains, Labone would be the one they all wanted to lead them out. He should have been a World Cup winner but he loved his woman so much he didn't want to spoil her big day. They stayed together 40 years until Labone collapsed in the street near his Merseyside home after attending an Everton fans' awards evening in 2006. He passed away aged 66.

At first you think Labone choosing to turn down a World Cup, and getting married instead, is a heads-gone moment. But then you realise it's a true love story and it melts the heart. What makes it even more poignant is that Brian and Patricia Labone were newly-weds enjoying their honeymoon together, while England players were celebrating winning the World Cup at a banquet in London – *without* their wives.

Daphne Cohen, wife of full-back George, had to hitch a lift to Wembley for the final itself. She had not seen her husband for eight weeks while the players prepared for and played in the tournament. Wives were told to 'stay away', they couldn't even telephone the hotel, and her only communication with George was by post.

The wives expected to be invited to the banquet after the World Cup final victory, but instead were led off to a burger bar. Unsurprisingly, FA officials were allowed to take their wives, but as Daphne Cohen said: 'We were too scared to complain.'

The third example starts in 1977, in a luxury apartment in Barcelona. Armed raiders break in, tie up the husband and wife who live there, and hold rifles to their heads. The couple are thinking only about the three children who are also in the apartment: seven-year-old Chantal, her five-year-old sister Susila and the little boy Jordi, aged just three. They are helpless, but desperate for those children not to be harmed. Jordi is named after the patron saint of Catalonia, in clear contravention of General Franco's rule that made all symbols of Catalonian nationalism illegal. Maybe this was why the gunmen had broken in, who knows? The parents were tied up in their own home, helpless, not speculating on why it was happening. They were only worried about their children.

The incident ends with nobody seriously injured, but mentally and emotionally the couple are scarred. So much so that police give them protection for the following four months after the attack, sleeping in the house with them. The children are escorted to and from school by guards, the father is accompanied to work by a bodyguard.

The couple who were tied up were Johan and Danny Cruyff. At that time Cruyff was the best footballer in the world. He had scored twice against Argentina and once against Brazil to help Holland to the 1974 final where he was brought down for a penalty inside two minutes. The Dutch eventually lost 2–1.

After qualifying comfortably from their group Holland were many people's favourites for the 1978 World Cup. But then came the bombshell.

In October 1977 Johan Cruyff announced he was retiring from international football and would not be going to Argentina with the Holland squad. He never gave a reason. The news rocked Dutch football: speculation was rife as to why Cruyff had walked away. His wife was blamed, so were the Dutch FA who had apparently had issues over his sponsorship. But the most popular theory was that Cruyff, a huge campaigner for Catalan independence, was equally motivated by the political struggle in Argentina. The theory was that he was so opposed to the military junta in Argentina that he refused to take part in the World Cup.

Only in 2008 did Johan Cruyff reveal that he refused to go to the 1978 World Cup because of the armed raid on his home and the threats to his family. Cruyff said on Radio Catalunya: 'All these things change your point of view towards many things. There are moments in life in which there are other values. We wanted to stop this and be a little more sensible. It was the moment to leave football and I couldn't play in the World Cup after this.'

Holland achieved the impossible by losing to Scotland at the 1978 World Cup but they reached the final again. Without Cruyff, Mario Kempes, who was also playing in Spain with Valencia, was the star of the tournament and scored two to help the hosts beat the Dutch 3–1 in that final. Cruyff, once described as 'Pythagoras in boots', eventually returned to international football with Holland and he also came close to joining Leicester City. Early in 1981 Cruyff was wanted by Leicester manager Jock Wallace. Talks definitely took place, but the move broke down because the Cruyffs had 11 dogs at the time (yes, a whole team), and didn't want to be without them while they were quarantined under the UK's strict laws on bringing animals into the country. So he joined Levante whose crowds increased by 20,000 overnight. Cruyff's debut ended in a 1–0 win, after which he said: 'I'm sure we can go up to the First Division as long as my team-mates adapt to my style and follow my recommendations. I think our game will be more effective when the side understands me better, plays faster, and makes better use of my passes.' After ten games Levante couldn't sustain their financial promises to Cruyff, they failed to achieve promotion and the Dutchman left the club.

Makes a slight mockery of one of Cruyff's most famous quotes: 'Before I make a mistake, I don't make that mistake.'

'Makes a slight mockery of one of Cruyff's most famous quotes: "Before I make a mistake, I don't make that mistake."'

I'll finish this chapter by mentioning a player who has his own chapter elsewhere. He never played at a World Cup. He had the chance to, he desperately wanted to, and probably everyone on the planet wanted him to. Except his national team's manager.

George Best was playing in the USA when Northern Ireland boss Billy Bingham was close to qualifying for the World Cup in Spain. Aged 35, Best knew the glory days at club level were behind him, but he felt this might be one last chance of playing at a World Cup. The previous summer with San Jose Earthquakes he had scored 13 goals, including some special Best classics, and he was off the drink at that time.

Northern Ireland had two qualifiers left, and the first was against Scotland, who were also well positioned in the group. Best and the Earthquakes had finished their season and came over to Britain for a tour. They played Best's old club Hibs (he was sacked by the Easter Road club for drinking), and in Best's own words: 'It was a pretty dismal performance by us and long before the end I was just going through the motions.'

Bingham saw enough to put him in the squad. Best hadn't played for Northern Ireland for five years. The following week Best played for San Jose in a 1–1 draw with Linfield. Bingham subsequently dropped Best from the squad saying that he wasn't fit enough for international football.

Meantime Middlesbrough, struggling towards the foot of the top flight at that time, wanted Best to help save them from the drop. Boro' boss Bobby Murdoch, one of the famous Lisbon Lions who won the European Cup with Celtic in 1967, spoke with Best and told him if he showed his fitness it could help change Bingham's mind. But Best decided not to join Middlesbrough, partly because his wife Angie had given birth to their son Calum in February 1981. This is what Best said in his autobiography: 'The timing wasn't right, what with . . . the new baby. I couldn't imagine that Angela would fancy moving to Middlesbrough and I didn't fancy playing in another poor team, nor stepping back into the media circus that my return to England would have become. So I said thanks but no thanks, although I was sorry for Bobby, who was shattered when I told him.'

Middlesbrough ended the season bottom and relegated, Murdoch was sacked and never managed another club. Best went back to the States and started drinking again. In June 1982, while Gerry Armstrong was becoming an all-time Northern Ireland legend scoring the winner against Spain in Valencia, Best was being snapped by the paparazzi embarking on a very public affair with former Miss World Mary Stavin, which brought an end to his marriage to Angie Best.

A little twist of the story here and there and ultimately

you realise that George Best chose Miss World over a World Cup. Angie and Calum Best lost a husband and father, Best fell in love with Miss World and booze (again), Middlesbrough were relegated and Murdoch's managerial career ended. In the space of less than a year, Best left a trail of casualties with his decisions. Yet in an interview with *Four-FourTwo* magazine a few years before his death in 2005, Best was asked what his biggest regret was. He replied: 'I missed a penalty against Chelsea at Old Trafford. It's the only penalty I remember missing, so I wish I could take it again.'

PART 4

'You can say . . . these other players are better than me, not a problem. Everyone's got opinions; that's football. Not a problem with McClaren's opinions if he plays someone else, not a problem with him at all, but don't ever call me a bottler on radio in front of thousands of people listening to you.'

Football magazines

Back in the 1970s when I was a boy and really getting into football, there was only one football magazine with any credibility and that was *Shoot!*

Match Weekly began in 1979, and for the football purist has always been looked upon as a kids' comic. I went to buy a copy for use in writing this part of the book but once I saw a cover advertisement for a feature about 'football farts' I thought I wouldn't bother wasting my money. A special mention for *When Saturday Comes*, the fanzine style magazine which is serious and funny at the same time. There have been some consistently high-quality articles and interviews in *FourFourTwo*, which came later, and the more recent addition to the shelves *TwentyFour7* looks like a well-put-together authentic and serious football publication. But for people of a certain age, *Shoot!* was the No.1.

One particular edition from December 1982 was special to me because it featured that man again – Mark Heeley. At this time Heeley was in Division Four at Northampton Town.

This edition of *Shoot!* featured a picture of Spurs' Glenn Hoddle tackling Luton's Paul Walsh on the cover, and inside had a double-page article called 'Wing Wizards In Waiting'. The piece highlighted Heeley as one of six 'wingers waiting to be discovered in football's less fashionable outposts', players who could be good enough to play in the top flight.

Yes that's right, an article about lower division wingers.

Heeley was featured first with a picture of him taking a shot against Blackpool. The article then discussed his strengths and weaknesses, before getting a quote from his manager and giving him a rating out of ten:

> Strengths: Very quick from a standing start and always dangerous when he takes on a full-back. Good crosser of the ball, can work on the left-wing as well as his usual right.
>
> Weaknesses: Lacks a bit of strength in the tackle, and his finishing is wayward when he gets in goalscoring positions.
>
> Manager Clive Walker's verdict: 'Mark proved he could be a First Division player at Arsenal before he joined us. He's got tons of ability, but he is his own worst enemy at times. When he gets his attitude right he'll be a great player.'
>
> First Division potential rating: 7

Wingers were coming back into fashion: Tony Morley at Aston Villa had just tormented the Greek defence in a European Championship qualifier in Salonika which England won 3–0. Stoke City's Mark Chamberlain had just got into the England squad as well.

The other wingers featured in the article were 21-year-old Welshman Daral Pugh of Huddersfield, who had a good career but all in the lower divisions and went on to coach in the Leeds United Academy (Pugh scored the highest rating, 9, from *Shoot!*); Graham Houston, a 22-year-old Preston wideman, who played 150 games for the club before moving on to Burnley, Wigan, Northwich and

Carlisle (all Houston's football was played in the lower divisions); and Colin Morris, who was 29 at the time of the article and playing at Sheffield United in the Third Division. He had played at Burnley, Southend and Blackpool before

'Even as a young football reporter I always pushed the boundaries.'

arriving at Bramall Lane where he stayed until a move to Division Four with Scarborough in 1988.

Also included was Brian Marwood, who was at Hull City. Marwood, 22 at the time, was the only one who did go on and reach the top flight. Eighteen months after the article was published he was signed by Sheffield Wednesday, who had just been promoted to the First Division under Howard Wilkinson. He then won the title with Arsenal in 1989 and played for England. He was most recently at Manchester City, brought in as part of Sheikh Mansour's revolution at the club.

The saddest story was that of the final winger featured in the article: 23-year-old Bristol City fan Micky Barrett of Bristol Rovers. By the end of the 1983–84 season, Barrett was a regular in the side and had played over 100 games for Rovers scoring 18 goals. But he struggled during pre-season training in 1984, and tests showed he had cancer. By the middle of August that summer he was dead. He was 24, and passed away six weeks before the birth of his son Liam.

Elsewhere in that copy of *Shoot!* was an interview with Spurs and Ireland defender Chris Hughton, worryingly titled 'Less Attacking – More Success'; a rather timeless piece with Scotland manager Jock Stein declaring his team wasn't good enough after a 2–0 defeat to Luxembourg; and an inexplicable photograph of Arsenal manager Terry Neill with Frida from Abba, the caption claiming she was a big Gunners fan.

Shoot! also offered a free gift at the start of every season – the league ladders. I recently bought some of these on eBay. They were cardboard sheets with slots for 'team tabs', little bits of card with each team's name and stadium name on. In the days before the internet this was the best way to keep up to date with the league standings. I pinned mine to a lump of wood I found in the back garden, and those league ladders were special to me.

Shoot! also gave line-ups and goalscorers for every single game. For a football anorak like me this information was priceless.

There were some terrific articles: Peter Reid declaring, 'I'm not soccer's Mr Greedy!'; a front cover asking 'Who Is The Super Supermac?' – Ted MacDougall or Malcolm Macdonald; Kevin Bond, who later became Harry Redknapp's driver, on the problem of being the manager's son; a feature called 'World Wide' with information from around the globe (again this is all pre-internet); and loads of lower division articles – one *Shoot!* from March 1979 has features with Luton's Bob Hatton, Charlton's Dick Tydeman and Brighton's Teddy Maybank. And if there was any mention of Peterborough United I was in heaven. I still have a copy of a *Shoot!* piece with Alan Slough from summer 1977 when he had just joined us from Fulham. 'IT HAPPENED OUT OF THE BLUE' was the headline, and Slough went on to explain how he hadn't expected to join Posh. Well, who would, two years after playing in an FA Cup final? At Fulham he was alongside Bobby Moore, George Best and Rodney Marsh. Eight-year-old me thought: 'He must be *really* famous if he's in *Shoot!*'

Top players had columns in the magazine: one-time most expensive signing Andy Gray (who said he left Villa for Wolves in 1979 because 'Villa are on the decline', and he had 'a better chance of success with Wolves'; he won the League Cup but then Villa won the title and the European Cup, and Gray was relegated with Wolves), Bobby Moore, Alan Ball, Ray Wilkins and Bryan Robson. And George Best. Top football writer Chris Davies was the young scoop who ghosted Best's column and imagine how difficult this was. No mobiles, no email, and Best of no fixed abode. That's proper journalism! Chris told me: 'George was terrific to work with. I miss our fish 'n' chips lunch when we did the column and then picked our team to represent the world against the moon . . . George absolutely loved football, obviously not his only passion.'

Chris, who had 13 years at *Shoot!* before going on to write for the national newspapers, tells the story of one guy who loved the magazine so much he used to stand in the road waiting for the delivery van to arrive 'because I just couldn't wait to read it'.

The evergreen 'You Are The Ref' feature started in *Shoot!* Remember this one? 'The ball is heading towards goal, the goalkeeper is beaten when he takes off his cap which has a lead-lined peak . . . the cap hits the ball and deflects it wide . . . what do you do?'

One of the most exciting things about *Shoot!* back in the 1970s was the fact that it included full-page, colour, glossy pictures of players and team pictures. But colour newspapers and sports supplements with the daily papers emerged in the 1980s, and by the end of that decade *Shoot!* was up against it, having led the way for so long with ground-breaking features and ideas, and a circulation of 600,000.

It may be nostalgia but I can't help thinking football is a poorer place without *Shoot!* It ceased publication in summer 2008, with sales a fraction of what *Match* was registering. Farts and football – the new teeth and tits.

Ten random *Shoot!* articles

10) The issue of *Shoot!* dated 12 November 1977 features Brian Kidd and Dennis Tueart on the cover celebrating a Manchester City goal together. Inside is an article on the rising cost of goalkeepers after Peter Shilton had joined Nottingham Forest from Stoke for £270,000 the previous summer. Manchester United winger Gordon Hill's article, called 'My Soccer Scene', highlights strikers who could solve England's goalscoring problem (England were about to fail to reach the World Cup finals for the second time in succession). Hill suggests Ray Hankin of Leeds, Peter Ward of Brighton, and Bob Latchford of Everton, who would go on to be the First Division's top scorer that season. (For the record Hankin never got a cap, Ward played five minutes in a friendly against Australia, but Latchford played 12 times for England scoring a respectable five goals.)

Gordon Jago was the Millwall manager at that time and he wrote an article called 'Save Our Soccer', suggesting football stadia in England were dilapidated, the fans were treated badly, and clubs would have to step up their service on and off the field on a match day if football was to thrive. He concludes the article with this: 'People today have more money to spend and attitudes have changed . . . . We have to keep pace with modern trends and unless we compete on a more equal footing with other forms of entertainment, football as we know it today could be very very dead in a few years' time.' Among his many proposals is a plan for all-seater stadia. It would be almost another 12 years before 96 deaths at Hillsborough finally forced the issue and saw Gordon Jago's ideas bear fruit.

9) 25 October 1980 saw Ray Clemence on the front cover of *Shoot!* He was previewing the Mersey derby. But it was the letters page, 'Goal-Lines,' in that edition which caught my eye. David Harvie of Teynham wrote in to wish Alan Dicks all the best after his sacking as Bristol City manager. Mr Harvie wrote: '. . . even a friendly, likeable club like Bristol City succumbs to the modern practice of axing the boss the minute the team hits a bit of difficulty.' Dicks had been manager for 13 years. The author of the letter had a point: Bristol City went on to suffer successive relegations after Dicks was sacked. He was the last manager to take the club into the top division.

Elsewhere on the letters page Helen Benton of Cardiff had a complaint about ticket prices: 'I have been watching Cardiff City for a few years, but now that the cheapest tickets are £1.60 my father and I will not be going so often.' She then proceeded to say how wonderful and cheap it was to go and watch the local amateur rugby team instead. A one-liner from letters page editor Steve Carter killed her argument: 'You don't need gate receipts if you aren't paying the players.' The edition of *Shoot!* from 3 May 1980 featured an article from regular contributor Andy Gray saying football needed full-time referees (it took another 20 years before Gray's wish came true) but in the letters page was this classic from Stephen Cochrane of Hartlepool, who wrote: 'In seven years' time, Hartlepool will be a leading force in Divison One.' Division One in today's world is the Premier League. Stephen's prediction didn't come true; it was based on his admiration for young manager Billy Horner who had been given a seven-year contract.

Hartlepool didn't get promotion by 1987. But Horner was a legend for keeping them going, and sometimes even making them competitive on a shoestring. In his time they had to apply for re-election to the league three times after lowly finishes (there was no automatic promotion/relegation between Division Four and the Conference). He was relieved of his duties in 1983, John Duncan came and went, as did Mick Docherty before Horner returned. In fact Hartlepool had four managers in nine months, and two of them were Horner.

8) The issue dated 21 October 1978 features Forest's Martin O'Neill chasing a ball pursued by QPR's Stan Bowles with Viv Anderson in the background. Inside is an interview with Peterborough manager John Barnwell. Denied promotion to the second tier the previous season on goal average, Posh broke their transfer record fee received, but also their record fee paid and Barnwell's interview was full of optimism: 'The future for Peterborough United is looking very, very bright indeed . . . there's nobody in this division who frightens me. I think the team we've got here is capable of winning promotion.' Less than a month later Barnwell quit after a row with the board of directors and Posh were relegated at the end of the season.

Seven pages further on is a piece about Ipswich Town's FA Cup-winning midfielder Brian Talbot. It is headlined with a quote from Talbot: 'I never really wanted to leave Ipswich.' Talbot had been linked with other clubs, including Arsenal. He told *Shoot!*: 'I felt for a while a change might have been good for me. Then I decided I wanted to stay with the club. I'm really happy I made that decision.'

Two months later Talbot moved to Arsenal.

Amazingly, in the article Talbot said this: 'To me, there are two glamour clubs in England – Arsenal and Manchester United.' As he said it, Liverpool were still wallowing in the glory of back-to-back European Cup wins.

7) Player ratings. *Shoot!* used to give the details of every game in all four divisions, and Scotland (and for a while Ireland) back in the 1970s and 80s. Included in the rundown were marks out of ten for each player. These then became commonplace in newspapers and are still popular today.

I was a young radio reporter covering a game at Orient (I think) back in the early 1990s when after the final whistle a fellow journalist, an older more experienced national newspaper writer, asked me if I would be kind enough to give the marks out of ten for each Posh player. I happily did so. It felt like a massive moment because I knew what these marks would mean to players.

One of the Posh players at that time, the captain Mick Halsall (an absolute and total club legend at Peterborough, and a fantastic man off the pitch too), was so upset about criticism of his performances at one point in his London Road career that he went slightly over the top when he was awarded a 9/10 mark in the paper after one particular performance. He cut it out, taped it to his forehead, and went to training. He wore it the whole day.

This almost matches the performance of another former Posh player, centre-half Paul Price. A Welsh international, Price won the FA Cup with Spurs in 1982. He dropped down the leagues four years later to join Peterborough in what was then Division Four. The manager at the time was the former West Bromwich Albion centre-half John Wile, famous for smashing heads with Brian Talbot of Ipswich in an FA Cup semi-final in 1978. Both players got bandaged up and played on, blood streaming out of Wile's wound for the rest of the game. Wile was having a tough time at Posh; a bottom-half finish in 1985–86, and then several new signings, including Price, got off to a flyer with a 2–0 home win over Southend, but a dreadful run followed after that. Wile's job was on the line after a 1–0 home defeat to Lincoln at the end of October (I was there, we were pathetic). Around that time, according to the players, Wile had started launching scathing attacks on their performances, with some justification.

I had made the trip to Hartlepool for a brilliant 2–1 win a week before the Lincoln game, but apart from that there were few signs of life from a Posh outfit that didn't play much football. Incidentally, at Hartlepool I travelled on the supporters' coach and stood on the away terrace and my memory may be playing tricks but I recall only around ten Posh fans travelling to the game. They were the hardcore usuals who went away to support Posh, and there weren't many of us. My recollections suggest most of us stood in a line along a terrace, and at one point one guy said, 'Spot the weirdo,' and nodded backwards with his head. Literally all of us in the line turned around to stare at this one man who was standing there eating a sandwich. We had never seen him on a Posh trip before and we never saw him again, but he sure felt uncomfortable at that moment, the poor chap.

So Wile was hammering the players after games and in training, as well as preaching to them and lecturing to them about having a long and rewarding career at the top level, something Wile had clearly enjoyed at The Hawthorns. Paul Price was getting a bit fed up with this. He had played and scored for his country, and had lifted the FA Cup at Wembley just four years before his ill-conceived move to Posh, and he didn't need a struggling lower-division manager who had enjoyed a less-decorated career telling him he was useless. So after the Lincoln defeat, and more ranting from Wile, Price arrived at training with his FA Cup winner's medal taped to his forehead, in an act of rebellion against the manager. Price was aged 32 at the time.

Before the next game Wile was sacked and never managed a club again.

It turned out the player ratings I gave to my press colleague that day at Orient upset one ex-professional. The former Spurs, Palace and Brighton defender Gary O'Reilly had just quit playing and was pursuing a (now very successful) career in the media. He was sitting alonsgiside me as I quickly read the marks out loud. When I had finished O'Reilly launched a minor verbal attack on me, saying that I should take more time considering my judgement of players' performamces (he wasn't aware I had actually spent a good fifteen minutes doing just that). He finished by adding: 'Players really do care about these marks.' Gary, I know only too well that players and their egos can't handle low marks or criticism.

Even as a young football reporter I always pushed the boundaries. I was never scared to criticise, and never scared to say what I thought about players. Stuff like 'Scunthorpe's Andy McFarlane hung in the air like a bad smell,' and 'he managed to achieve the impossible by playing a one-two with Steve Claridge,' or 'Steve Butler, more misses than Henry VIII.'

Most of it passed players by, largely because they didn't hear it. But one player did catch up with me. I had a spell reporting on Cambridge United matches. Gary Johnson, later at Bristol City and Yeovil, was the manager at the time. After the regular Friday pre-match interview with Gary at the Abbey Stadium, I packed up my things and prepared to leave. Gary suddenly said: 'Daishy's gunning for you.' I replied: 'Why?' Gary simply said: 'I don't know, but he definitely wants a word.'

Liam Daish was a brick outhouse of a centre-half who never smiled. He was quite scary, and very miserable. The previous Saturday, Cambridge lost 2–1 at Bristol Rovers with Daish and his centre-half partner Danny O'Shea to blame for both goals. In my full-time report I described them on the radio as 'dodgier than a pair of used-car salesmen'. Back in Cambridge their team-mate Gary Clayton was injured and listening. He thought it was hilarious, and proceeded to mock the pair all week. O'Shea was calm about it, a total professional. Daish was wound up and hated it. As I drove back from interviewing Johnson, I figured this would be the subject of the conversation Daish wanted to have with me.

So the following day I'm in the press box at the back of the main stand at Adams Park, Wycombe an hour or so before their FA Cup tie with Cambridge, when a voice bellows up from pitchside: 'Down here!' It was Daish, so I duly bounded down the steps and offered a handshake. Daish declined and growled: 'I don't need you taking the piss out of me so don't do it again,' and made to head back to the dressing room. I replied: 'To be fair, Liam, you were at fault for both goals last week.' He turned back, with a look that indicated challenging him on the matter wasn't my wisest move: 'Listen, clubs are interested in me and I don't need you taking the piss!' And with that he was off.

Cambridge lost the game 1–0. Liam Daish was at fault for the goal. He and O'Shea left a cross to each other and Tony Hemmings swept it into the net. Needless to say, I pointed this out during my reports. Two months later Birmingham manager Barry Fry paid £500,000 for Daish. As one Cambridge player told me: 'The day Daishy went, the whole dressing room got a lift.' To be fair to Daish he went on to have a decent career, including a booking as Birmingham captain for playing a trumpet to celebrate a goal. The trumpet had been thrown onto the pitch by a Blues fan, Daish's booking took him to 41 points and a three-match ban.

6) 30 December 1978 and *Shoot!* comes out with a picture of a young Ray Wilkins dressed as Father Christmas on the front cover. Inside there was a feature on a European Youth Tournament in Monaco, at which England went out in the first round. The article, written by Max Marquis (a referee who also wrote an episode for an early series of the TV show *The Avengers*, a book about Sir Alf Ramsey, and who turned the scripts from the 1970s hit TV series *General Hospital* into several novels) concludes: 'But it was clear, agonisingly clear, the coaching of the England outfield players was markedly inferior to that of countries like Yugoslavia (the eventual winners), France and Italy. The whole system and quality of youth coaching in England needs urgent re-examination and probably restructuring . . . on the evidence of Monaco, it's true that talent is being coached out of our young players.' Sound familiar?

5) In the same edition there is a feature on Bobby Moore, England's World Cup-winning captain. The title of the piece is: 'BOBBY MOORE, HAPPY HE'S STILL OUT OF FOOT-BALL.' Twelve years after lifting the World Cup as England captain Moore had no role in the game. He quit playing in the summer of 1977, after exactly 1,000 senior games, and at that point announced he wanted to go into management.

One afternoon that summer at the Howard Hotel in London, two of England's most famous people sat down to have lunch. Football icon Bobby Moore was sitting opposite legendary popstar Elton John. At the end of the meeting, the pair shook hands, and John, who had just taken over Watford Football Club, told Moore he had the job and he would call soon to confirm.

Three weeks later Moore, still waiting for the phone to ring, read in a newspaper that Graham Taylor had been appointed manager at Vicarage Road. The directors shouted Elton John down and appointed Taylor, who chose Fourth Division Watford ahead of top-flight West Bromwich Albion, who appointed Ron Atkinson instead.

In the article Moore says: 'The longer I am out of League football the more likely it is I will stay out.' But he seems happy enough: 'For almost the first time in my life I can make my own decisions. All my life as a footballer I had to ask people permission for everything I wanted to do. Now

I am my own man. I suppose it becomes less likely every day I will get a full-time manager's job – but I'm certainly not bitter. I like being able to pick and choose what I do and when. I can look at every offer on its merits, decide if it is something I would like to do, and either take it or turn it down. That sort of freedom is priceless.'

Six months later Moore took a job in the eighth tier of English football at Oxford City (with former West Ham team-mate Harry Redknapp as his assistant). They were relegated and Moore left. The next opportunity in England came with Southend United, where there was seemingly always a financial crisis, so much so that the football was almost an afterthought. His widow Stephanie told the *Observer* in 2005: 'It must have been very stressful for Bobby working there. They didn't know how they were going to pay the players. They'd get to the end of the week and somebody would say, "Oh, we've got a game tomorrow." Bobby was involved in all this other stuff, the last thing he was allowed to do was really pay much attention to the team. He was too busy trying to keep the club afloat.'

It was during this spell that I first encountered the great man. Posh went to Southend at the end of March 1986, and I made the trip with a handful of others. Arriving early, a few of us went into the supporters' bar for a drink, and there he was, Bobby Moore, standing on a small stage making a speech to the fans.

Posh won 1–0 thanks to a late strike from permanently permed frontman Jackie Gallagher, who went on to play for Wolves. Frank Lampard Senior, brought in by his old friend Moore to help with coaching, played in the game.

A month and four defeats later Moore was relieved of his duties.

No club wanted him as manager, so the *Sunday Sport*, a newspaper filled mainly with hard-to-believe stories and even harder-to-believe huge breasts, paid him £25,000 a year for a few hours' work each week as the Sports Editor.

He then worked with Capital Radio in London, commentating on games with Jonathan Pearce. I later worked at Capital myself and learned a huge amount from JP. The pair came to Posh to watch Brentford win the Division Three title on the last day of the season in 1992. I was also working on the game, a young reporter in local radio at the time. The 14,539 fans seemed to stop what they were doing for a moment when it was announced that the great Bobby Moore was at London Road that day, and the press box seemed frozen by the presence of such an England hero.

Less than a year later, after suffering from bowel and liver cancer, Bobby Moore died at the age of 51, the first of the legends of 1966 to leave us.

It is a source of much debate and consternation that he never succeeded as a manager. The bigger concern is that nobody gave him a proper chance. Later on when he was working for a less-than-respectable newspaper, it seems absurd that the Football Association or West Ham United didn't give him a significant role in the game. In the *Observer* article in 2005, Pearce talked about '. . . this huge effect Bobby had on people – whether it was for 30 seconds or 30 years – for the game never to have employed that and to have never benefitted from that is a scandal.'

The reality is that Moore's relationship with West Ham wasn't always good; the *Observer* article claims he 'was never fully welcome back at the club'. In fact the club almost prevented him from playing in the World Cup final in

1966. Moore's contract with West Ham ended on 30 June, the day before the final. He wanted to move to Tottenham, where he thought he had a better chance of winning the title. But West Ham wouldn't let him (this was long before the Bosman ruling and freedom of contracts). So on the day of the World Cup final, Moore was technically not under contract with a club, therefore not affiliated with the Football Association, and not eligible to play for England. Alf Ramsey had to bring Moore and West Ham manager (later England boss) Ron Greenwood together at the England HQ in Hendon, North London to thrash the situation out. Four years later, Moore wanted to move again, but Greenwood intervened this time too.

When the time came for Moore to finally leave West Ham in 1974, the club promised him a free transfer, which would have meant he picked up any fee the 'buying' club would have paid. The Hammers didn't see it through, and took £25,000 off Fulham, when they eventually sold Moore.

A year later Moore and Fulham lost to West Ham in the FA Cup final at Wembley.

It makes me wonder what would have happened had Elton John made that telephone call in the summer of 1977. Moore takes the job at Watford, takes them all the way to the First Division, but goes one better than Graham Taylor by overhauling Liverpool and finishing first rather than second to win the title in 1983, and a year later beating Everton to win the FA Cup final. Bobby Moore, not Taylor, is appointed England manager in 1990, and the World Cup semi-finalists go on to take both the European Championship crown in Sweden in 1992, and the World Cup in the USA two years later. Do I like that . . .

4) A double Christmas and New Year edition at the end of 1980 included a feature on players *Shoot!* predicted would be 'England's Superstars of the 80s'. Aston Villa's Gary Shaw was the first. A European Cup winner and a Division One champion with Villa, but remarkably he never played for England. Next was then Everton midfielder Steve McMahon. He won countless trophies as a tough midfielder with Liverpool, but couldn't translate that class onto the England stage. He got 17 caps, but his most memorable appearance was as a substitute in the Italia 90 group game against the Republic of Ireland. He came on, miscontrolled the ball and the Irish equalised.

The article says Terry Venables was among many who believe goalkeeper John Lukic would be an England star. He won the title with Leeds and Arsenal, but never played for his country.

Sammy Lee was the next player tipped for international glory, and he would go on to win three titles and two European Cups at Liverpool. The midfielder scored on his England debut, and won 14 caps, but he had an impact when coaching England from 2001. A few months after joining Sven-Goran Eriksson's team, England went to Germany and won 5–1 in a World Cup qualifier. All the goals were scored by Liverpool players – a hat-trick for Michael Owen, and one each for Steven Gerrard and Emile Heskey. Lee was also coaching Liverpool at the time. Coincidence? Maybe. But a few days later England beat Albania 2–0 and again the goals were scored by Anfield men – Owen and Fowler. Lee was well liked as a coach; in the words of Jamie Carragher, he was 'top man.'

Next up was Manchester United's Mike Duxbury, whose ten caps came in an 11-month period between November 1983 and October 1984.

Among those tipped in the article who never won a cap are Forest's Gary Mills, Remi Moses, Adrian Heath and Newcastle full-back Chris Withe (brother of Peter).

The magazine also listed (with no detail) five players from the lower leagues who they felt might go to the top. Unbelievably three of them played for England – one played at the 1986 and 1990 World Cups for England. That was Peter Beardsley, then at Carlisle. The others were Paul Walsh (Charlton), and Gary Mabbutt (Bristol Rovers). The two who didn't quite make the top grade, but enjoyed decent careers in the lower divisions, were Brentford striker David Crown (now an accountant), and Chesterfield winger Alan Birch, brother of former Villa midfielder Paul who played in the Villa side who beat Barcelona in the European Super Cup in 1982, and who died of bone cancer in 2009.

Shoot! also highlighted Middlesbrough's Craig Johnston, a South African-born Australian, who also qualified for Scotland and England among others. His story is very special.

In 1959, a young Aussie failed to make the grade on trial at Dundee United, so he decided to meet up with a young South African woman he had met on the journey to the United Kingdom, who had told him to join her in London if things in Scotland didn't work out. So they got together, and he became a Fulham fan. She became pregnant, and one day they went to Craven Cottage to watch the great Johnny Haynes play. At the ground, this young man patted the swollen stomach of his new wife and declared that the boy (he was guessing) would grow up to be a professional footballer. They then headed back to South Africa where Mr and Mrs Johnston gave birth to their son, who they called Craig.

When he was still a boy they moved to his father's home-land Australia where six-year-old Craig was badly beaten up resulting in him contracting osteomyelitis. It was so bad his mother signed the papers for doctors to amputate his leg. Before the operation, a specialist, touring and lecturing down under, intervened, and saved Craig's leg. It was pure good fortune this specialist was in the right place at the right time.

When he was 14, his parents sold their house after he wrote to Middlesbrough asking for a trial and they agreed. The family paid for him to move to England. Within weeks Jack Charlton, the Boro' boss at the time, said Johnston was 'the worst player I've ever seen'. Johnston agreed, saying, 'I was crap.' Charlton told him to go and never come back. Senior pros Terry Cooper and Graeme Souness took pity on him, and said they would pay him to clean cars and boots and do odd jobs around the club, but warned him he had to stay out of the way of Charlton.

Johnston didn't want to let his parents down, so he earned his money doing jobs, and at the same time worked on his game ferociously, hour after hour kicking a ball in the car park at Middlesbrough's Ayresome Park ground. He drew crosses in each corner of the wall, and practised hitting the crosses, not allowing himself to return to his digs until he hit each cross twenty times. He also watched and studied the first team train and play.

Cooper had played with Jack Charlton for Leeds and England (Cooper said: 'I played with him for 13 years and he still didn't know my name'), and told the Boro' boss he had got it wrong about Johnston. Charlton left, replaced by John Neal. When he first saw Johnston, he said: 'Who's that bloke in the car park with all the hair? Is he any good?'

At one point a virus swept through the Boro' squad, so Johnston was called up and sat on the bench for a reserve game at Scarborough. Boro' were 2–0 down at half-time, Johnston came on and scored from a dead ball, from a volley and a chip just under the bar – claiming he had worked on all three techniques in the days building up to the reserve game – and Boro' won. For a year and a half he had coached himself, and done odd jobs to earn his keep. It all paid off in that second half in Scarborough.

Souness helped secure Johnston a legitimate contract at Middlesbrough and Johnston was a first-team regular.

Johnston wanted to play for Australia but couldn't afford to return during the close season. He wrote to Aussie soccer chiefs explaining the situation and asking for help, but they replied saying they had never heard of him and that they weren't a charity. So Johnston chose England, saying that playing international football for Australia was 'like surfing for England'.

In 1981, Johnston was wanted by Brian Clough and Bob Paisley, two of the most successful managers English football has ever seen. He chose Anfield and won five league titles, an FA Cup and a European Cup. He was always 100 per cent committed, and had a lot of quality in his game too – you didn't sign for Liverpool and get into the side by accident. It amazes me that he never played for England, but Johnston never sold himself, he said he was 'the worst player in the world's best team. I never ever considered myself a proper footballer. When you look at Hoddle or Maradona or Cruyff, Messi and Modric, I never considered myself a proper player. God gave them a gift. It's just the magic when the foot touches the ball.'

My main memory of Johnston is some footage of him running back to help Liverpool defend a corner. The camera behind the goal is close to Johnston as he holds on to the post waiting for the ball to come in, and he clearly is coughing his guts up and looking extremely ill. Such was his commitment to the cause, and his desperation to hold on to a first-team place at Liverpool, he hadn't even told his coaches that he was ill.

But at 28 he retired to return to Australia and care for his ill sister. Dressed as Dame Edna Everidge and all ready for the Liverpool Christmas party, Johnston took a call from his mother saying his sister was in a coma.

He then did a huge amount to help the bereaved families after the Hillsborough disaster. Later he developed Predator boots, invented a hotel minibar system and devised a TV gameshow. In 1999 he was worth £3 million, but five years later he was homeless after another business venture, a grassroots coaching programme, went wrong. Johnston says the whole ordeal cost him his marriage. So he went into photography.

In an interview in 2008, Craig Johnston said that he wanted to be remembered as: 'Just that bloke from Newcastle, Australia, who tried really hard. I know that is the way I am remembered by the hardcore Liverpool supporters who paid the money they couldn't afford. Forget the inventions, forget the photography, forget everything else. If you play football in England there is a surreal bond between you and the fans, and if you try your hardest, you are respected for evermore. I guess that might be on the tombstone: "He didn't have that much natural skill, but, boy, did he try."'

Craig Johnston's story is inspirational in so many ways. Work hard and you have a great chance of achieving your goals. But never forget to always try to do what's right and decent.

3) November 1979 saw a *Shoot!* feature on the record transfer of midfielder Steve Daley from Wolves to Manchester City (even before the gazillionaire Sheikhs took over City!). Daley cost £1.4 million, signed a five-year-deal and banked £64,000 as his cut. He was a two-footed, goalscoring midfielder. The article asked several top names in the game if he was worth it. Bobby Robson said Daley was 'not in the same class of Liam Brady'. His former Molineux team-mate John Richards said it was a 'ridiculous fee, but typical of the transfer market.' Richards also predicted Steve would find it difficult to adjust at Maine Road. Dennis Mortimer said Daley was 'as good as any midfielder around'. He also said big transfers were 'ruining the game'. Middles-brough defender John Craggs said: 'No player is worth that amount . . . this type of transfer isn't good for the game.' And Daley himself was asked for his opinion: 'By today's standards I am worth it. [Man City] will see the best of me.'

City never did. Twenty months after joining City he went to play soccer in the USA before his career faded out at Burnley and Walsall.

In 2009 Daley told the *Guardian* he was making a living out of after-dinner speaking: 'I basically stand up and take the mickey out of myself. That's all I can do. I can't go to a function and talk about things that I've won, because I never won a thing in my career. I've won no trophies, no cups, no medals. The only thing I can talk about is the things I haven't done in the game. When I am on my own and I think about football, and I think about what happened in my career, I look back and think I wish I could have that time at Manchester City again. I make light of everything, but it doesn't hurt anybody more than it hurts me.'

2) November 1979 and Ron Greenwood, England manager, features heavily in an extraordinary *Shoot!* interview where he declares that his new formula for England may not include a centre-forward. This is 26 years after Nandor Hidegkuti was nominally Hungary's centre-forward but kept dropping deep to destroy England 6–3. And Greenwood's 'new' philosophy came more than 30 years before Barcelona bamboozled the game with their false No.9.

The article suggests the 'wind of change is blowing gently through the oak-panelled rooms of the Football Association's headquarters.' Greenwood says: 'Do you need a centre-forward? I'm not sure you do. What I am saying is that my mind is open on the issue.' Only trouble is Greenwood never saw it through. At the European Championships the following year he went with David Johnson, Garry Birtles and Paul Mariner – all orthodox centre-forwards. England didn't get out of the group.

1) A flick back through some copies of *Shoot!* from the 1970s and 1980s reveals a shocking difference in attitudes to black players compared with the modern game. A letter with the title 'Be Prepared!' sent to the magazine by J Klotz of Buckinghamshire in 1977, read as follows:

I am an American, but have lived in England for five years. Even before I left the States it was an accepted fact that stars of baseball, basketball and American football were – and still are – negroes.

However, and this is the real point of my letter, they are seen in the same way as white athletes. Here players such as Viv Anderson and Laurie Cunningham are looked upon as being very different.

My point is greatly emphasised when, in a commentary, colour seldom fails to be dropped into the discussion, often seemingly in spite or jealousy.

I'm sure there will come a time when the higher percentage of superstars in England will be black. The public must be prepared for this.

In the context of today's world it's an extraordinary letter. The editor's reply is equally shocking:

America has a history of outstanding black players at most sports while the negro is only just making his mark over here. But in ten years I expect blacks to be much less of a novelty in our sport.

This was in 1979. Back in the 1950s thousands of Italian immigrants came to live in my birthplace Peterborough; they were leaving behind poverty-stricken rural parts of southern Italy and filling jobs in the expanding brickworks in Peterborough, with raw materials needed for the rebuild after World War Two.

In the midst of this immigration, the local newspaper published a form on the front page asking residents to fill in a questionnaire and send it to the council. The question being asked: 'Do you want an Italian family living on your street?'

It seems incredible, but that was how attitudes were then.

Garth Crooks was interviewed by *Shoot!* later that year in a piece headlined 'NO COLOUR BAR ON THE FIELD'. The Stoke City striker started by saying: 'In football, being black is just one more problem, an extra barrier. The only way things are going to get better is if there are more and more black players throughout the League. Black players are capable of overcoming those barriers. I've got through them – there's no reason why others can't.'

Crooks claims he had 'never come across a racist on the pitch', but he does admit that 'things are said in the heat of the moment (but) after the game they are always the first to come and shake hands – that's one of the beauties of professional football.'

The article concludes: 'He is naturally skilful and intelligent. So next time you're standing next to someone who's giving Garth Crooks some stick because of his colour, remember one day he could be playing for England in the World Cup.'

So if he doesn't have a chance of playing for England in the World Cup, would that make racial discrimination acceptable?

Tackling racism was in its infancy then, but still the problem persists.

Don Revie's 'Dirty' Leeds United

Dirty Leeds? Or the dominant force in English football in the late 1960s and early 1970s? Or both?

What I can say without fear of contradiction is that Don Revie took a club doing nothing in the second tier and changed everything: the kit, the youth system, and the fortunes on the field.

He took over in 1961 and eight years later Leeds were champions of England. They won the championship again in 1974, and were runners-up five times under Revie. He took them to an FA Cup and a League Cup triumph, and they reached three other FA Cup finals. They made the Fairs Cup final three times, winning twice, as well as reaching a European Cup Winners' Cup final.

Leeds were an almighty force under Don Revie. He quit for the England job in 1974, but even then he left a side that went all the way to the European Cup final.

Many years ago when I first discovered how successful Revie had been at Elland Road, I was shocked. All I had heard up to that point was 'Dirty Leeds'. I hadn't even started school when Leeds won the title in 1974, so I don't remember seeing that side first hand.

Brian Clough said this about Revie's Leeds: 'I despised what they stood for – systematically putting referees under intolerable pressure with their violent behaviour, both physical and verbal, their overreactions, and the unsavoury spectacle of skipper Billy Bremner running alongside the harassed referee, constantly yelling in his ear. They angered and offended me to such an extent that I took every opportunity to condemn their cynicism, which for me, devalued so much of what they achieved and the marvellous football of which they are capable – a high level of skill and organised teamwork that I, like millions, admired. Leeds in those days cheated – and I was more than happy to draw people's attention to the fact.'

From what I now know I think Clough's words sum Revie's Leeds up perfectly. They had some stunningly talented players, notably Eddie Gray, but all too often the ill-discipline would overshadow the football.

Certain Leeds players actually backed this view up. Johnny Giles said this in an interview with the *Irish Evening Herald*: 'I became as big an assassin as there was, and as dangerous in my own way . . . you do it coldly, you do it clinically, but you let everybody know in the game there are no liberties taken here. I was given the choice of becoming a lion or a lamb and I was determined not to become a lamb.' Giles later said he was 'thoroughly ashamed' of 'the bad things I did'.

Norman Hunter confirmed it. After the infamous 1974 Charity Shield (this was actually Brian Clough's first game in charge of Leeds, but it was seen as Revie's team, so much so that Clough asked Revie to lead them out at Wembley, but he declined), Liverpool's Brian Hall said: 'Norman [Hunter] kicked me all over the pitch. I was counting my bruises in the bar afterwards when this big arm wrapped around my neck and Norman leaned over and said, "Sorry about that Brian, I thought you were Steve Heighway."'

That Charity Shield, with Leeds players clearly violently targeting Kevin Keegan, shamed Wembley Stadium, and was the worst example of Leeds' cheating.

Revie had started with good intentions. The book *The Unforgiven* quotes a Revie article in which he 'defended his team against accusations of gamesmanship'. Revie wrote this: 'Some time before Leeds United won even the first of the several honours that have come our way, I told a gathering of our players that it was not sufficient merely to become champions. Of equal importance in my book was to behave like champions, off as well as on the field.'

Revie claimed accusations that Leeds were over-physical were 'totally unfair'. George Best in his autobiography *Blessed* described a Giles' over-the-top challenge as being so hard it went through his shinpad and into the bone. Best described Leeds as 'masters of the dark arts'. He did also say Leeds had 'players of great individual skill'. Leeds players were talented, but violent. They also hassled referees more than most, and this in turn fed the fans with fury at certain decisions.

The worst example of this was in a game in April 1971. Leeds were going for the title, and had what should have been a routine home game against West Bromwich Albion. They lost to a goal from Jeff Astle that caused Don Revie, as well as fans (some wearing collar and tie), to come on to the pitch.

I've not heard anyone say this so I will be the first to state the obvious – there is absolutely nothing wrong with the goal. Nothing wrong with it whatsoever.

Hunter is in the West Brom half, he plays a poor pass inside, Tony Brown sticks a leg out and connects with the ball, sending it forward into the Leeds half. Brown then chases it. All this time, West Brom's Colin Suggett is coming back from an offside position, he makes no contact with the ball, he doesn't go for the ball, and he doesn't even join the attack after Brown chases through, runs with the ball to the box, and then squares it for Astle to slot home. The bitterest Leeds fans have suggested Astle was offside. No, he wasn't; he was behind the ball when Brown played it.

It's a perfectly good goal. The ref, Ray Tinkler, was manhandled by Leeds players and fans in the ensuing chaos. Revie wandered onto the field, bizarrely with a tartan blanket tucked under his arm, and fans invaded the pitch. It was almost as if they were claiming it's against the laws of football for the opposition to score at Elland Road.

Truth is, the linesman put his flag up, and as Barry Davies, the *Match of the Day* commentator, said at the time: 'One must add that they played to the linesman and not to the whistle.'

There were more police on the field than players as Davies said: 'The Yorkshire spirit's really coming to the fore.'

The goal rightly stood, and Arsenal won the title. The players' lawlessness and violence (at one point Davies says 'there's a wrestling match going on in the centre circle') was copied by the fans, and so the reputation of dirty Leeds on the field stuck, as did the endless links between the fans and hooliganism.

An article written at the time of the Astle 'offside' goal by David Miller in *The Times* could be seen as pompous, or it could be a reflection of what many people thought at the time. Miller described the aftermath of the goal going in as 'the definitive moment of moral corruption in English soccer, from which point the domestic game moved steadily downwards. Leeds United under Don Revie stood for everything that was reprehensible in sport from gamesmanship to physical intimidation and were blatantly beyond the effective control of either the Football League or Football Association.' Miller wanted the Leeds players to be the subject of a police investigation.

Leeds fans would say it was an example of the media being anti-Leeds. My view is that Revie was well liked by the media generally, until he failed in two qualification campaigns with England, and then walked out on the job to take money in the Middle East. That for me was the turning point in Revie's relationship with the press, probably because he sold his story to the *Daily Mail* for £20,000, and apparently he let the newspaper have his letter of resignation before he had given it to the FA. The public outside Leeds turned against Revie when it was revealed that without mentioning any offer from the Middle East, he had offered to resign if the FA gave him a £50,000 pay-off. The FA banned Revie from football for ten years for bringing the game into disrepute. Revie appealed to the High Court, which overturned the ban – but the judge was scathing about Revie's integrity.

I think Leeds were dirty but I also think they didn't get the credit they deserved.

They could be brilliant: in March 1972 they hammered Southampton 7–0 at Elland Road and they were sensational. Six or seven passes led to the first goal; more brilliant passing for the second with movement bamboozling Saints' players, and then Lorimer's clever run finding space for the finish; Clarke showing quick feet for the third; Bremner tenaciously winning the ball before a fierce Lorimer strike for 4–0. Lorimer struck one of those again for 5–0 (Lorimer reputedly had the hardest shot in football in the 1970s); one centre-back, Norman Hunter, crossed perfectly for the other centre-back, Jack Charlton, to head home the sixth (Hunter had been offside seconds before he crossed, but came back to an onside position – funnily enough, no Leeds fans ran on the pitch to complain a year on from the scenes against West Brom); and Mick Jones was a fox in the box for number seven after a deep cross was headed back by Lorimer. Then Leeds capped the display with a stunning show of possession. Every player seemed to touch the ball as Leeds played out time against Southampton. Giles and Bremner showed neat flicks, Madeley gave it away but immediately won it back, and Leeds basically stood there laughing at Southampton. It was a brilliant display from Don Revie's Leeds United.

So why wasn't this stunning football highlighted more? My view is that Leeds were a victim of the era. They could be brilliant, but this was a time when Brazil in 1970 had shown the world football that was even better, and they didn't foul or cheat or hassle referees.

The Leeds players also failed to replicate their quality on the international stage: after taking a two-goal lead England lost to West Germany in the 1970 World Cup quarter-finals, conceding the equaliser seconds after Norman Hunter came on as a substitute for Martin Peters. Hunter's mistake in 1973 at Wembley against Poland robbed England of a place at the World Cup the following year and cost Alf Ramsey his job. Hunter needlessly lost possession on the halfway line, Poland raced clear to score. Allan Clarke was one of England's main strikers as we failed to qualify for successive tournaments in '72, '74, '76 and '78.

There was also the Gary Sprake factor: having literally thrown the ball into his own net against Liverpool in 1967, Revie stuck with him. Sprake later said: 'It went over my shoulder right into the net in front of 30,000 people and right in front of the Kop.' He let a Peter Houseman shot slip under his body in the 1970 FA Cup final against Chelsea. Revie stuck with him. Against lowly

Colchester in the FA Cup in 1971 Sprake was at fault for the three goals which saw Leeds knocked out. For the first, he came and got nowhere near the ball; for the second he was slow off his line and Ray Crawford scored while lying on the floor; and for the third Sprake and Reaney failed to communicate properly, got in a mix-up and the ball ended up in the back of the net.

> 'I think Leeds *were* dirty but I also think they didn't get the credit they deserved.'

But Sprake's biggest 'crime', according to the Leeds fans, came after more than 500 games and ten years at the club, when he sold his story to the *Daily Mirror*, accusing Don Revie of being involved in match-fixing. Former Forest keeper Jim Barron backed up Sprake's claims: he said opposition players were asked to 'take it easy', and if they did there would be some 'holiday money' in it for them. Barron claimed it was the former Leeds captain Billy Bremner who went into the opposition dressing room to make the offer, which Barron told his team-mates he wanted no part of.

In *The Doog*, the biography of former Northern Ireland striker Derek Dougan, details of a game between Wolves and Leeds at the end of the 1971–72 season show, according to the authors, that 'the evidence is credible . . . [of] . . . murky goings-on in the days leading up to the game.'

Leeds were challenging for the title with Brian Clough's Derby County and Liverpool, but they had been asked to play the game at Molineux (in front of over 53,000 fans, 15,000 more than for the first leg of Wolves' UEFA Cup final with Spurs the previous week) two days after winning the FA Cup final at Wembley. According to the book 'there are members of the [Wolves] team who will always steadfastly maintain that they were asked directly to do things to help Leeds' cause . . . word of the approaches was relayed to [Wolves' boss] Bill McGarry and the manager decided he needed to address the players on the morning of the match. He called them out to the centre circle of the Molineux pitch as if he feared the dressing room might have been bugged. Then he told them in no uncertain terms that if any player gave the impression of not giving 100 per cent that night, they would never play for Wolves again.'

Wolves won 2–1, Liverpool failed to win at Arsenal, and Derby won the title while Clough was on holiday in the Scilly Isles.

Peter Lorimer's response to all the allegations was to say Leeds 'didn't need to bribe teams to beat them'. Billy Bremner launched legal proceedings against one newspaper and won £100,000. Revie's son Duncan said the accusations were 'ludicrous', adding that lots of games must have been fixed for Leeds to be so successful for ten years. World Cup winner Alan Ball claimed in his autobiography *Playing Extra Time* that Revie tapped him up after the World Cup in 1966. He also believed Revie was the man behind regular payments of £100 being delivered to his door by a mystery man who said: 'No names, no pack drill, here is an investment.' In the end, Ball went to Everton, and was fined by the FA for his part in this tapping-up scandal.

The one claim that leaves doubt in the mind is that of Bob Stokoe, who was manager of Bury in 1962, when Leeds were trying to avoid relegation to the third tier of

English football. Until his death in 2004, Stokoe repeatedly claimed, without receiving payment from any newspaper, that Revie had asked him to 'go easy' against Leeds, and had offered him £500. When Stokoe refused, Revie asked if he could speak to the Bury players. Stokoe always maintained Revie was an 'evil' man. Stokoe got his revenge in 1973 when he led Sunderland to an unlikely FA Cup final victory against Revie's Leeds.

One thing is for sure, Revie never left anything to chance: he had dossiers compiled on all the opposition, and not all the players were happy with them. Peter Lorimer said this in *We Are the Damned United*, Phil Rostron's factual account of the Clough era at Leeds: 'I had come to loathe Don Revie's dossiers. Such was the detail in his analysis of players we were up against, he could make Hartlepool United sound like Real Madrid. It was all very tedious . . . it was just Don's way. He felt you had to know everything, and that if you didn't he hadn't done his job.'

Those dossiers, and Revie's insistence on bowls' nights, are believed to have played a part in the England players losing faith in Revie at the end of his reign.

In his time at Leeds he was talked about in the Manchester United boardroom as a possible successor to Matt Busby. He was offered jobs at Birmingham, Everton and in Greece – in fact one newspaper actually ran the headline 'REVIE ACCEPTS EVERTON JOB' on 15 May 1973 – the day before Leeds lost the European Cup Winners' Cup final to Milan. Revie had travelled to Liverpool to speak with Everton about the job and left them in no doubt he was going. He apparently changed his mind when the Leeds board improved his contract.

The judge in that High Court case Revie brought to overturn the FA's ten-year ban after he walked out on England, ordered Revie to pay two-thirds of the costs. Justice Cantley said: 'Mr Revie . . . presented to the public a sensational and notorious example of disloyalty, breach of duty, discourtesy and selfishness. His conduct brought English football, at a high level, into disrepute.'

There was good reason for people to dislike Revie: whether it was accusations of match-fixing, the allegations of Leeds being dirty cheats with sharpened studs, or the way he walked away from England.

But his Leeds players were brilliant at times, and they won a huge number of trophies. Plenty to criticise, but in my view as a football fan, there was even more to admire about Revie's Leeds.

Who was better: Peter Shilton or Ray Clemence?

In the summer of 1976 Peter Shilton told England manager Don Revie he didn't want to play for his country again. Eventually he changed his mind. Good job he did because he went on to break the all-time caps record for England.

Shilton had been on standby for the 1970 World Cup as a 19-year-old after a season in goal for Leicester that had seen them lose the FA Cup final and suffer relegation.

He made his England debut that autumn as a Second Division player, and with Leicester crowned champions in

1971 he returned to the top flight. He was a fierce trainer, a perfectionist, and a brilliant keeper.

He also had breathtaking confidence in his own ability. Shilton conceded *the* goal of the 1973–74 season when Leicester went to Craven Cottage for a Cup-tie with Fulham. It was a stunning volley from the edge of the box by Alan Mullery that flew into the top corner of the net. At half-time, Shilton ran up to Mullery, tapped him on the shoulder and said: 'I got my fingers to it.' Mullery replied: 'If you'd got your fingers to that one, Peter, your hand would have landed in Hammersmith.'

By 1975, with more than 20 caps to his name, Shilton decided to quit the international game. He spoke to Revie during the Home Championships, and told him he didn't want to go on the forthcoming tour to America. Shilton was tired of being second best behind Liverpool's Ray Clemence.

At the time Shilton said: 'I know a lot of people are saying it can't be bad to be considered the second best keeper in England. And when you consider the depth of goalkeeping talent we have in the country they have a point. But it was against my nature to simply sit back and accept it – my pride would not allow me to do that. I have always aimed at being the best, and this sort of thing eventually affects your thinking. I don't mind having to fight for a place. In fact I welcome it, for competition puts an extra edge on my game. But I was just not getting the chance to prove myself.'

Not likely to prove yourself if you don't bother joining up with England, are you Peter? The trip to the States – for the Bicentennial Tournament, which FIFA actually listed as competitive, saw two keepers – Jimmy Rimmer and Joe

Corrigan – win their first caps. So had Shilton gone on the trip he would have had that chance to prove himself. It was a bizarre decision from 'Shilts'.

Incidentally Rimmer won two caps that day – his first and last. He let in two goals and was substituted (Corrigan came on) against Italy, but England recovered to win 3–2. Rimmer must be the only keeper with two European Cup winner's medals to have only one international cap. But then he only played nine minutes in the two finals put together. He was an unused sub for Manchester United in 1968, and he started for Villa in 1982 but had to go off injured. In the USA, Brazil won the Bicentennial Tournament, after beating England with a goal from the explosively named Roberto Dinamite.

Shilton missed a chance to win more caps when he fell out with hometown club Leicester City. He wanted a move, they didn't want him to go, so manager Jimmy Bloomfield put him in the reserves. In the end Stoke City paid a record £350,000 for him in 1974. He was brought in to replace the legendary Gordon Banks, who had been injured in a car crash. Tony Waddington was the Stoke manager: 'Some managers thought I was mad when I spent such a sum on a keeper. Peter was worth ten points a season to us.' (These were the days of two points for a win.) In fact Arsenal under Bertie Mee enquired but refused to pay such a big fee. It was at Stoke that Shilton decided to turn his back on England. Waddington's most famous quote was genius. He said: 'Football is the working-man's ballet.' Certainly it summed up the game at that time.

Shilton looked after himself financially. For the talks with Waddington he turned up with an accountant and a solicitor and the whole process lasted over five hours. He was one of the first to agree a lucrative personal kit deal that compromised footballing tradition. Having been signed up by the kit manufacturer Admiral, Shilton wore an all-white kit, at a time when every goalkeeper was wearing a green jersey. When Stoke needed to pay for storm damage to their stadium, they agreed a fee with Manchester United for Shilton. United offered to make him their highest-paid player, but Shilton refused to sign. He was relegated with Stoke the next season.

Only then did he move on, this time to Brian Clough's Nottingham Forest. The *Guardian* had it in their list of the ten most inspired transfers of all time, and in his first season, Shilton won the league title, and the European Cup in successive seasons after that.

At the same time Forest were signing Shilton, Clough was being turned down by a teenage midfielder from the north-east. Peter Cartwright rejected Forest's offer in favour of taking up a job sorting out roadsweeper routes for Northumberland County Council. Three years later Cartwright said: 'I regretted not signing for Forest soon afterwards when I realised that life with the council wasn't all that exciting.'

While Cartwright was at his desk in the Highways Department, Forest won the title, then the European Cup twice. Cartwright would later say: 'I know now it was a mistake to turn Forest down and I thought I'd blown my chance of professional football for good. So when Newcastle came in for me, I almost bit their hand off.'

Newcastle had seen him playing non-league for North Shields, they signed him, he stayed four years and developed a habit of scoring against Sunderland. Spells with Scunthorpe, Darlington and back in non-league with Blyth

'The main reason I would put Clemence ahead of Shilton though is because of Maradona's Hand of God goal at the World Cup in 1986.'

Spartans followed before Cartwright became a teacher in the mid-1980s. His son Andrew is with the Sunderland Academy at the time of writing.

Meanwhile, success with Forest meant England manager Ron Greenwood gave Shilton more caps, and he was pushing to be No.1 ahead of Clemence. In the 1970s, apart from the period when Shilton 'retired' from England duty, Clemence and Shilton took turns to wear the keeper's shirt for England. By the time of the 1982 World Cup Shilton was the clear No.1.

Both men had won virtually everything at club level (although Shilton never won the FA Cup), but experts struggled to separate them. They shared duties at the 1980 European Championships (Clemence played twice, Shilton once) but many regard Shilton as the better keeper for two reasons. The first was his longevity – he played 125 times for England, played over 1,000 club games and continued beyond the age of 40. The second was that while Shilton played in three World Cups, Clemence never actually played in one.

Shoot! magazine once asked England World Cup winner Martin Peters to assess both keepers and decide who was best. They separated it up into ten 'rounds'. The first was handling ability: Peters decided they were 'absolutely level'. Then it was distribution: Peters said they were 'both accurate', and 'use the ball'. Bravery: 'They are both brave, but agile enough to get away with it.' (My view is that Clemence was slightly braver: he was prepared to come off his line and get involved with the game more – my mother used to call him 'tea-break Clemence'.) Round four: Temperament – 'no obvious differences . . . both very sound.' Five: Command of the area – 'on a par with each other.' Six: Agility and Reflexes – 'level pegging again' (Peters apologised at this point for not favouring one over the other). Next up, one-on-one reactions – Peters admits they approach one-on-ones differently but concludes 'both men react brilliantly in this tricky situation.' Round eight: confidence for England – Peters actually gives Clemence the edge here, but only on the basis that he was, at the time of the article (November 1978), 'the man in possession'. He added though: 'they both believe they are the best in the job.' Round nine: Concentration – 'even-steven on this one.' And finally Round ten: Positional ability – 'they don't do it the same way but they both definitely do it well.'

Peters concluded: 'I just wouldn't say anything to put either Ray or Peter ahead of the other.' It sounds like Peters is sitting on the fence, and he probably is. But they were two very good and extremely successful goalkeepers. One particular Shilton performance – a clean sheet in an absolutely vital qualifier in Katowice against Poland – stands out head and shoulders above the rest. Shilton simply wouldn't concede that night. But then again he made a few high-profile errors.

Shilton actually claimed he only made one mistake for England in his 125 games. That came in the 1973 qualifier against Poland at Wembley. England needed to win, but drew 1–1. Shilton seemed to dive late for the Poland goal. He claimed in his autobiography he was trying to make the perfect save, and got it wrong. The error was made to look even worse because the Polish keeper Jan Tomaszewski – who Brian Clough once famously called a clown – was having the game of his life keeping everything out (apart from a late Allan Clarke penalty).

Shilton unquestionably made a mistake in his final game for England, dallying on the ball in his own box. Roberto Baggio robbed him, Shilton then went to ground when he shouldn't have, Baggio fired into the roof of the net, and Italy won the third-place play-off at Italia 90.

I also felt sorry for Chris Woods, England's No.2 keeper when Shilton was the undisputed No.1. He travelled everywhere with England knowing he wouldn't get a look-in – it had been the same position for Shilton when Clemence was favourite. Woods carried on, Shilton turned his back on England. Woods actually won a trophy at Forest before Shilton, the League Cup in the 1977–78 season. Shilton had moved to Forest after playing a few games for Stoke that season, one of which was a League Cup defeat to Bristol City, meaning he was Cup-tied. In fact, Shilton knew he had to get out after the first league game of the season – a 2–1 defeat at Mansfield Town. Stoke fans rampaged through the town centre, and the game was stopped by two pitch invasions. As Shilton said in his autobiography: 'It had all gone horribly wrong for me at Stoke.'

So he went to Forest but couldn't play in the League Cup. His understudy at the City Ground was teenage prospect Woods, in his first full season as a professional. He kept five clean sheets in the competition, including one in the final and another in the replay at Wembley against European Champions Liverpool. Ahead of the final Woods said: 'I've never even been [to Wembley] before, and I always said I'd like to make my first visit as a player. He [Peter Shilton] has been a great help to me. He tells me what to do. I'd be a mug not to take the advice of someone like him.' So Woods won the League Cup in 1978, picked up a European Cup winner's medal the year after just for sitting on the bench and then moved on to Norwich, where he won the League Cup, and then to Glasgow Rangers. He won four titles, four League Cups and broke the record for going the longest time without conceding a goal – 1,196 minutes.

It was while he was with Rangers, that Woods was called up for Italia 90 – as Shilton's understudy again. Many thought Woods would come on at half-time in that third-place play-off game. Everyone knew it was Shilton's last game, and a 'handover' seemed appropriate in such a game. Furthermore, Woods was the wrong side of 30, and this would probably be his only opportunity to play at a World Cup with David Seaman fast emerging as a brilliant keeper in line for the England jersey.

But Shilton lasted the whole 90 minutes, and made the error that put Italy in front.

The main reason I would put Clemence ahead of Shilton, though, is because of Maradona's Hand of God goal at the World Cup in 1986.

Clemence used to stand off his line, and I have no doubt would have got to that ball before Maradona had even thought about punching it in. Yes, I know Clemence was finished with England by then, and injuries ended his career early, but I'm talking hypothetically. I have a print of the moment Maradona handles the ball framed on a wall in my home (some people think that's weird, I think it's an iconic moment in England's football history). The picture is also on the back cover of Shilton's autobiography. Shilton is obviously sure he is getting the ball, but he's barely off the ground, he doesn't clear the situation right out. Shilton said:

'The one question I have been asked repeatedly is: "Why didn't you go straight through him?" The answer is simple. I couldn't have gone straight through him because I was over-reaching for the ball. It wasn't my style to go through a forward . . . In over-reaching for the ball, and given Maradona's position, even if that had been my intention, it would have been physically impossible for me to have taken him out.' It's a far from compelling explanation. Maradona cheated, but could Shilton have done more? Yes, I think so.

England supporters

I simply have to bust the most annoying myth in football.

A journalist at an England game once saw a Union Jack with Bristol Rovers written across the middle. Then another flag with Bromsgrove Rovers on it. Then one with Rotherham United. And another with Aldershot. He then wrote an article saying these flags prove that only fans of small clubs support England and somehow people were stupid enough to believe it.

It absolutely does my head in.

I've been to England games with fans of the following clubs: Leeds, Arsenal, Ipswich, Man City, Millwall, Everton, Chelsea, Liverpool, Manchester United, Spurs and West Ham among others. Think it through: when Wembley is full, and 75,000 fans are there to watch England, do people honestly think not one of them supports a big club? What an absolute joke.

The truth is, fans of all clubs support England, some more passionately than others. But to see a Bristol Rovers flag and claim it's only small clubs' fans who support England is ludicrous.

One caller to talkSPORT suggested fans of smaller clubs don't have much to look forward to and that's why they support England. Excuse me? What exactly is there to look forward to when supporting England? If anything England compound the agony.

These days fans of smaller clubs have far more opportunities for big days at Wembley than big clubs, with play-offs and Johnstone's Paint Trophy finals, so logic that says they also need to support England to get their football kicks is at best patronising, and at worst ignorant. He was a Spurs fan that caller. Spurs have been weighed down with trophies in recent years, haven't they?

So why do you see only flags made by fans of small clubs at England away games then? Fair question. But it isn't true. I've seen West Ham and Chelsea flags travelling with England recently, and club shirts from the top to the bottom of the football pyramid are seen at tournaments involving England.

But the truth is, if you're a Manchester United fan, you're going to spend your money travelling to see United in Europe, ahead of spending it on going to qualifiers or friendlies with England. That is putting club before country. But actually most fans put club before country. On international weekends I would choose to go to watch Posh play a League One game over going to watch England. That doesn't mean I don't love England.

What some people can't grasp is that you can actually support your club *and* England at the same time, regardless of whether you write the name of your team across a Union Jack.

Anyone disagree? Any English fans of football out there who reckon they don't care about England? These people were probably right in the middle of the passion during Italia 90 and Euro 96. Let's see you remain unmoved if ever England have a big game in the latter stages of a major tournament. Impossible. It's in your blood.

Should Gary Lineker have scored?

Five England hat-tricks is some achievement. Okay, one was against Malaysia (in fact he scored all four in a 4–2 victory, one with his left, one with his right and two with his head; the second Malaysia goal came from a ridiculously awful David Batty backpass, he shinned it straight to the centre-forward who made no mistake). But Lineker also scored all four in a win in Spain, two hat-tricks against Turkey in qualifiers, and a crucial, and brilliant, hat-trick against Poland at the World Cup in 1986. That tournament is central to this chapter on Lineker.

Even though England went out at the quarter-final stage Lineker won the Golden Boot. Impressive in itself, but when you throw in the fact that England failed to score in the first two games of the tournament you realise how huge Lineker was in Mexico.

But he didn't click into gear until Bobby Robson changed things for the must-win final group game.

England went into the tournament with a partnership up front of Mark Hateley and Lineker, on paper a fantastic duo. Hateley had won the Under-21 Championships in 1984 (England retaining it, having also won it in 1982), scored four against France in that tournament, and was named UEFA's 'Golden Player'. I worked with Hateley in television after he retired, and he had a habit of getting his words the wrong way round. On one show instead of saying 'ifs, buts and maybes,' he actually came out with 'ifs, mutts and babies'. Genius.

With 40 goals in 57 games for Everton in the 1985–86 season, Lineker was a certain starter for England. When England lost 1–0 to Portugal in the first game I remember tearing off my England shirt and throwing it on the floor. With Bryan Robson off injured and Ray Wilkins sent off, England laboured to a 0–0 draw with Morocco (who eventually won the group). Neither Hateley nor Lineker had impressed, and with Hateley playing deeper, helping out midfield in the second game after Wilkins' red card, he took most of the criticism and was dropped.

Peter Beardsley hadn't had time to strike up any kind of understanding with Lineker; indeed his England debut had only come in January before the World Cup when he came on as a substitute in place of Lineker. When they did play together, Chris Waddle scored the only goal in a win in the USSR. Robson went with Beardsley and Lineker for the crucial Poland game, and Lineker's 25-minute first-half hat-trick won it for England. After retirement, Beardsley was full of praise for Lineker: 'His ability to keep finding the target was the main thing – even if he didn't score, he'd always force the keeper to make a save. You can teach players many things, but you can't teach them to be in the right place at the right time. He could place his finishes, blast them, whatever was required. We were perfect together because we never got in each other's way. Gary was always in the box and I was running about, working the channels.'

In total for England the partnership of Lineker and Beardsley produced 33 goals in 39 games, arguably the best partnership England has ever had. They played together in both a World Cup quarter-final and semi-final.

Beardsley was almost a fantasy-player, almost a No.10, and Lineker benefited from his partner's style: 'As a goal-scorer, you want a fellow striker who does not get in your way and who is preferably unselfish, someone who is prepared to drop deep and confuse defenders in order to give you more space. For me, that player was Peter Beardsley. We just hit it off and became the catalyst for the team.'

With Poland unable to defend against Beardsley's clever movement and passing, and England playing some fantastic football, Robson's men blew their opponents away. Lineker showed strength to hold off his man and fire home the first, he then met Hodge's cross perfectly on the half volley for the second, and capitalised on a goalkeeping error at a corner for the third. It was the perfect display of goalscoring from England's main striker.

After the Poland triumph, Lineker then scored two and Beardsley the other in a 3–0 win over Paraguay before the quarter-final with Argentina. After the Hand of God goal (Peter Shilton said: 'It hasn't gone away – it has accompanied me through life to this day' and Terry Butcher said: 'I'll never forgive him'), and then the solo effort (Glenn Hoddle, who was awful throughout the game, gave the ball away in midfield and Peter Reid, who shouldn't have been playing because of an ankle injury but 'was never going to miss this one', couldn't keep up with the cheat), John Barnes and Chris Waddle came on – two players I loved watching. They started to run at Argentina's tiring defenders and Barnes in particular was getting a lot of joy. He beat two men then crossed for Lineker to pull one goal back.

And then the moment that leaves me doubting Lineker's greatness. Maradona was surging away upfield again, and Steve Hodge, whose back-pass had led to the Hand of God

'Was he brave enough to throw himself at the ball and make sure it went in?'

goal, raced back to stop him. The former Forest midfielder, who went on to win the title with Leeds, said: 'I saw No.10 flash away from me, I heard Brian Clough's voice echoing in my head, "Get the ball back", so I got my head down and sprinted back to slide in on the halfway line and get the ball back.' It went to Barnes who took on his defenders, with stepovers and bursts of acceleration. He made room for the cross, and with the keeper in no man's land the ball was half a yard away from the goal ready for the onrushing Lineker to bury it for 2–2. But incredibly Lineker didn't make contact. Instead Argentina defender Olarticoechea got there first to make a spectacular clearance.

Who wanted it more? Lineker rolled around in the back of the net. Was it his wrist again? Or was it his pride this time?

In his autobiography Hodge wrote: 'The ball arrived and I was looking at Gary as he'd found a little bit of space and in my head I thought, "Yes! He won't miss from that range", but the lad flicked it away from close in with some brilliant defending. It just wasn't our day.'

Gary Lineker – one of England's finest strikers ever, no question. But answer this: was he brave enough to throw himself at the ball and make sure it went in?

If you think I am being harsh, then what about this question: why the hell didn't Lineker punch it in? I'm sick of people saying he was never booked or sent off and he was an honest player. Sod that. Lineker would have known by then that Maradona cheated, so he should have done the same. He could have changed the history of English football. That was the difference between going home or staying at the World Cup. I can't forgive Gary Lineker for not cheating against Argentina in 1986.

It is a chance he should have taken in my opinion, even if it meant clattering into the post, or taking a boot in the face. And even if he feels to this day that he was certain he would get his head to it, the truth is he didn't. So he should have made sure by cheating. It's not something I would normally advocate, but Maradona had done it, so it was only right that England should seek to even things out.

But little has been made of Lineker's terrible miss because of the Hand of God controversy and the subsequent Maradona wonder goal.

Lineker finished unerringly four years later in the semi-final against Germany, and he scored his penalty in the shoot-out.

But then came the only other black mark against Lineker in his England career.

Poised to equal Bobby Charlton's goalscoring record for England, Lineker stepped up to take a penalty in the tenth minute of a Wembley friendly against Brazil. Inexplicably Lineker tried to chip it. The keeper saved easily. Like all good strikers, Lineker said it wasn't his fault, he blamed the pitch: 'I saw Carlos [the keeper] make a move, and I tried to chip him, but I got my foot stuck in the turf which is a bit long.'

Had he taken that penalty properly, he would now be England's joint record goalscorer. That's how costly his decision to chip the penalty was. A month later England went to Sweden for the European Championships, Lineker failed to score, England finished bottom of the group and that was his international career over.

Lineker had scored the crucial goal against Poland to seal our qualification, but it had all gone wrong after that. Graham Taylor substituting him in the final group game when we needed a goal has to go down as one of the worst decisions an England manager has ever made. Taylor says it was a 'footballing' decision.

Gary Lineker was phenomenal at club level, and was one of the very best for England.

But he missed a sitter in 1986 that could have changed the course of England's footballing history.

Pep Guardiola's Barcelona

It all started so badly. Guardiola's first game in charge of Barcelona ended with a 1–0 defeat away to small-time Numancia. The goal was scored by Mario Martinez Rubio, a man who at the time earned roughly half in a year what Thierry Henry was earning a week. And after a free-kick from a long-haired, alice-banded Messi smacked against the post in injury time, suddenly Pep's decision to let Ronaldinho and Deco leave that summer because of the 'disorder' of their lifestyles, was being questioned.

By the end of the season, Rubio had not added to his goal tally, Numancia were relegated, and Barcelona comfortably won the title. In Guardiola's first season they also won the Copa del Rey, the Champions League, and then went on to win the Spanish Supercopa, the UEFA Super Cup and the World Club title. It was the most successful season in Barça's history. And so the story continued, trophies were won, and superb football was played. But was it down to Guardiola – or did he just tell some extremely talented players to go out and play football? Was it easier to succeed than fail at Barcelona?

I cannot subscribe to that view: Guardiola increased the intensity of what Barcelona players were doing to a level football has never seen before. Rinus Michels' 'circulation' football – which for me forms the basis of everything good about Barcelona under Pep Guardiola – took on a whole new meaning.

Barcelona won their first ever European Cup in 1992 under Johan Cruyff at Wembley. It was an awesome display of football, in which opponents Sampdoria played their part. Guardiola, aged just 21 then, lined up in midfield that night.

Cruyff took his football philosophy from Michels, having played under him for club and country. Both these Dutchman are inked into Barcelona's history, and as Guardiola said when he took the job at the Nou Camp: 'The style comes dictated by the history of this club and we will be faithful to it.'

But in his biography of Guardiola, Guillem Balague claims he 'revolutionised football because he used a Cruyff idea and made it a method: always accumulate more players than your rival right from the start of a move to gain the initiative.' When Barcelona had one point from two games at the start of Guardiola's reign, it was Cruyff he went to see.

So Guardiola changed things from what was happening before: he asked more of the players, the centre-halves became creators, keeper Valdes was a passer of the ball – almost an outfield player; wingers were never on the periphery; and in time the out-and-out striker would be discarded by Guardiola, in favour of a 'false No.9', a player who didn't wait in an attacking position like a traditional centre-forward but instead positioned himself between the centre-halves and the central midfielders, planting indecision in their heads, and opening up opportunities to attack for the false No.9 and his team-mates. With Messi as the false No.9, Barcelona went to Real Madrid in May 2009 and won 6–2. The sixth goal highlights how 'total' the football was. Eto'o raced down the right wing after being released by Messi, who was in a central midfield position. Eto'o squared low for Gerard Pique – a centre-half in a centre-forward's position – to finish.

So why did Guardiola leave? The young man who took the job in 2008 had turned into an old man when he departed in 2012. My opinion is that the sheer hard work of maintaining the standards required on and off the pitch to produce a team as dominant as Barcelona were under Guardiola had left him exhausted. I also felt his spirit had been broken by Jose Mourinho.

Arriving to take charge of the B-team in 2007, Guardiola told the young players: 'Giving everything while competing with dignity is a victory, whatever the scoreline suggests.' His assistant with the B-team and then the first team was Tito Vilanova, the man Mourinho poked in the eye on the touchline during an El Clasico. Not much 'competing with dignity' from Mourinho, a man once branded 'the enemy of football' by the head of UEFA's referees committee. A succession of similarly undignified actions from the then Real Madrid coach proved too much for Guardiola. It stopped being about football. So he left.

What Guardiola achieved at Barcelona is stunning, as was the football. His place among the tactical greats is firmly established.

Own goals

Is there anything more counter-productive than an own goal? Quite often it's an act of unforced ineptitude that makes your own job of winning the game even more difficult. Having said that, who doesn't love a good laugh at a ridiculous own goal?

Yet in the laws of Association football, there is no specific reference to own goals. In fact, up until 1997 the laws clearly stated that the ball had to come off an 'attacking player' for a goal to be awarded. And check out Law 13, free-kicks. It states: 'If a direct free-kick is kicked directly into the team's own goal, after the ball is in play, a corner-kick is awarded to the opposing team.'

So if a misplaced backpass from a direct free-kick by a defender to his goalkeeper goes in the back of the net, the defender, for no apparent reason, is spared the embarrassment of his mistake, and the opponents denied what seems a perfectly good goal.

In sport generally there seems to be an unwillingness to celebrate the ironic beauty of a cock-up – a player, who's supposed to make the ball go in one net, actually putting it into his own by accident. What a plonker!

In ice hockey for example, own goals do not exist. The goal is awarded to the last attacking player to play the puck. It's almost as if they don't want to acknowledge one of their players is capable of such nonsense.

We've all got our favourites and here are my top ten in no particular order:

1) First up **Jamie Pollock**. Back in 1998 anything but victory for Man City against QPR would send them down to the third tier for the first time in their history and keep the London side up. At 1–1, Jamie Pollock scored a cracking own goal. Remember Gazza's wonder goal against the Scots in Euro 96? Very similar. Pollock looped the ball over a Rangers attacker about 20 yards out from his own goal and following it into the box he looped a header over his own keeper. It ended up 2–2 and City went down.

2) The 1877 FA Cup final between Wanderers and Oxford University. **Lord Kinnaird** – formerly of Eton and Cambridge and part of the family banking business that became Barclays – volunteered to go in goal because Wanderers didn't have a keeper.

Yes, we really are meant to take old football seriously despite the fact that Wanderers turned up to an FA Cup final without a goalie.

During the game Kinnaird collected the ball but stepped over his goal-line – own goal. Luckily for him Wanderers ended up winning 2–1. But Kinnaird was so embarrassed he appealed to the FA to have the goal wiped from the records – and they agreed! It gets worse because Lord Kinnaird then served as President of the Football

Association for 33 years; indeed he was so revered they presented him with his very own FA Cup. All that time he ran football in this country, his own goal was obliterated from the record books. Eventually the own goal was officially recorded in the 1970s, around 50 years after Kinnaird's death.

3) World Cup winner **Jack Charlton** tried to invoke the Kinnaird rule as a Leeds United player, when his teammate, keeper Gary Sprake, threw the ball into his own goal at Liverpool in 1967. (He had intended throwing it to Terry Cooper, but at the last moment noticed Cooper had been closed down, and in trying to hold onto the ball, actually hurled it into the net.) Charlton said to the referee: 'You're not going to give a goal for that?!' The ref gave it. No doubt Leeds claimed it was a conspiracy and another disgraceful decision that went against them.

4) Bury defender **Chris Brass** tried to hook a ball away as Darlington attacked, but smashed it into his own face and it went in. He broke his nose.

5) **Bernard Parker** buried a bullet header past his own keeper in a crucial World Cup qualifier in June 2013. From the edge of the box it arrowed into the top corner and denied South Africa a place in Brazil 2014.

6) **Andy Linighan** is famous for scoring the winner in the last FA Cup final replay for Arsenal against his old club Sheffield Wednesday in 1993. But he scored an even better goal for Wednesday while he was playing for Norwich. He should have dealt with a through ball calmly, but he didn't.

He ended up rounding his own keeper and smashing the ball into the top corner from about two yards out. Linighan is now my local plumber.

7, 8 and **9)** Wolves against Den Haag in the 1971–72 UEFA Cup. Molineux enjoyed another fantastic night of European football in the greatest traditions of the game. Derek Dougan had already put Wolves a goal up when the Dutch side took out a massive blunderbuss and blasted their feet off. Comedy of the highest order, better than any BBC3 sitcom you care to name. And all three OGs were scored in the same half, a world record. The first was headed in by **Wiener**, who was lying on the ground at the time (Dougan celebrated with him only to be pushed over by a Den Haag player); Dutch international **Aad Mansveld** grabbed the second, poking it in at the near post as he raced back to help clear the danger; and the third came from full-back and club legend **Theo van den Burch** who sank to his knees for no apparent reason as the ball came towards him, it spun off his thighs and into the net. Wolves went through 7–1 on aggregate, and were eventually beaten 3–2 over two legs in the final by Tottenham. But the Den Haag coach that night was Vaclav Jezek, who less than five years later would lead the Czechoslovakian national side to victory in the 1976 European Championships. Jezek, and his assistant at that tournament, Josef Venglos – later manager of Aston Villa – were rigorous and detailed in their preparation. They even got a crowd together at training sessions to whistle and jeer as the players practised for a penalty shoot-out. It paid off. The Czechs won the shoot-out in the final against the penalty gods of West Germany, culminating in Uli Hoeness smashing his kick into orbit, and Antonin Panenka chipping his down the middle out of reach of the already prostrate Sepp Maier. Venglos and Jezek had refused to watch because they knew Panenka was going to play that trick. Jezek lost his job after the Czechs failed to qualify for the 1978 World Cup, despite being European Champions.

10) FA Cup first-round day and for all non-league sides who make it that far, it is massive; win that tie, and they're just one game away from being in the Third Round draw with the big boys.

Back in 2000 Forest Green Rovers were optimistic. The club was on the up, firmly established at that time in the Conference, but in need of any revenue they could find. A home tie with Morecambe was seen as a game they could win.

Morecambe missed an early penalty, and maybe Forest Green thought that would mean it was to be their day. Five minutes before half-time Forest Green won a corner. But with defenders up for the set-piece, Morecambe cleared it and broke away.

As the move developed down the left, Forest Green centre-half **Wayne Hatswell**, who had been up for the corner, was sprinting hard to help out. He outpaced the striker he was chasing as they entered the box. The striker stopped his run to hang out and wait for the pull-back, but Hatswell thought he was still on his shoulder. As the ball came across, keeper Steve Perrin, a former Wiltshire cricket captain who refused to play for them again after being controversially dropped for the Minor Counties final at Lord's in 2005, fumbled it into Hatswell's knees. The ball fell a yard in front of the unmanned goal. Left-footed

Hatswell was alone, but crucially he thought the striker he had been tracking was right on his shoulder. Thinking he had to hurry the clearance, he swung his left leg and lashed the ball into the top corner of the goal. It went like a rocket, nearly ripping the net off. One of his team-mates had his head in his hands but at the time Hatswell simply thought: 'Let's get on with it.' Years later he said: 'Just a few centimetres further to the right and it would have missed the goal.'

But Forest Green were knocked out 3–0. Hatswell was named Forest Green's man of the match and one local paper said: 'Hatswell . . . shone in an otherwise dour display.'

Match of the Day had the FA Cup rights, and showed the goal, and so it has become very familiar to a lot of football fans. It really is one of the funniest own goals of all time. The following week Hatswell scored both goals in a win at Dover and *Match of the Day* mentioned him again. But what happened to him?

He had been a non-league player way down the pyramid before the move to Forest Green, and just a few weeks after the own goal Oxford United paid £35,000 to take him into the football league.

From there he went on to Chester, Kidderminster, Rushden & Diamonds and Cambridge United, and was captain at most of them. At Kidderminster he was player of the year, and it's where he met his wife. It's also where he had his toughest time. Wayne has no brothers and is very close to his only sister. Whilst he was at Kidderminster, his niece was diagnosed with a brain tumour and died. She was just eight years old.

'My life goes on, whether it's heartbreaking stuff, or the good times. But through it all, people who don't know me only remember the own goal,' Hatswell told me. 'I'll take it to my grave I suppose, and I've learned to accept it and in the right environment I can laugh about it, but only if my mood is right, according to my wife. I am a hot-head, and if a random passer-by in the street mentions it, then it can be annoying but if something goes wrong you have to pick yourself up and get on with it.'

Hatswell, who hates Wembley, having been there three times and lost on every occasion, wasn't the greatest player the world has seen, but at a certain level, he was the guy managers wanted to sign for his leadership qualities and his attitude.

In a short spell in management at non-league Stamford he won promotion, despite having only one player under contract and being a long distance from his wife and family. At the time of writing he is assistant manager at League Two Newport County.

He will probably always be remembered for that own goal – even he acknowledges that. But if you get a chance check out the 40-yard screamer he scored (at the right end – but also against Forest Green) for Cambridge.

1966 World Cup final

Which player had the ball in the net first in the 1966 World Cup final? Helmut Haller you think? Wrong.

It was actually Bobby Moore but it was disallowed. Geoff Hurst flattened the keeper, the ref waved play on and then blew up for something far more innocuous as Moore rifled home. But step away from this World Cup final and the fact that England won it, and assess whether it was any good. For the purposes of this book I sat and watched the game twice, that's 240 minutes of England winning the World Cup, including the agony of the late equaliser in normal time.

First of all, there was an annoying vuvuzela-type car horn noise all the way through extra-time that would have driven most people mad. But what about the game? West Germany kicked off and within two seconds Wolfgang Overath had booted it high and long out of touch for an England throw in. (When England kicked off the second half it took five passes before Wilson thumped it to an opponent.) The Germans were useless on the day, truly awful. Emmerich literally did nothing good all afternoon, Seeler couldn't control the ball, Beckenbauer's talent was stifled by the fact he was told to hold Bobby Charlton's hand all day (or as the captain of an opposing team said to a player who was bizarrely man-marking me in a charity game once: 'Grab hold of Ginger's nuts and take him for walk!'), and they played on the break for most of the game.

After just ten minutes came the first goal, a calamity from England. Ray Wilson's ridiculous header straight to Haller – in the England penalty area – gave Germany the lead. Their second was equally fortunate: a terrible free-kick broke luckily for the Germans and they poked it in to make it 2–2 with time running out. Jack Charlton complained it wasn't a free-kick, but if he'd shown a bit more composure he would have let the German win it and kept tight to steer him away from danger. But Charlton piled in and gave away a free-kick with a minute left. Germany played little football, they didn't create chances, and scoring two goals flattered them.

Here is something else I noticed: Martin Peters was a 1960s' version of Frank Lampard; he has four long-range shots in the first ten minutes. Every time he gets the ball he shoots, but the one time he didn't he laid it off to Charlton, went for the return ball 25 yards out . . . and had a shot. He took his goal well though; a woeful defensive clearance ballooned up in the air and Peters slammed it towards the net from close range. It helped that the keeper and the defender dived out of the way of it – brave as lions.

Gordon Banks made some decent stops but had a relatively quiet afternoon. The England legend did have two heads-gone moments though. Firstly, when England scored their second goal to lead 2–1 there were still 12 minutes of normal time left, yet Banks ran the length of the field to celebrate with his team-mates. Not his wisest move.

Second heads-gone moment for Banks came in extra-time. Germany's second goal to make it 2–2 came from a set-piece with 30 seconds of the 90 left. With around 30 seconds of extra-time left, England led 3–2, and Banks actually punched a corner. Yes, he punched a corner. Watching it I shouted (both times): 'Catch the thing, Banks man!'

Commentator Kenneth Wolstenholme was excellent. My personal favourite moment from him is one which summed up Alan Ball's performance, deep in the first half of extra-time: 'Here comes Mr Perpetual Motion again.' And just before the third goal Wolstenholme said Ball was 'running himself daft'.

With England holding on at 3–2, the Germans were penalised for handball and Wolstenholme remarked: '97,000 referees gave that decision.'

The commentator's curse struck in the 87th minute. Hurst lamely dragged a shot wide and the commentator said: 'Three minutes left, it doesn't really matter.' And then the Germans equalised.

But what struck me most about the commentary was that there was no analysis or comment on the third England goal – was it over the line or not? There was only one TV angle and no replay, and obviously it's easier for commentators and pundits to pass opinion if they see it again. But once the goal had been given, that was it, Wolstenholme moved on. He instantly thought the ball was over the line, and his commentary seems a little familiar: 'And now Hurst, can he do it? He has done – YES!'

Incidentally the commentary also points out that had the two teams been level, there would have been a replay. All those who had kept their ticket stub for the first game, would have the opportunity to buy a ticket for the second game, before the rest were put on general sale.

The standout players on the day for England were Bobby Charlton who always tried to use the ball so well; Hurst, not just for the hat-trick, but for his movement up front and his ability to hold the ball up; and Bobby Moore. If ever you're in doubt about Moore's excellence, watch the World Cup final. All the clichés trotted out by the old timers who were around to watch him are true: he moved with such elegance, he could pass the ball, always calm and controlled, and he showed true leadership. He was miles ahead of anyone else on the pitch. I'll pick out two special

'"Here comes Mr Perpetual Motion again." And just before the third goal Wolstenholme said Ball was "running himself daft".'

moments from Bobby Moore's World Cup final. Five minutes before half-time Moore is on the ball but under a bit of pressure from two Germans in his own half. He finds a perfect pass into the opposition half to the feet of Roger Hunt, who has the touch of a pinball machine and sends the ball rocketing back into the England half into the path of Emmerich. Moore calmly strides across to make a last-ditch saving tackle, or the German would have been clean through. And then in the last five minutes of normal time, Moore stays calm when he has the ball deep in his own half and England lead 2–1. He doesn't smash it into row Z. He controls it, treasures it, respects it. He passes it when penned in by his own corner flag, and sets in motion a move that leaves England three-on-one against the ragged Germans. A fantastic opportunity to seal victory but Hunt makes a mess of the pass and the Germans are let off the hook.

Moore did exactly the same in the 120th minute, but this time he not only calmly brought the ball out of defence, he also picked out an unmarked Hurst in the German half and the England striker made it 4–2, sealing his hat-trick. Moore even popped up on the left wing twice during the course of the afternoon.

England were by far the better side on the day; it takes the bitterest Scot to deny that. But maybe that fourth goal shouldn't have stood. There were some people on the pitch, they thought it was all over . . .

The Daily Arsenal

In 2006 I came away from the Champions League final in Paris mystified by Arsene Wenger and questioning the direction Arsenal were going in as a club.

Title winners two years previously, not only had they started running scared of Jose Mourinho and Sir Alex Ferguson, they finished a massive 15 points behind Liverpool in the 2005–06 season (a campaign in which Marlon Harewood was the Premier League's seventh top scorer, remarkably). The champions Chelsea were 24 points ahead of the Gunners. In fact they only finished in a Champions League place because Spurs players ate a dodgy lasagne.

It was at that point that I started to seriously question Wenger. Bergkamp was retiring, Henry was itching to leave, that was inevitable, and Sol Campbell was past his best. Wenger still couldn't sort the goalkeeping out, and that cost them in the Champions League final. There were so few positives for the future.

So I started to tell a few Arsenal fans some home truths on the radio and they hated it. I was slaughtered for it, but it's become familiar for Arsenal fans to tell me I was right about the situation all along. Over the next few years, it seemed that every day we were talking about Arsenal on the show.

In fact I conducted a secret survey over a three-week period, and found that only two days out of 15 were Arsenal talked about as the main topic. But the reputation stuck, and so I decided to prove everyone right by talking about the Gunners every day. And so 'The Daily Arsenal' was born. Twice the subject of killing it off has been raised, and both times 'The Daily Arsenal' has come back even stronger. We've had comedy, ranting, live music, Spurs fans, Arsenal fans, special guests and gossip in that slot. But most of all we've had positives as well as negatives about Arsenal.

I've suggested in the past that 'The Daily Arsenal' may reach its end when the Gunners finally win a trophy. But I'm beginning to think people would miss it too much . . .

Brazil's first visit to Wembley

I can't really ask if Brazil are all that now, can I? But they took a beating the first time they came to Wembley. England scored four and missed two penalties, and Stanley Matthews teased them all afternoon.

It helped that the Brazilians had inexplicably put Flavio Costa back in charge of the national team; he had led the Brazilians to an almost impossible defeat in the 1950 World Cup final in front of 200,000 fans at the brand new Maracana stadium in Rio de Janeiro. They had even been leading 1–0, and the way the tournament worked back then, a draw with Uruguay would have been enough. But they were beaten and Flavio Costa immediately lost his job. Rio de Janeiro reportedly sunk into a depression. There were rumours that defensive midfielder Danilo (who had celebrated a move to a big club so hard as a youngster he was hit by a car and broke his leg on the way home) had tried to commit suicide, and it's more than rumour that some fans actually did kill themselves at the stadium after the defeat. Jules Rimet himself remarked that the silence 'was morbid, almost too difficult to bear'.

Flavio Costa said: 'I can never forget that match, the people will not let me.' But most Brazilians didn't blame the coach. They turned their anger towards the goalkeeper Moacyr Barbosa. The winning goal came with just over ten minutes left: Alcides Ghiggia went past the left-back Bigode (who never played for Brazil again) and Barbosa moved off from his line to anticipate a cross. But Ghiggia fired goalwards, and Barbosa was beaten at his near post. Uruguay lifted the World Cup.

The Brazilian players were abused in public, and Barbosa suffered more than most. Shortly before he died in 2000, he said: 'The maximum punishment in Brazil is 30 years imprisonment, but I have been paying, for something I am not even responsible for . . . for 50 years.' In 1963 he was given the old square wooden posts from the goal frame in the 1950 final. He burnt them. And then in 1993 he was told he wouldn't be allowed to commentate on a Brazil match, and was refused permission to watch the Brazil national team train ahead of the World Cup. He was told he would be a jinx on the team. He died in misery, penniless.

By the time Brazil arrived for their first ever visit to Wembley on 9 May 1956, they were still recovering from that shattering defeat in 1950, and their subsequent mauling in the 1954 World Cup in Switzerland. In November 1953 England were thrashed 6–3 at Wembley by Hungary. Six months later England lost in Budapest 7–1, the England centre-half Syd Owen saying: 'It was like playing people from outer space.' It was a humiliating time for the nation that invented the game. That match in Hungary was a warm-up for the World Cup where England were beaten 4–2 in the quarter-finals by Uruguay, Brazil lost by the same scoreline to Hungary in a fiery game which saw players fighting and stamping, while Nilton Santos, arguably the world's finest ever left-back, and Humberto Tozzi were sent off for Brazil. Hungary's Jozsef Bozsik was also dismissed.

So the wait for World Cup success went on for both England and Brazil.

As Brazil warmed up for the 1958 tournament in Sweden, they organised a friendly against England at Wembley. Walter Winterbottom told his England players to stop the Brazilians getting the ball, saying: 'When they get the ball, they're fantastic, so don't let them have it.' And Stanley Matthews had a small bottle of Babycham before going out onto the pitch to settle his nerves.

Within 90 seconds England led after Johnny Haynes laid the ball back for Tommy Taylor to score. Two minutes later Sheffield United's Colin Grainger, on his debut, tapped in the second. Grainger went on to sign a recording contract and was nicknamed the 'singing winger'. He performed on the same bill as The Beatles and sang at the London Palladium. It was 2–0 at half-time.

In the second half it was Brazil's turn to score two quick goals – Paulinho's shot from an acute angle deflected in on 53, and then two minutes later Didi, nicknamed the Cobra, fired one in from 25 yards which the keeper Reg Matthews, playing in the Third Division (South) with Coventry, fumbled into the net for 2–2. Taylor headed in after a good run and cross from Stanley Matthews for 3–2. Grainger sealed it with his second and England's fourth with seven minutes left, again Matthews the provider.

The penalties were ridiculous: Tommy Taylor rugby tackled in the box, and then a blatant handball virtually on the penalty spot which somehow the Brazilians persuaded the French referee was outside the box. The linesman intervened and the spot-kick was awarded. But both were missed – John Atyeo of Bristol City saw his shot saved by Gilmar, and then Roger Byrne's penalty was also saved.

England had beaten the emerging Brazilians in 1956. So what changed by the time the next World Cup came around, and Brazil and England fought out the first ever goalless draw at a World Cup? Stanley Matthews retired from England duty in 1957 at the age of 42. And tragically the Munich air disaster, a few months before that World Cup, took the lives of Roger Byrne, Tommy Taylor and Duncan Edwards who had all played in the England team that had beaten Brazil at Wembley.

In Sweden, England failed to win a game and came home early. But Brazil won that World Cup in 1958 thanks largely to Garrincha and Pele who emerged as world talents as the tournament went on. Neither had played against England in 1956.

Since that 4–2 win for England, the World Cups have stacked up for the Brazilians . . . latest score Brazil 5 England 1.

Calling a professional footballer a 'bottler'

9 July 2007, 5pm. Liverpool centre-half Jamie Carragher calls into my radio show on talkSPORT.

Carragher: Just phoned up on me way to training listening to your show, normally a good show until you start rabbiting on this afternoon about being a bit of a bottler. Be interesting to see if you've got any bottle and come down to Anfield or Melwood and say it to me and we'll see what happens, won't we?

Durham: I'd say it to your face and I'll say it to you now . . .

Carragher: Oh would you mate? I tell you what, come down to Anfield on a Champions League game or whatever and we'll see, won't we?

This wasn't a good start to our relationship. I'd spent the first hour of the radio show calling Jamie Carragher a bottler after his decision to retire from England duty. In his autobiography Carragher said he was 'raging' after he heard me use that word.

Believe it or not, I don't just throw these words in randomly, I actually think them through. I used the word 'bottler' because Steve McClaren, then the England manager, had set a challenge to Carragher to make a place in the England starting line-up his own, and to make himself undroppable. Carragher had decided against that, and chosen instead to give up international football. In my opinion he had not faced up to a massive challenge. And that to me is bottling a challenge, hence the term 'bottler'. People might disagree but that was my view of the situation.

The live on-air argument between Jamie and myself continued, with Micky Quinn acting as peacemaker, sort of:

JC: You can say whatever, you can say these other players are better than me, not a problem. Everyone's got opinions; that's football. Not a problem with McClaren's opinions if he plays someone else, not a problem with him at all, but don't ever call me a bottler on radio in front of thousands of people listening to you.

AD: So why are you even thinking of quitting international football?

JC: Because there's that many people who he's played ahead of me. As I say it's a game of opinions, but when you're at my age, they're all younger than me and they're all going to improve which maybe I won't at that age. I played in the Champions League final, there's not much more you can do in club football – obviously win it but we did that a couple of years ago. He played Ledley King who's a top player but he's been injured all season, so how would you feel in my situation there, what would you do?

AD: I'd feel like proving myself and getting the stomach for the fight going, and going for it!

JC: Proving yourself? I'm 29, I've been doing it for eight years and obviously I haven't proved it enough. So it's not going to change now, is it? It's not as if I've just got in the squad and jumped out, so when you talk about proving yourself – and who's the other fella who was saying, 'Oh, he's probably jacked it in cos he's got his contract at Liverpool for a hundred grand a week?' Who's he?

AD: He reads our sports bulletins. [Jamie was referring to Andrew 'Macca' McKenna.]

MQ: He's the newsreader.

JC: Is he that . . . ?

AD: . . . hang on, Jamie, he's a fan, he's a football fan . . .

JC: He's a fan . . .

AD: An England fan who's entitled to his opinion.

JC: And none of 'youse' are more of a football fan than

me, so don't try and make out that I'm someone who's more interested in money than playing football.

MQ: Jamie, in some senses when some of these lads who work here haven't played professional at the highest level . . .

JC: Ah no . . .

MQ: No Jamie . . . but don't understand. I mean I've been in a position, not as big as your decision you've made but on a club level where I wasn't getting a game and I had to move on, and that's what players do at club level – they move on, get a transfer cos they're not in the first team. It's a similar thing at international level, but at 29 will you ever regret this decision?

JC: Well, time will tell won't it, but I mean who knows? But as I said the main thing for me now is to concentrate on my Liverpool career. It's football, it could be anything, even a radio presenter or whatever, if you didn't feel you were getting your chances you'd move to another station wouldn't you, if you wanted to be the top man on your radio . . .

MQ: I tell you what Jamie, five minutes ago he nearly did move to another station! He bottled it when you came on! (*laughter all round*)

JC: I just heard another caller saying he bottled it with [Leroy] Lita as well so he's not the bravest is he? (*more laughter all round*)

AD: Nah, I didn't bottle it with Lita. I tell you what, I've never played professional football, I've hardly played amateur football, but I don't understand, as a fan – an England fan as well, Jamie – I don't understand how anybody who's in their twenties cannot want to win the World Cup.

JC: I'd love to. I tried to win last year (the World Cup). I'd have to wait til next time and I'll be 32 then, so if I'm not getting a game now at 29, there'll be no chance of getting a game at 32.

AD: (*exasperated*) How do you know that? I don't understand how you know that?

JC: Cos everyone the manager has picked ahead of me is younger than me.

MQ: And I tried to explain that he's never played you in your right position.

AD: No, no, no, no, it doesn't make any sense . . .

JC: I'm not having a go at the manager for that, as I said . . .

AD: It doesn't make any sense . . . he's brought back David Beckham – he picked right-sided midfielders who are younger than David Beckham, so what's to say he won't pick you?

JC: But David Beckham has been captain, he's been a regular for England – I've never done that in the first place. So move on to your next point, cos that was wrong.

MQ: There you go.

JC: Beckham's always been a regular.

AD: Well he hasn't, he was retired from international football by the manager, who then decided to bring him back.

JC: The manager said the door was always open, which it was, cos he came back.

AD: Oh come on!

JC: He came back, didn't he?

AD: Hang on, what are you saying now because one of your quotes is: 'If the England boss comes calling, I'll play.' Which is it – are you retiring or not?

JC: At the moment it's not 100 per cent official because I've still got to speak to the manager before the next game, but at the moment it is looking like that. And as I said if there's a major injury crisis where the four centre-halves who he obviously picks ahead of me are all injured, and he's absolutely desperate, of course I would, yeah.

AD: But would you understand if a manager, an England manager thought: 'Well, if Jamie hasn't got the stomach to fight for his place, why would he have the stomach for, say, a World Cup quarter-final?'

JC: Well I've had the stomach to fight for me place for the last eight years. What do you want me to do, keep going or . . .

AD: Yeah, simple as that.

JC: All right, well there's nothing more I can say to that, is there? All I can do is play as well as I can for Liverpool, I've never really played centre-half for England, and to be honest I've never really played that well for England because I've played a lot of the time at full-back. But at centre-half I don't think I've really played as much as maybe I think I maybe deserve, but as I said that's opinions, that's the manager's choice, and if he has chosen other people ahead of me I don't think anyone can really complain if then I think I'd rather concentrate on Liverpool and try to do as well for them, and save myself for Liverpool games. And I don't know what you're so worried about Adrian, to be honest mate, cos you went through all the players before who were better than me, so I don't know why you're so bothered.

AD: I was reading out a text.

MQ: Jamie, you look at players who have retired from

international football – the likes of Scholesy, the likes of Alan Shearer – and their clubs really did benefit from them and it could elongate your career as well, get another two or three years out of it.

JC: Well, yeah, hopefully that'll be the way I look at it, but also, there is a difference in that I'm only basically a squad player. They were making the England team, so I'm sure the England team were missing Paul Scholes and Alan Shearer a lot more than they're missing Jamie Carragher. So I'm not sure why people are so worried about it, to be honest.

AD: I'll tell you why we're worried Jamie. Cos when I read it, I was massively disappointed. And I thought to myself, 'Jamie Carragher has played in Champions League finals . . .'

JC: But you weren't disappointed with Shearer, you said before, why not?

AD: Well, cos he's had two and a half years' worth of injuries, that's why.

JC: Well, I had a knee operation.

AD: Everybody has their injuries . . .

JC: Exactly.

AD: . . . but I think Alan Shearer probably had it worse than most, but I think you're a terrific player and I wanted you to be in there fighting for your England place.

JC: I'm a terrific player? You were slaughtering me before, that's why I rang up.

AD: Hang on, saying you're not as good as John Terry or Rio Ferdinand – that's not slaughtering you.

JC: Woodgate as well, you said.

AD: I think Woodgate is a better player but this is a guy who's also had injury problems, he might be out for a year, who knows when, then you're back in the pecking order. I'm disappointed you don't wanna be in there.

JC: And the other fella who said before that he might not play me because me and John Terry are too similar . . . when John Terry was out I never played, Woodgate played, so . . .

AD: I would have to say I never understood the Ledley King one, why he was picked ahead of you. But I mean, all I'm telling you is my view today, when I heard the story I didn't believe it for a start, and secondly I was disappointed because a good player has decided not to play for England. As an England fan I cannot understand that. As England fans, those who have never played, we would all give anything to play for our country and have the three lions on the chest, and here we have a player still in his twenties saying no, I don't wanna do that any more.

JC: I know you're an England fan, and I was as a kid, but for me when I was a kid growing up it was always – obviously I was an Everton fan as a kid, and now I'm a Liverpool player – the club is always more important for me. And as I said, I'm trying to make sure I give as much to Liverpool as I possibly can over the next few years. It's more to do with that – cos I don't play that much for England anyway, so I can't really say it's tiredness, I'm more thinking about the going away from the club and away from the family. I know some people will have a different opinion, but I've no problem with your opinion at all. It's just the fact that you called me a bottler – I'm not having that at all.

AD: So you wouldn't agree with that at all?

JC: No, not at all, no.

AD: Well, all I'd say is I think there are people out there who look at the decision, maybe don't know the details you know, because obviously you're on the inside of that decision, and they look at it and think, 'Who the hell does he think he is?'

JC: To be honest, I've been in the game a long time. I don't think people think I'm some big-time Charlie. I think my reputation over the last ten or 12 years will stand up to that, not just this one decision . . .

AD: Have you spoken to Steve McClaren yet?

JC: Yeah, I spoke to him a couple of times.

AD: Has he given any reaction to it at all?

JC: Yeah, he still wants me to be part of the squad. I'll speak to him before the Germany game. I told him my feelings and I didn't think they would change, but we decided to speak before the game with Germany.

AD: Jamie listen, I appreciate you calling in.

JC: All right, see you at Melwood, or Anfield on a Champions League night.

MQ: Jamie, I'll drag him down, don't worry.

JC: Make sure he brings boxing gloves, Quinny!

The reaction was phenomenal. The phone lines went into meltdown. To this day, it is still what most people want to talk about if the conversation turns to talkSPORT matters. In February 2013, after Carragher announced his decision to retire from professional football at the end of that season, the *Daily Telegraph* printed a feature on 'Carragher's Finest Moments.' One of the six 'moments' – squeezed in between the 2005 Champions League final, and Jamie raising £1 million for his charity set-up, the 23 Foundation – read:

'Talksport, July 2007. After announcing his international retirement Carragher takes radio presenter Adrian Durham to task for criticising the decision. Still as amusing six years on.'

The most common thing people said to me was that they agreed with what I was saying, but didn't like the use of the word bottler.

So do I regret using it? No, because I felt I used it in context. Most people misinterpreted it, thinking I was accusing him of running scared. But I was actually referring to his apathy. He couldn't be bothered to fight for his England place. In my life it's been a fight for everything and I don't remember giving up on something I really wanted.

It's only in the years since that Carragher phone call in 2007 that I have got to know him better, and with the knowledge of the man I now have, there is no way I would describe him as a bottler.

As an England fan I was massively disappointed. Anyone who retires from international duty is actually turning down any chance, no matter how remote, of winning a World Cup. Why would a professional footballer choose to do that?

The response from Carragher was understandably hostile, and so was the reaction from the whole of Merseyside. I had questioned the commitment not just of one of their own, but of a player who is, in Steven Gerrard's words, '. . . prepared to take his body to the limit and prepared to do whatever it takes to win a football match.' Anfield regulars could see his commitment in a Liverpool shirt, but actually so could opposition fans, including Evertonians.

That in itself is remarkable: it's well known that in his boyhood years Carragher was in his own words 'Everton-mad growing up . . . a regular at all the away games as well as at home.' As a seven-year-old he raced onto the pitch after Derek Mountfield scored the winner in an FA Cup semi-final in 1985, emulating his father Philly who'd got on to the pitch at Wembley after the FA Cup final in 1984 and kissed Graeme Sharp. Jamie even wore an Everton shirt when training at the Liverpool School of Excellence, and was told off by the Liverpool coaching staff for openly celebrating an Everton goal.

So for such a staunch Evertonian to be totally accepted by the Liverpool fans, Carragher had to do more than just put on the shirt. He had to prove his passion for the red half of Merseyside over and over again.

He is clearly passionate about being from Liverpool, and specifically from Bootle – 'my heart and soul were born and bred in Bootle.' Carragher's love for Everton Football Club died a long time ago – he has talked openly about a 'Goodison persecution complex' and how he 'loathe(s) Evertonians calling Liverpool fans "murderers" in reference to . . . Heysel' and goes on to say it's 'disturb-ing' and is also 'a big reason why my relationship with Everton has turned sour'.

Despite turning his back on Everton, a club he loved as a boy, you sense that most Everton fans still have at least a grudging respect for Carragher. One staunch Everton fan I spoke to on the subject said this: 'He's been a great player and ambassador for football. I don't think many Blues don't respect him.'

Most England fans would rather a player with Carragher's commitment had been in the team, but then at the same time they would almost certainly have picked Rio Ferdinand and John Terry ahead of him at the time Carragher retired. As he said himself: 'If I'd been England manager, I'd have picked Terry and Ferdinand as first-choice centre-backs. I was too similar to Terry. He's a better version of me.'

So the hostile reaction I faced from the moment Carragher called in to the show was predictable. But if people listen closely to the interview then they'll under-stand why I used the word 'bottler'. After asking me to go and see him at Melwood or Anfield (later suggesting I take my boxing gloves) he then said: 'I tried to win (the World Cup) last year and never, I'd have to wait til next time and I'll be 32 then so if I'm not getting a game at 29, there'll be no chance of getting a game at 32.'

He was so wrong. At the age of 32, Carragher was taken to the World Cup by Fabio Capello in South Africa and even though we were abysmal, we never conceded a goal while Carragher was on the field in an England shirt.

I went up to Liverpool to go head to head with Jamie, as he requested. We met at his bar in the middle of Liverpool, and a few people tried to make life a little uncomfortable for me, but Jamie himself was first class. I was hosting a radio show from the bar, and Jamie joined us, talking to listeners and giving opinions. It was a fantastic day. The *News of the World* even ran an article about me heading up to confront Carra, headlined: 'ADRIAN'S GOT SOME BOTTLE.'

Jamie's good friend Danny Murphy later told me that going up to Liverpool and sitting there fronting up to Jamie and his family, on Jamie's own territory, was the best thing I could have done.

I gave Jamie a framed photo of him playing at Wembley for England; he gave me a signed shirt he had worn at the 2006 World Cup. In fact it was in a carrier bag he threw at me as he walked over to where I was sitting.

After that day we stayed in touch and he invited me up to Anfield for a game, which I was happy to accept. We met again in the players' lounge afterwards, which was when I started to reconsider my view of international retirement. Liverpool had won the game comfortably, Steven Gerrard scoring a hat-trick in a 5–0 thrashing of Aston Villa. With World Cup qualifiers coming up, Gerrard and most of the players disappeared straightaway. Except Jamie Carragher, who walked in smiling, spent time with his wife and children, spoke to his dad about the game and then came over to say hello. Only then did it sink in that there was a serious attraction to staying with the family, rather than spending the next seven or eight days away training and sitting on a bench in Estonia or Kazakhstan.

I still feel uncomfortable about players retiring from international duty, but that afternoon gave me some perspective on the difficulty of the decision. I don't regret what I said that day back in 2007. I am a passionate England fan. And as most people realise, the lines are open for people to give their own opinions too – and that included Jamie Carragher.

Off the field I can say without fear of contradiction that Jamie Carragher is a fantastic person; his passion for his hometown, for his family and for football is obvious.

On the pitch I'll let Steven Gerrard do the talking. He takes up the story of the 2005 Champions League semi-final second leg at Anfield. Liverpool were 1–0 up thanks to a controversial Luis Garcia goal that Chelsea claimed wasn't over the line.

Mourinho went long ball, sticking Robert Huth up front. Gerrard takes up the story in his autobiography: 'We survived because of one man – Jamie Carragher. I looked at Carra and saw a man hell bent on not letting the lead slip. He was prepared to offer the last drop of sweat and blood in his body to get us to Istanbul. Carra knows his history and knew what it meant for Liverpool to reach the final. He did everything to prevent Chelsea ruining Liverpool's dream. He tackled, blocked, headed. Good at the Bridge, Carra was a colossus at Anfield. "If I get a booking," he kept saying, "I will miss the game." But he didn't. In fact, Carra was awesome all the way through the tournament. No wonder Inter Milan were interested in him. He kept stifling some of the best centre-forwards in the world. He saw off Zlatan Ibrahimovic when we played Juventus. Didier Drogba didn't get a sniff either.'

High praise from the captain, and Gerrard was equally generous when describing the final, that astonishing game in Istanbul where Liverpool were 3–0 down at half-time and came back to win in a penalty shoot-out. Extra-time saw Liverpool defending for their lives as AC Milan piled on wave after wave of attack. Gerrard wrote this in his book: 'Everyone fought. Bonds of friendship kept us together. Inevitably, Carra was a commanding presence, putting his body in the line of fire, getting blocks in, even with cramp gripping him too. An incredible desire to win consumes every fibre of Carra's body. He's a big leader for Liverpool, helping people, giving advice, often brilliant advice on football because he knows so much about it. Carra's like having another captain behind me. We needed him in Istanbul big-time. He gave everything. At one point, I saw him pushing against the post, stretching his calves to take the sting out of the cramp. Carra remarked afterwards that playing with cramp was worse than playing with a broken leg.'

Jamie Carragher's advice to Jerzy Dudek before the shoot-out was to copy Bruce Grobbelaar's 'spaghetti legs' from the last time Liverpool had won the European Cup, the shoot-out against AS Roma, in Rome. Dudek wobbled on the line, Serginho missed, and Liverpool went on to win the Champions League.

It was an unbelievable night of football, and unquestionably the pinnacle for Jamie Carragher.

Paula Carragher says she's sure someone has been watching over her son Jamie since the moment he was born. Well, whoever it is was watching over him and the rest of his Liverpool team-mates that night in Istanbul.